SELF-EDITING FOR SELF-PUBLISHERS

Self-editing for Self-publishers

Incorporating: A Style Guide for Fiction

Richard Bradburn

First published in 2020 by Reen Publishing, South Reen, Union Hall, Skibbereen, West Cork, Ireland

Cover Design: Finn

Formatting and Typeset by Reen Publishing

ISBN 978-1-8380165-0-0

www.editorial.ie

Making your words work, beautifully

Contents

Introduction

This book is not a tutorial on writing; it's a tutorial on self-editing. Learning to self-edit effectively can improve your writing, saves time and money when hiring freelance editors and helps you achieve your vision of the book you wanted to write. It's aimed primarily at self-publishers because they're the writers who have to cope without the support network of a traditional publishing house, but many of the techniques suggested are equally applicable to those writers who intend to pursue the traditional agent/publisher route. These days, publishers and agents want, more often than not, a finished product—something they can deliver immediately. The closer your draft is to a finished product, the easier the decision for an agent to agree to represent you, and the more receptive a publisher is going to be to the idea of publishing you.

Many books on writing include editing as part of the creative process. This isn't how the process works in the traditional publishing model, where the publisher edits your book. Their team of professional editors is objective, acting as advocate for the reader, moulding what they regard as raw material into something that readers will like, that will sell. Critically, they are not interested in creating anything—they are refining what is already there. The creation of the story is quite removed from the editing of it.

In the self-publishing model the author is trying to be both things, creator *and* editor, which is the reason that many self-published books end up as a bit of a muddled mess. Approaching self-editing in the structured way that this book suggests might help writers get to grips with this difficult task.

The book is in three parts. Part I is an introduction to the concept of self-editing as a separate process: when your book is ready for self-editing, how to prepare yourself and your manuscript (abbreviated to "MS" in this book), an overview of the process, and when to know you're done.

Part II of the book focuses on the big issues in a novel, such as character, plot and pacing. It's a chatty, informal section, designed to be read rather than studied—these are conceptual issues. This is editing, not writing, so the aim is to look a little more analytically at your writing and see possible flaws in the plot and characters that you've created. Each section will summarise the modern thinking on that subject, followed by things to look for in your own work. It includes a section on memoir writing—elaborating on which of the fiction structural issues can be applied to a memoir, and which can be ignored.

Part III is more detailed, analysing problems at a sentence by sentence level, recognising them and correcting them. This part can be read but is designed also to be used as a reference section. There are many rules and guidelines that apply to writing even the most straightforward fiction. Professional editors have textbooks to hand and constantly refer to them. As an author, you don't need to try and memorise the *Chicago Manual of Style* (for American authors, seventeen editions and counting, around 1,200 pages of *very* small print), or even the more concise but equally dry *New Hart's Rules* (the British English writer's equivalent guide). This part of the book aims to be *a style guide for fiction*, if you like: a useful compendium of the most common mistakes, questions and queries that I've come across in the course of editing countless books, hosting a couple of popular writers' websites, and moderating several author groups on social media.

What is the aim of this book?

This book describes a key stage in the creation of a book that's often either overlooked by writing classes and "how to write" books, or treated as part of the general creative process. This isn't right, and I'll explain why. I think this significant failure to understand a key element in the creation of a book is one of the main reasons a high percentage of self-published books are commercial failures, and why most authors wishing to traditionally publish fail to get signed. That key element is self-editing.

Who is this book for?

This book is for anyone looking to publish, be it non-fiction, memoir, genre fiction or the highest highbrow literary masterpiece. It is expressly aimed at the vast majority of authors in this digital age who choose to go it alone and self-publish, but the material and methods described will hugely assist authors looking to go down the traditional route of agent and publisher, and could make all the difference between getting a deal and languishing in the slush pile. Much of the focus is on fiction, but the general principles of the method suggested here for achieving objective distance from your work apply equally to non-fiction. The style guide to punctuation and sentence construction in Part III is intended as a useful concise reference guide for all writers.

What exactly is self-editing?

Self-editing is the process of looking at your book as a reader (or an agent or publisher) will, being able to assess its flaws clearly, and having the ability to correct those problems that to you as author were utterly invisible. Being able to look at your work objectively is an extremely difficult skill to master, but this book will give you proven techniques on how to achieve that objectivity, and then describe a structured approach to the process of correcting the flaws you discover.

What this book isn't

This isn't a "how to write" book. It won't tell you "how to write a bestseller" or "how to write epic fantasy," because those things can't be "taught" in the way that, say, French irregular verbs can be taught. It won't tell you how to avoid "writer's block" (although it will tell you a common cause of that problem and how to avoid it). It will, however, vastly improve your writing, making it tighter, more focused, gripping, empathetic and believable.

How to use this book

Read the book all the way through from beginning to end. This will give you a thorough understanding of the process of self-editing: when you need it, how to do it and when you can consider the process finished.

When the time comes to self-edit your book, read through Part II again. You'll now be able to look at your characters with a fresh understanding, be able to see how they might be made stronger, more empathetic. You'll be able to look at your plot more analytically, recognise the pacing problem with that dull bit in the middle, understand why you feel like skipping scenes at certain points. You'll have a set of guidelines to rewrite these problem areas to make them more compelling and entertaining.

When you're happy with the story, you can work through your MS on the fine details, using Part III as a reference guide. How much detail you'll want to go into on this pass through the MS is up to you, but if you applied everything in Part III to your MS, you'd have a very tidy and well-written book of a standard that's head-and-shoulders above a lot of self-published work, and top of the heap in an agent's or publisher's submission pile.

Before we begin

Many authors use Microsoft Word as an electronic typewriter, but it's actually a much more powerful tool than that, and professional editors use a raft of functions that "amateur" users probably don't know exist. There are other writing software packages out there, but none come even close to the power and editing flexibility that Word does. (Apple, a company famous for being extremely defensive about their proprietary hardware and software, have tacitly acknowledged this by allowing a Word for Mac version to run on their machines.) Because of that, most professional editors use Word, and a lot of them won't countenance working on some other software package. If you do engage an editor, they will almost certainly want a Word doc to work on, and the work they do, in editing and commenting on your manuscript, may well not survive a conversion process back to some other software.

Another result of this market dominance is that you will find, when the time comes, that a Word document will interface very easily with design and formatting applications like InDesign or Vellum, whereas there may well be glitches with newer, less-proven packages like Google Docs.

There's nothing stopping you writing in your own software package, but be aware that at some point in the process you will probably need to look at a Word doc version of your book. It will pay to be familiar with that software even if you don't use it on a day-to-day basis while writing.

I will make the occasional reference to some of the more advanced features available on Word in this book. I can't anticipate every piece of writing software other than Word that people might use, so if I reference a function that's available in Word but not in your software of choice, apologies, but take it up with the programmers of your chosen software—don't complain to me!

Notes on the text

This book is written in a kind of mid-Atlantic style, as a nod to readership on both sides of "the pond." I use mostly UK spelling conventions and vocabulary, but consciously tried to avoid usages that were particularly idiomatic.

In terms of punctuation conventions I've used a mix that appeals to me personally. I use the US convention on quotes (double quotes, other punctuation inside quotes) for example, but I don't use the serial (or "Oxford") comma unless it's needed for clarity. By the time you've finished this book you will be able to identify the differences in style available between US and UK writers, and also understand the various alternatives open to you.

Acknowledgements

For a profession who generally work alone, sitting at a desk, editors are a remarkably helpful, supportive and convivial bunch. Many people have helped me in my editing career with advice and guidance, particularly the crowd at EAE Backroom over on Facebook, tolerating my dumb questions and weird sense of humour.

Among the people who helped specifically with this book, critiquing, beta reading, copyediting and proofing, I'd like to give particular thanks to: Sarah Anderson, Amanda Berthault, Hannah Close, Diana Dexter, Lynda Dietz, Judi Heidel, Kimberley Hunt, Andrew Pelechaty, Jennifer Warren, and a special mention to Kia Thomas, who went beyond the call of duty.

Any remaining errors, after all that editorial input, are my own!

Dedicated to Joan, Finn and Laragh – my tribe

PART I: THE CONCEPT OF SELF-EDITING

Self-editing

The majority of writing classes and the multitude of books on writing craft usually concentrate their advice on the initial creation of a book: where to find inspiration, how to create empathetic and believable characters, how to plot, how many words a day you should write. Once you've got to the end of your book, their job is done and you're on your own.

Finishing a book is definitely a very satisfying moment. You feel great, and so you should. It's a wonderful achievement to have completed a full-length work. Many try. Few succeed. Desk drawers and computer hard drives are full of half-completed novels the world over.

The trouble is that many first-time authors don't realise that when you type "The End" on the final page of your first draft, you haven't *finished* at all—the process of writing the book is far from over at that point. It's completely normal to rewrite many drafts of the same MS, especially if you're new to writing, but we live in a world of immediate satisfaction. Writing a book may have been the single most complex and concentrated task you've ever undertaken, equivalent in time and mental energy to completing a degree course. You've had to make sacrifices—perhaps given up some commitments to family time or social life. Having now got to the end, you want results. People ask whether you've finished your book, and when you say you have, they want to read it.

Additionally, there's an unfortunate emphasis in some writing circles on speed—write your book in a month, have a quick read through, and then stick it on Amazon as an ebook the following month. Bingo! You're a published author. Write the next book. Write a series. The more books you write in a year, the bigger chance you have of making money. It's as if by flooding the market you can drown out all the other authors, and get readers to buy your book instead of the hundreds of thousands of others that are published each year. In contrast, the idea of going over and over the same book—revising, changing, rewriting—doesn't carry anywhere near the same magic as seeing the word count steadily grow on a new project. Writing is fun, creative, exciting; editing is hard work.

Ernest Hemingway famously said, "All first drafts are shit." Perhaps he was being a little melodramatic, but not even many bestselling authors can bang out a draft straight off, send it to their publisher for a quick tidy up and then publish immediately. If they do, dare I say it usually shows? The book is likely to be generic and not particularly original or compelling—in short, formulaic. There's lots of money to be made by accomplished authors writing to a formula but the chances are, if you've picked this book up, you're not an accomplished author, or you haven't found a formula that works, yet.

For you to rush to publish that first draft as soon as you've finished it and get on with the next book might seem a good idea, but may I suggest it rarely is. If you publish a first draft, it's likely that there will be mistakes. (As a rough idea, most average length novels I do a first copyedit on have between five and ten **thousand** corrections. Yes, you did read those numbers right. Some of those will be almost invisible to the average reader—two spaces instead of one after punctuation, for example—but many hundreds will be glaring and obvious.) Readers who pay even a little money for your book will write scathing reviews about poor punctuation, bad grammar, nonsensical plots and unbelievable characters. Those reviews will be there forever, putting other potential readers off your writing. Far from forging a career as a writer, you might have done a good job of shooting yourself in the foot.

So what is the process that changes that rough first attempt into the polished jewel that is your final draft? That process is called self-editing. This book sets out a structured approach to self-editing, one that replicates, as closely as possible, what would happen to your MS if you were working with a traditional publisher and the team of editors they would use to fine-tune your novel. I'll explain the process from start to finish, giving tips and techniques on how to self-edit and showing you what kinds of problems you're looking for and how to correct them, so that at the end you can feel confident that your book is the best you can make it.

Firstly, a word about editors

You might ask, why is a professional editor writing a book about self-editing? Surely he's putting himself and all his colleagues out of business? Not really. Go back and read the last line of the previous page again. "The best you can make it"? Does that sound a little underwhelming? What about "The best that it can be"? That, I'm afraid, is simply not possible on your own. The process of self-editing creates your final draft, the version of your book that is as complete and polished as you can make it alone. In order for it to be the *best book that it can be*, it would need to have another pair of eyes on it—an editor, in other words.

It comes as a shock to newcomers, but writing is a collaborative art form. Every successful novelist has an editor. Stephen King has an editor. J. K. Rowling has an editor. Clive Cussler, Annie Proulx, John Irving, Murakami, George Martin. These are all accomplished writers, entirely capable of writing a book that will sell in the millions. Why do they have editors, then? Because it's impossible to see all the faults in our own work. In fact, it's surprising what you can miss; the eye sees what the mind wants it to see. We are often too close to our work to see holes in the plot and inconsistencies in the narrative. In the process of revision, names may get changed, scenes shuffled around, minor and even sometimes major plot points cut. If you're too familiar with the book, you may not notice that when you changed the main character's house from a detached house in the suburbs to an apartment in a city-centre high-rise, there is a scene halfway through the book where a cat jumps in at the kitchen window—quite an achievement if the apartment is twenty floors up.

At a detailed level, we glide over missing words, our brain filling them in automatically. We may be oblivious to the fact that we're misusing a word, so no matter how many times we read it we won't pick up that it's an error. An ambiguity of sentence structure might not be apparent to us, because we know what we mean, but it might be utterly confusing to someone who doesn't know the story.

Most books published these days are self-published, and it is self-publishers who have to cope without the support structure of a traditional publisher (hence the focus of this book). In our eagerness to self-publish, it's very easy to throw the baby out with the bathwater. In dispensing with the traditional model of agent and publisher and royalties, we forget that publishers did do something other than just sell our book for us—they actually helped refine it. Perhaps four different editors would get involved in the production of a book, acquisition (or commissioning), substantive, copyeditor and proofreader. They would all have some say in the final work, so the idea of a solitary writer slaving away in a garret and *bing*, a masterpiece is born, ready to publish, is just nonsense.

"Okay then. If I'm going to need an editor anyway, why do I need to bother with self-editing?" Saving money, primarily.

> *The more work an editor has to do, the longer the job will take and the more they will need to charge.*

The most time-consuming and expensive type of editing is called developmental (or substantive) editing. It's a fantastic experience (or at least, it is with the right editor), and I would always recommend to a novice author that they get one developmental edit early in their career—it can pay enormous dividends with their future writing journey. But it shouldn't be something that you necessarily need with every subsequent book you ever write.

Developmental editing can cost thousands. It goes deep into the structure of the book, how the plot hangs together, the development of characters, pacing, the handling of conflict, point of view (PoV) and so on. For a novice writer whose first attempts have serious flaws, that could be perfect. They might need guidance as to how to plot; they might have too many characters; they might need help understanding how PoV works, or the balance between action and exposition. But if you have a book that is already well-written, doesn't contain any significant plot problems, is well-paced, and has clear and compelling character arcs, then an editor won't need to get involved in those issues.

If you go through Part II of this book applying what I'm going to show you so that your plot flows smoothly, the characters are well-rounded and developed, PoV is consistent and pacing is great, then you may not need any developmental editing. In short, self-editing can save you money.

The same goes for subsequent rounds of editing: the copyediting and proofreading stages. If you work through Part III of this book it will help you eliminate a lot of the technical problems that a copyeditor or proofreader then won't have to fix. Most editors charge by the hour, effectively, so if your MS is very "clean," leaving the editor only minor changes to make, they will charge you less.

There's one more question that frequently pops up about editors, and that's miss-rates.

Miss-rates

"I decided to self-edit because editors still get things wrong. I've seen edited books with errors in them, so editors won't make my book perfect. Why should I pay for an editor when I might still find mistakes in my finished book?" Editors aren't machines. There's what's called an acceptable "miss" rate in publishing, on the grounds of efficiency and cost. Let me explain it in a series of steps.

An author contracts with a freelance editor to copyedit their finished manuscript of 120,000 words. The editor's fee, for the sake of argument, is $1,500—the book needs a fair bit of editorial intervention. The editor works away and delivers the copyedited MS back to their client, with 8,000 amendments and alterations. (That is by no means an unusual number of amendments on that length a manuscript, as I've already mentioned, but it will include relatively inconsequential things like two spaces instead of one at the end of a sentence.) In terms of corrections and the editor's fee, that works out at 12.5 cents an error.

The author goes away and works on their book, and comes back for a final proofread. The editor quotes a price of $800 for the proofread, and delivers the edited MS some weeks later, with 400 errors for the author to correct (note that it isn't necessary for an author to go through these one by one!), some of which would have been things missed in the copyedit, some of which will have been new mistakes introduced by the author when revising. The standard "miss-rate" talked about in publishing is 5%. That means there might be as many as twenty errors still remaining in the MS. Some of those errors won't be visible to anyone but an editor, but a few of those twenty errors could well be typos or duplicated words that should have been picked up. Who knows why they weren't? Perhaps, as the editor was reading that page, the doorbell rang, and when they came back to their work they skipped a line. In efficiency terms, although the proofread was much cheaper than the copyedit, the error-cost has grown to $2 per error, a sixteenfold increase.

The author notices one of the twenty remaining errors, complains that their manuscript isn't perfect like they expected it to be and wants another proofreading pass, from the same or perhaps a different editor. That editor will also charge a similar fee—let's say $800—they do their proofreading pass and they pick up 95% of the remaining twenty errors. The cost for finding those nineteen errors is now an astronomical $42 per error, and there's still at least one error remaining in the book. Perhaps $42 per error might sound realistic to someone looking for as close to perfection as they can get, but if you extrapolated that error-cost back to the first pass copyedit, the copyediting fee would have been $336,000, which is a *little* steep.

At some point in the process, a book is as close to being perfect as it needs to be. Only the author (or the publisher) can decide when that point has been reached and further passes of editing would be too expensive to warrant the investment. In the scenario above, the author has spent over $3,000 on editing their book, and there's still an error in it. It might well be that no one will ever notice it. It might also be the case that the error is on page one and one of your first readers notices it and points it out in their review. That's called Murphy's Law. In an ebook you can quietly go in and alter the file. In a print edition, unfortunately, you can only laugh it off.

One final point: I'm aware that some writers will use this book as a substitute for commissioning professional editing of any kind. That's fine. Some writers just can't afford third-party editing and are prepared to accept that their book won't be as good as it might be. That's fine too. Writing should be an inclusive art form, not only open to those with deep pockets. If you work though this book, subject by subject, you will have a book that, although it might be flawed, you can still be proud of. But I will say this just once. If you want your book to be *the best that it can be*, then you will need to employ an editor at some stage, however diligently you follow the advice of this book.

Is self-editing different from writing?

Yes. Thanks for asking. You've just hit the nail on the head, and the reason why this book is called what it is, rather than yet another "how to write" book. When you write, you're the author. It's the story inside your head that needs to get put into words. When you self-edit, you're trying to look at your book as a reader. This is what a professional editor does. Although an editor is employed by the writer, they are an advocate for the reader, telling the writer what's wrong with the book from the *reader's* likely perspective.

"Okay, no biggie. I'm just going to pretend I'm a reader."

Ah, but it's not that easy. You can't just pretend that you're a reader, because you *did* write the book. You know all the characters. They speak with your words, act out your scenes. You might know things about your characters that your readers will never find out (I hope so—more on the "iceberg principle" later). You might know what is going to happen to that character in books two and three and four of the series.

A crucial prelude to self-editing is getting out of the mindset of the writer and getting into that of a reader—essentially looking at the text with fresh eyes.

> *The secret to editing your work is simple. You need to become its reader instead of its writer. (Zadie Smith)*

If it were possible to forget you'd ever written the book, you'd be in a great position to self-edit it.

The self-editing mindset

So how do we try and achieve this, this forgetting we ever wrote the book in the first place? We need to make the MS as unfamiliar to ourselves as possible. There are quite a few practical ways of doing this, some of which will work better than others for different individuals.

Time

Perhaps the most simple and easily accomplished method is to put some time between finishing writing the draft and beginning the edit. Books are written very much in the moment. As writers our writing style tends to evolve over time, both with the increased mastery of our craft that comes with experience, and with the lives we live. We have experiences that colour the story we've written. We are part of a civilisation that goes through regular social and political upheavals. A book that you might write at the beginning of one year will not be quite the same as if you had started at the beginning of the following year. Personal life intrudes. A book written when you're single might have a rather grim and gloomy tone. Fast forward two years and you're happily married and the story might have a much more positive feel (it might also be completely the opposite way round, but the less said about that ...!).

So put your first draft away in a drawer and forget about it.

"For how long?"

A year.

"A *year*? I can't leave it a year!"

Well, Jane Austen used to literally lock away her first drafts in a drawer and give a friend the key, with strict instructions only to let her have it back after twelve months had passed.

But okay, six months then. I can guarantee that when you take your MS out after six months to a year of doing other things, you will look at it in a new light. However much you thought it was just perfect when you put it away, there will be sentences on the very first page that stand out as awkward, descriptions that you realise are clichéd, dialogue that you suddenly realise sounds wooden. You might have fallen out of love with one character and realised that another character is considerably more interesting than you thought. Although you might not feel it, you've changed as a writer.

But it needs some time to get to this state of perception—a couple of weeks are rarely sufficient. A couple of months would be a bare minimum—really, six months for a significant change.

"I can't not write for six months!"

Whoever said you couldn't? One of the best things to do while letting that first draft sit maturing in your subconscious (you'll never really forget about it, and it's absolutely fine that your subconscious is beavering away anyway—that's where all the best writing comes from) is to write another book, either the sequel to this one, or, even better, a completely different book. This both occupies your mind and keeps your writing "muscle" exercised.

Format

Looking at the draft in a physically different format can be a great help. If you can manage it, print your book off and read it in hardcopy. If it's a 200,000-word fantasy epic, that might not be practical (congratulations—you've just found out why 200,000-word fantasy epics are not too popular with publishers either). But you could experiment with font sizes or line spacing to compress the book as much as possible so that it's still legible but a lot less of a page count (you're going to need to make notes though, so *too* condensed is just not going to be practical).

If you want to be very thorough, why not get a single copy printed off by an online printer? There are dozens of firms who will take a file and create a book out of it for you. Seeing the work in book format will almost certainly throw up a whole raft of changes you'll want to make.

If you want to keep it electronic, even just changing the font or font size might be a good jolt to the brain, bumping you out of the familiar. Change the text to "justified" from "left-aligned" (or vice versa) to make lines split at different words (many simple copyediting mistakes are concealed "in plain sight" at the end of a line). Change the document to display in landscape format, rather than portrait. Read it on a different device. If you composed it on a laptop, read it on a desktop. If you're ambitious, download the text into a different app, or convert the file to a basic e-reader file and read it on your e-reader/kindle (the only problem with this is that you won't be able to edit the actual e-reader file, only highlight areas that you want to check on your actual manuscript).

Audio

Some people set great store by listening to their book being read out, using proprietary audiobook software. That should certainly catch incorrect word usage, missing words or poor sentence construction, but it might not catch missing or incorrect punctuation, and won't necessarily point out some of the more "big picture" issues like character development or point of view problems.

Place

It can also help to remove yourself physically from the environment you wrote the book in. Take it on holiday. Go and stay at a friend's place. Do a house swap in some exotic location. Sit in a public library, or, if they'll tolerate you, a local coffee shop. If none of these are viable alternatives, just try and avoid sitting at the same desk in the same room at home.

Summary

Let's quickly recap. There are four simple ways of trying to achieve that objectivity about your manuscript that is so important to self-editing.

The most important is time. Give yourself time to forget the exact details of your book, what each character does in every scene. You won't forget the entire plot, or the ending, but you might forget scenes that you realise are ... well ... forgettable. That's a good hint in itself that something in that scene might need tweaking.

Place is a luxury that not everyone has, but think creatively about where you might get a different perspective. One playwright I know writes his plays at his desk but does all his editing in bed.

Formatting is just trickery, but it does work. Seeing your work in a different layout or font, or on a different screen or even hardcopy, can fool your mind into thinking that it is looking at a different script.

And audio is really just another formatting option, but appeals to some writers who set a great deal of store by how their work sounds, as well as how it reads.

When is the book ready to self-edit?

So do you start self-editing as soon as you've typed "The End" for the first time? Well, no, not if you remember the advice about leaving some time between finishing the writing and starting the editing. But more importantly, that very first version (I won't even honour it with the title of draft) is likely, unless you're a very experienced novelist, to be rather raw and rough around the edges. It's quite likely that you will need to redraft, cutting some scenes, even some characters, adding other material. This is a book still in its creation phase.

"Hang on. I'm *redrafting* here, not self-editing? What's the difference?"

It's a subtle difference. While redrafting, or revising, or rewriting, whatever you want to call it, you are still in the *creative* phase of the book. Most established authors would do at least a couple of rounds of rewriting before they considered they'd got a finished first draft. It's only then that they would put the MS away in that drawer to start the self-editing process.

The first time you get to "The End," I would advise leaving some time before going back to your completed work and rereading it. It's exactly the same concept as that gap that you're going to leave before finishing your first draft proper and moving on to self-editing, except that here the idea isn't to forget about the book, just to give your mind some perspective on it.

If you've left the book a couple of weeks, or a month, when you go back to it you'll already see things that you could improve, areas where the pace slows, scenes that you could perhaps leave out. This is rewriting, not self-editing. You're just as likely to be adding scenes, fleshing out characters and giving more background, as cutting scenes, deleting subplots and eradicating needless exposition.

The self-editing process should begin when the majority of the creative work is done. Remember that difference in mindset between writing and editing?

> *You don't want to be trying to create when you're trying to correct.*

(The reverse is equally true—you don't want to be trying to correct when you're trying to create.) The first draft should be your completed story, all scenes written from beginning to end, plot resolved, journey accomplished. As far as you're concerned, *writing* the book is now finished.

Don't start to self-edit as a method of jump-starting a rewrite. You don't want to be trying to create fresh material, at a full scene level, when you're editing. The odd sentence is fine, perhaps a rewritten piece of dialogue, but you want to be trying to refine what's already there, not write new material, when you're self-editing.

"But it's not cut and dried, is it?"

No, it isn't. Nothing in writing is cut and dried. What happens if you *think* that the book is finished and you start your self-editing and realise that a whole chapter—or even worse, character—doesn't really work and needs to be rewritten? It happens, particularly with new writers, and you've just got to get on with it. Part of the experience that writing a lot of books gives you is that you're better able to identify what doesn't work earlier in the writing process so that when you come to start work self-editing your first full draft, you won't get nasty shocks like this. But if you're new to the writing process you're more likely to discover things about your book that you really don't like when you come to self-edit. It might be that you identify that the point of view is too distant, or that you're consistently telling instead of showing, and that to correct these flaws is going to necessitate rewriting large chunks of the book. Don't be disheartened. By going through this iterative process, every version of this book is going to be better, and in every subsequent book you write you're probably going to avoid making those mistakes in the first place.

The idea that you write an excellent first draft and then self-edit a few minor problems out of it to produce your perfect final draft is the paradigm you're aiming to achieve. In practice, the process is often much messier than that—be adaptable—but keep in mind that, in a perfect world, the self-editing process should be as discrete from the actual writing of the book as you can make it. You've written the book all the way through to the end. You've left it for a while, then reread it, changed a few things, added some bits, deleted other bits, reread it again. Perhaps it's ready? Lock it away. Forget about it. Lose yourself in the new job/summer holidays/major DIY project. Your book will be ready to self-edit when you get back.

What is the self-editing process?

In this book I suggest approaching self-editing in a reasonably structured way, replicating the workflow of a publisher's editing team as closely as possible. That's the way publishing has worked for centuries—why rock the boat? When you become adept at self-editing, or you're an experienced novelist with many successful books under your belt, you might be able to go through your MS in one pass and pick up most of the problems with it as you go. However, I suggest breaking it down into a three-stage process because I think it's easier to manage, especially if you're new to the concept. Although I suggest that there are three discrete stages, bear in mind that in practice there will most likely be several reiterations of the same stage before you can move on to the next, so we could be talking five or six or more passes through the book.

So, it's been a year (or six months at least) since you last did any major revisions of the text. You've settled in at your new job, or are back from the summer holidays with a tan, or are sitting in your new home-office that you converted from the old pig-shed. You're eager to begin.

The first stage: overview

Read-through

The first stage of the self-editing process is to just read your book, as a reader would do, from beginning to end. You are trying to get an overall feel for the book as a whole. If it's non-fiction, does it get the message that you wanted to deliver across? If it's fiction, is it a compelling story? Do you find yourself immersed in the book, or did you find yourself thrown by certain phrases, or plot points, or sentences where the meaning was unclear? Did you find yourself getting bored or confused? How keen were you to read on and finish the book?

A good idea is to have a highlighter pen (if you're reading in hardcopy) or the highlighter function in Word at the ready. Any moment at which you stop reading, or find yourself going back and reading a sentence or a paragraph again (apart from a conscious decision for a toilet break or something), highlight that passage. That's what I call later a "sentence stumble." There's something in that passage that has caused confusion, or has thrown you out of the story enough for you to think, "I'll just pause here while I put the kettle on." It might not even be obvious to you what the problem is at this stage but, in later rounds of editing, with the tools from this book that will be at your disposal, you can focus on these passages and establish exactly why your reader experience faltered at that point.

This read-through should give you a good general overview of where you might need to make some revisions, even if you don't know exactly what form those revisions will yet take. It will also have given you a reminder of what the book is actually about. It's a good idea to write this down, in what the industry calls a synopsis.

Summarise—write a synopsis

So what book have you actually written? If it's non-fiction, the answer to that question should be obvious. Perhaps it's a self-help book, or an instructional on a particular craft or hobby. The purpose and "mission statement" of the book should be laid out very clearly, early on. In the introduction to this book, for example, I state what the aim of the book is, who it's for, what it's about and how to use it.

If it's fiction, you might have also thought the answer to this question was going to be obvious, but it might be that now you've sat back and let some time pass, you suddenly see a whole new facet of your book that you hadn't considered before.

It may have been that you started off convinced you were intending to write a romance, but when you reread it you realise you've actually written a much darker book about the abuse of power in relationships. You may have started off thinking you were writing a crime thriller, but funny lines and situations kept coming to you and now you realise you've written a comedy.

This is the first stage of your understanding of your book *as a reader*. You're not the writer any more. You're assuming the role of a reader. What kind of reader is going to pick your book up? What are they looking at when they see the title, and look at the cover, and read the blurb on the back? If they do buy your book, based on the concept you've sold them, are they going to be satisfied? Satisfied readers come back for more. Satisfied readers recommend your book to their friends and write great reviews.

When you start editing, it's important to understand what kind of book you've written, because the answers to a number of questions that you'll be asking yourself, to do with length, voice, plot complexity and so on, will depend on your understanding of what your book *is*.

> *Crucial to being able to sell your book to readers who will enjoy it is understanding the book you've written.*

So how would you summarise your book? Are there aspects to it that you hadn't realised you were expressing when you were writing it? Is your overall impression now, as a reader, that the book is much more nihilistic/funny/romantic when reading it than you thought it would turn out to be? In order to summarise your book, I recommend writing a synopsis.. This is an extremely useful document that, should you decide to try the traditional route of agent and publisher, you will need anyway. In Appendix I you'll find detailed instructions on how to write a synopsis. I suggest, if you haven't written one, to go off and have a try round about now.

If you haven't got a synopsis, or tried to write one and failed, *don't panic*. It is one of the hardest things to do, and if you just can't manage it, then you can still move on. Even trying to write down the most rudimentary summary of your book will have encouraged you to think about your writing in a slightly different way, an analytical viewpoint closer to that of a reader than a writer, which is what you wanted to achieve. If you have got a synopsis, then great. The second stage of self-editing is the big-picture perspective, and you'll refer to your synopsis quite a lot during this stage.

The second stage: big picture

The big-picture stage of self-editing corresponds to the developmental editing I mentioned before, where an editor goes deep into the structure of your book, looks at the resolution of conflict in character arcs, looks at the pacing, weighs up the balance of minor characters and subplots to the main thrust of the book and so on.

This is where, if there are problems to be found, they could well necessitate substantial rewriting. Are there sections that drag? Why do they drag? Can you perform some simple, brutal surgery and cut those sections out? If not, if they fulfil some purpose in the story, then what purpose is that, exactly, and can it be expressed more succinctly?

How many characters are in the book? If you had to make this into a movie or a TV mini-series, how many actors would you have to employ? (A bit early to dream about movie adaptations, perhaps, but no harm thinking about it!) Do you need all those characters? Particularly important is the number of characters whose point of view we get to share. These are characters that you are expecting the reader to make an emotional investment in. Can a reader realistically keep all those characters' stories in their head, and will they want to? In some genres, particularly epic sci-fi or fantasy, a large ensemble cast is appropriate. In romance, however, it would be peculiar to ask the reader to empathise with more than three or four characters at most.

What point of view do you use in the book? Do you have a very distant "narrator" style, or are you immersed in the action in a very close first-person perspective? (I'll explain all these terms in the point-of-view section in Part II and in detail in Appendix II.) What's more appropriate for the story?

If you've written non-fiction, is the message or method you intend to promote or explain clearly stated? Is there a logical sequence to the chapters? Do the conclusions you come to arise naturally from the text?

All these issues are, if you like, the skeleton of the book, the bone-structure on which the flesh of the story hangs. Without a skeleton, the book would be a puddle on the floor. With a misshaped skeleton, the book might have seventeen legs (too many characters), or no head (lack of a central theme). If the skeleton is too distorted the book is going to require major surgery, but to extend the skeletal allegory, it's much easier to amputate than it is to graft more limbs on. This is why you shouldn't worry too much that your first draft is messy and over-written. It's much easier to cut material than compose new.

The third stage: detailed level

The third stage of self-editing is to look at your book on a sentence-level, word-by-word basis. This corresponds to the copyediting stage of a professional editor's workflow. You've fixed everything there is to fix about the book's structure. You have a central theme; you have a few well-developed characters whose stories are immersive and engaging, supported by a cast of minor characters and subplots that keep the book ticking over. Pacing is good, quickening to climaxes, slowing for contrast in other sections, and point of view and language are consistent.

Now is the time to start at the detailed level. Now you're looking at every word, every sentence. Is that the right word? Is there a better way of expressing that thought? Could you say this more vividly?

What you're looking for here are problems that might throw the reader out of a scene, that make them become aware that they are reading a book. Your aim should always be to get your reader immersed in your story, so much so that they miss their stop on the bus, or their toast burns. Anything that throws them out of that immersion needs to be ditched.

Other complications might be dialogue, where there are too many "he said, she said" exchanges, or situations in a multi-part conversation where it might not be obvious who is talking. There are few things more irritating when reading than losing track of a conversation and having to spend time working out who said what.

"Why couldn't I do all this detailed work at the same time as the big-picture pass—save myself some time?" you might be wondering. Professional editors always separate these tasks, and there are two good reasons.

You can't concentrate properly on big-picture problems if you're also concentrating on picking up spelling mistakes and correcting punctuation errors. Judging whether a character arc comes to an emotionally satisfying conclusion requires a distant, holistic perspective. Making sure that every opening quote has a matching closing quote requires a completely different, intense focus. Metaphorically, it's as if one task requires you to be holding the book at arm's length, while the other requires your nose to be almost touching the pages.

The second reason is a purely practical one. There's no point checking text for spelling mistakes and punctuation problems if you're going to be cutting it anyway. You'll save yourself real time, and effort, if you only start on the detailed editing when you're pretty sure that all the remaining text is going to feature in your final draft.

When is the process over?

When have you finished the self-editing process? It's a valid question, because you can edit forever. Editing a book is like that maths conundrum—if every step you take halves the distance to your destination, you'll never actually arrive. You can continually tweak an MS—perfection isn't possible—and sometimes it can be difficult to know when to stop. If you're self-publishing, in particular, there is no third party who gently prises your MS from your clutching fingers and says, "It's ready. Let it go." How can you be sure that you've done enough? The answer is that there is no answer (this is an irritatingly common response to many questions about writing). When you're experienced you'll know, intuitively, when you've done as much as you can with an MS. There's a law of diminishing returns that means that on every pass over an MS, you change less and less (like the editor I mentioned earlier who was looking for errors). There are fewer objective mistakes to find and correct and there are fewer subjective decisions to be made that you haven't already thought about.

At that point, the only way forwards is to get it out there to other people. That might be a professional editor, or, if you're not going down that route, it might be beta readers. Either will give you feedback, based on their own perspectives, on any problems they can see with your book. The professional editor will have the most unbiased and objective viewpoint, and also should be able to give you advice on how to fix the problems they do identify, but that advice will cost money. Some beta readers charge a fee, but many don't. They are not professionally trained and they will bring their own biases and predilections to their critique of your book. Unless they're very good, the points they raise might even be objectively incorrect, or questionably subjective opinion that you'd do better to ignore, but they are a second opinion.

The response from editor or beta reader is going to give you a reasonable idea of whether your book needs more work. For a more in-depth look at hiring beta readers, how to hire them, what to look for, what questions to ask them, and how to assess the feedback that you get, read Appendix IV: Beta readers, uses and misuses.

That's the end of this introduction to the subject of self-editing. It should have helped you understand a few things that are necessary to appreciate the rest of the book.

- You should understand what self-editing is, and why it's a very necessary part of producing a final draft.
- You should understand when in the writing process it takes place (but also be aware that it's not always a clear-cut process, and that boundaries between writing, rewriting and self-editing can blur).
- You should know how to prepare yourself and your MS for the self-editing stage (this might take trial and error, to see what works most efficiently for you).
- You should understand that if you can apply all the methods and techniques in the

> following chapters to your MS, you'll likely have a very good final draft. For many self-publishers, that's as good as they need, even though it might fall short of what the publishing industry would call a finished product.

We can now create a template for all the workflows described in the previous sections:

- Write a complete book
    - Leave for two or three weeks
    - Read through and rewrite
    - (repeat these steps as many times as you feel necessary)
- Prepare your rewritten first draft for self-editing
    - Leave for four to six months, even a year
    - Reformat and/or
    - Create an audio file and/or
    - Find a new place to work on it
- Self-edit your first draft
    - Write a synopsis
    - Do a big-picture pass
    - Rewrite
    - (repeat these two steps as many times as you feel necessary)
    - Do a detailed-level pass
    - Make corrections
    - (repeat these two steps as many times as you feel necessary)

- Give to an editor for editing, or a beta reader for story feedback.

Let's get started!

PART II: THE BIG PICTURE

Big picture elements

It's time to start working on your MS. You've read it through already, to remind yourself of what it's about, to get a feel for the general impression it gives the reader. Now you're reading it again, this time much more slowly, with a pencil in hand, or fingers on the keyboard.

In this first editing pass we're not looking for punctuation errors or spelling mistakes (although if there's a glaring error you might want to correct it—less to do later on in the process). We're looking at the story as a whole, to see how it hangs together. That initial rush of inspiration six months or a year ago should have faded, and now we're looking at the book as a reader might.

As you get more experienced in self-editing, you might be able to address all the issues in Part II—plot, character, pacing, point of view and so on—at the same time. If you're new to the process however, you might find it easier to focus on one or two issues only per read-through.

When talking about these big-picture story elements, I often reference films rather than books. You might think this an odd choice, since I'm talking about writing, not film-craft, but there are a few reasons.

Firstly, films share some fundamental qualities with books—story structure, character arcs, plot, pacing—that make analysis of them a useful tool to apply when trying to understand the structural elements of a successful novel.

Secondly, on a more practical note, there are a lot fewer films made than books written, so there's a good chance that you have seen and are familiar with a film I'm referencing, whereas you might not be familiar with a particular text (don't be worried, literary purists—you'll find examples drawn from Kafka as well). In that way the point I'm getting across is immediately obvious, rather than requiring you to go and get a book and read it to understand fully what I'm talking about. (There's the further related consideration that, if you're not familiar with a film I mention, then it's only an investment of perhaps an hour and a half of your time to get familiar with it, rather than invest the days or weeks it might take you to get through a 500-page novel.)

Book structure

Before we get in to the detail of plot and character there are some questions that come up time and time again about the practical structure of a book: the necessity of chapters, what length chapters should be, prologues and why they're commonly demonised in writing advice and so on. Let's start with prologues.

Prologues

In recent years prologues have developed a very bad reputation. There is a time and a place for prologues—they're a perfectly valid literary device—but most prologues written by first-time authors aren't necessary. Instead, they're used for all sorts of nefarious and dastardly practices. They can be "info dumps," where the author laboriously "sets the scene" for the coming story. They can be "false beginnings," where the author, mindful of being told to start with some action, drags a fight or an explosion or a car-chase from somewhere else in the story and makes it the beginning (meanwhile leaving the awfully dull chapter one still in place). Perhaps the worst misuse is describing a dream sequence, which is usually a vain attempt to create some mystery in what is otherwise (the author knows and is desperately concerned about) a rather dull and prosaic book.

What should *a prologue be used for?*

Probably the simplest answer is to tell the reader something that they will need to know to appreciate the story, but that cannot easily be told within the structure of the story without causing awkward leaps in perspective, time or place. This could be an incident in the distant past that sets up the current story. It could be a crime carried out by an unknown assailant that the rest of the book will seek to solve, or it could be a modern narrator looking back on incidents in the past.

This last is the classic "old man writing a memoir" type of prologue that, for example, Umberto Eco used in the prologue to *The Name of the Rose*, a book rare in that it actually has two prologues, describing a story within a story within a story. In prologue one, a modern historian describes tracking down the memoir of a medieval monk. In prologue two, the monk himself introduces, in his dotage, the story of events that transpired in his youth. It's only chapter one that then starts the actual story off, and even that is written as memoir.

Dan Brown started *The Da Vinci Code* with a prologue, and since that book has sold over eighty million copies, I think we can safely say that the prologue didn't harm sales. His use of the prologue conforms to the criteria set out above. It relates the assassination of Jacques Saunière, curator of the Louvre, by an unknown assailant. It is written from the perspective of Saunière himself. Since he dies, we never see things from this perspective again, and the rest of the book is related from the point of view of Robert Langdon, the sleuth who untangles the whole messy conspiracy hocus-pocus.

Many crime novels have adopted this pattern. In a prologue, you can narrate the crime from the murder victim's perspective, and then never hear from that character again in the course of the book. It's a useful trope because by definition the crime can be violent or shocking or chilling, and therefore create a great hook with which to capture the reader's attention.

There are well-respected authors who might include what is to all intents and purposes a prologue in their books, but disguise it. Whether that's out of deference to the lack of respect in which prologues are held generally, or some other reason, who knows, but the long monologue from Sheriff Bell at the beginning of chapter one of *No Country For Old Men* by Cormac McCarthy is a prologue in all but name.

Danger signs

When trying to assess if your decision to include a prologue is justified, what are the danger signs you should be looking out for?

The most common problem is using a prologue to describe the setting of your story, sometimes at great length. This can be a temptation when writing in the sci-fi, fantasy, or historical fiction genres, for example. You want the reader to understand, as quickly as possible, the environment in which your story will take place. It's much easier and more efficient to write "The Neptune Six was a revolving star station in close orbit off Andromeda IV-A, a small blue planet in the Ellyptian galaxy" than it is to work that information into the text in some kind of organic way. So when editors spend most of their time telling authors to cut unnecessary text, why should it be a bad thing for the author to tell the reader things in a really efficient way, minimising the word count?

It's not a bad thing, but it's about reader immersion in the story. That Neptune Six sentence above is essentially non-fiction; it's just relating facts. Non-fiction isn't *immersive*. It might be interesting, absorbing even, but it doesn't put the reader *in* the space station. The space station is only interesting if a character is in it, otherwise it's just an inert hunk of metal and plastic spinning slowly in space.

> Doris gazed through the window at the blue planet passing slowly beneath them. Andromeda, they had named it, Andromeda IV-A to be precise. She'd looked the name up on Neptune Six's Earth-history databanks and found the original Andromeda was a beautiful princess in Greek mythology.
>
> The two-inch thick glass misted with her breath. She was rubbing at it with the sleeve of her pilot's suit when her headset crackled.
>
> "Doris, can you get back up to the bridge? Fast."

Much the same information is included in this passage (with the exception of the name of the galaxy, although that could quite easily be fitted in at a later date). It's much longer, because it introduces a character and starts giving us a little information about her, but, crucially, it's much more immersive because it tells us close to the same amount of information *in relation to one of the characters the story is about*.

Have a look at your prologue. If you've written a fact-heavy prologue, consider whether the reader needs to know all that information, and if you've included those facts from the perspective of a character. Remember, you're not writing a Wikipedia entry. Any story in any genre is about the characters in the story, not about the setting. The setting might add lots of original and fascinating detail, but it isn't crucial to the story. Drama companies often stage enactments of Shakespearian plays in completely different settings (*The Merchant of Venice*, for example, is often transposed to Nazi Germany, because of its associations with persecution/vilification of Jews) without altering their impact.

Another curiously common problem is to start with a dream sequence, presumably to create a sense of foreboding or mystery. It's not a good idea, because your reader, not knowing at the outset that this is a dream sequence, will think they're reading real narrative. When they find out "and he woke up with a start, sweat covered and panicking. It had just been a dream" they will feel horribly let down, and quite possibly very irritated. It will almost certainly not intrigue them and make them want to read the rest of your book, because you will have broken, from the very first page, the author/reader bond of trust that says an author can't deliberately mislead a reader.

The third common problem is to have a really gripping, violent and/or explosive single-scene prologue meant to completely hook the reader, promising them a roller-coaster ride of intense excitement. That's fantastic, but if that scene does what it promises, why isn't it chapter one? The worst disappointment in the world is to have a gripping, violent and/or explosive prologue, and then turn the page and find an extremely dull and laborious chapter one. Your energies would have been better spent revising chapter one and making *that* really gripping and entertaining.

Final word on prologues

In fiction, if something works, then it works. There are no rules about prologues. They have come in to disrepute because they have been roundly abused in recent times but there's no law saying you can't have one. However, in the light of how badly they are currently regarded (trends might change in the future, but I doubt that it will happen quickly) you do need to really consider why you've got a prologue.

If you're including one because you think you *ought* to have one, because proper serious books have a prologue, don't. They're not required. If you're including one because your chapter one is really boring and you were told in your writing class that your story needs to start with some excitement on page one, then the thing to worry about is the first page of your chapter one, not a prologue. The reader is still going to get to page one of chapter one, and they're still going to find it boring, if it is.

Too much exposition is a reader turn-off in a prologue or chapter one, so instead of making your aim for the reader to appreciate your vividly imagined setting as fast as possible, make your aim for the reader to begin to be interested in your characters as fast as possible.

Finally, bear in mind the other little-acknowledged fact about prologues. Many readers skip over anything titled a prologue, thinking it boring front matter akin to a foreword ("I'd like to thank my mum, and my cat ..."), and go straight to chapter one. You might convince yourself of the need for a prologue, but a large percentage of your readers will never read it. If there's vital information in there that's necessary for them to fully understand the book, then they'll miss it, and their enjoyment of the story will be limited as a result.

Story structure

You've probably read before the idea that all stories are the same, and that authors endlessly retell the same tales. Well, the rumours are true. Using the old "boy meets girl" motif (feel free to substitute any gender or non-gendered combination you choose):

> *There are really only two stories: boy meets girl, boy loses girl, boy gets girl, (a comedy, in the traditional dramatic sense) or; boy meets girl, boy loses girl, everybody dies (a tragedy).*

As I said at the outset, this is not a "how to write" book, so it's beyond the scope of this volume to go into too much detail about all the myriad ways in which writers are advised to structure their novels. There's the three-act structure, or the five-act structure, or the Seven Stories (the "Hero's Journey" of Star Wars being one of the seven), the Hero With a Thousand Faces monomyth theory of Joseph Campbell or various diagrammatic theories of crisis points and at precisely what point in your story they should occur ("the inciting incident must occur on page two").

Study these by all means, but be very wary of books that try to sell you a "guaranteed" method of writing a brilliant novel or screenplay. Many people have spent a lot of time trying to analyse successful Hollywood stories to identify their common structural elements. It's a bit of a waste of time, because it doesn't mean that by artificially "constructing" a story out of those structural elements you're going to have a successful story.

> *Just because a house is built of stone doesn't make a house-shaped pile of stones a house.*

All of these structure theories overlap, to a greater or lesser extent. Ultimately, having absorbed what you can from those books, put them away and set to writing a great original story that you're inspired to write, not a by-the-numbers construct that you think satisfies someone else's magic formula.

However, it's good practice not to be ignorant of the general theory of story structure, so let's have a quick look at the basic principles.

All stories form a narrative arc. They begin in one set of circumstances, and finish in another set. Whatever has happened in the middle of the book will affect how the circumstances at beginning and end differ, but for a satisfying book, those circumstances are never the same. The status quo must have changed.

Someone who swears by the structural analysis of books will commonly tell you that the narrative arc can be described as being of five acts. (The process of splitting the narrative into five acts is, of course, completely artificial. Although Shakespeare's plays are now all presented in five acts—as are pretty much all plays right up to the twentieth century—they weren't written in five separate acts. That's the work of seventeenth century editors who had studied Greek drama theory, but let's roll with it.) Since a five-act definition helps with a detailed look at structure, we'll use that definition and take a look at Star Wars, that I mentioned above. Most people are familiar with the story, our analysis being from Luke's point of view.

Act One: A call to action. We meet the protagonist, Luke Skywalker, in his current state, bored out of his gourd in a backwater galaxy and dreaming of space travel. He quickly faces a call to action, finding Princess Leia's message, talking to Obi-Wan Kenobi and, returning home, finding that the Empire has killed his family and destroyed the farm. Nothing can be the same again. He must deliver the message to the Rebels on Princess Leia's behalf.

Act Two: Complications. Luke escapes from Tatooine. He begins to learn about the Force, the knowledge he will need to achieve his objective. He's not sure whether he can trust Han Solo, but they aim to deliver the message to Alderaan. Arriving at the point in space where Alderaan should have been, they are captured by the Death Star.

Act Three: Apparent success. Evading capture, Luke discovers that Princess Leia is a captive on the Death Star, and stages a rescue. Obi-Wan makes a dramatic self-sacrifice, allowing the group to escape and deliver both the plans and Princess Leia to the hidden Rebel base. Mission accomplished? Han Solo certainly thinks so, and heads off into deep space.

Act Four: Reversal. Their escape was not the success they thought it was. Although they delivered the plans to the Rebels, Darth Vader has outwitted them. The Millennium Falcon was tracked to the Rebel base and the Death Star materialises in orbit above them, soon to be in a position to obliterate the planet, and with it the last vestiges of the Rebellion.

Act Five: Climax. Analysing the plans, the Rebels decide on a plan of attack. Luke, using knowledge he has gained from his mentor Obi-Wan and, with last minute help from the returning Han Solo, fires the shot into the reactor that will destroy the Death Star. The Rebels are victorious and live to fight another day.

Almost every book, film or play can be broken down into this structure. The crucial elements are the *inciting incident* (in this case the Empire destroying Luke's family and farm), the *midpoint*, in this case probably Obi-Wan's sacrifice, allowing them to escape Darth Vader, and the *climax*, Luke's detonation of a torpedo in the heart of the Death Star, against all the odds.

Let's have a look at your book.

Review your story's structure

Have a go at breaking your story down into five acts. Firstly, can you identify an inciting incident? Where does the story start? Crucially, *why* does it start? Is this incident close to the beginning of the book?

Is there a midpoint, a turning point in the story, where perhaps the main character finally identifies the real problem they are facing and starts attempting to deal with it? Is that around the middle of the book?

And finally, presumably there is a climax, which is close to the end of the book? If you are able to do this easily, you've written a very classically structured book which bodes well for our examination of issues like plot later on.

If you can't easily identify these points, it may mean that your book has structural problems that will need sorting out, but it also might just mean that you need a bit more practice in analysing stories in order to tease out what your "act" structure actually is. Learning to break stories down into their individual structural components is a rather black art that some people excel at, and other excellent writers never bother to learn because structuring a story just comes naturally to them.

I wouldn't sweat, at this stage, about not being able to analyse your story to the satisfaction of a formula. As I mentioned before, I wonder if struggling to cram your story into a certain number of boxes stacked in a certain order is the right way to channel creativity. A beautifully structured story might also be ineffably dull if all the other components of a good book, gripping plot, entertaining characters, sparkling dialogue and fabulous imagination, aren't also present.

> *If there is a generalisation about structure to be made, it's probably that books have a beginning, a middle and an end. The beginning should be intriguing, the middle compelling, and the end satisfying. That's it.*

It's probably enough at this stage to be aware that such a thing as story structure exists. By the time we've finished with the plot and characterisation sections of this pass, you'll probably be much more able to work out what your story's structure is.

Plots

Having considered overall structure, we next look at plot. You might wonder if there is a difference between plot and structure. There are overlaps, and you will see some familiar terms pop up again in this chapter, but the key point is that while every book has a structure, not every story is plot-based—some are more character-driven. We first need to establish if your book is driven by plot, and, having established that it is, go on to focus on potential weaknesses in your plot, and how you might fix them.

Plot in general

What kind of book have you written? This is where the synopsis/summary that you wrote in the *overview* phase should help. From your synopsis, what genre do you believe your book falls into? This is an important question, because not all genres are plot-driven, and different genres have different plot conventions. Many works of literary fiction have very little plot and are all about character development. If you've written what you think is literary fiction, then this plot section may not have too much relevance to you and the section on character development will be far more important. However, if you've written something that closely resembles genre fiction, say crime, or romance, or cosy mystery, there are certain plot expectations for that genre and you flout those conventions at your peril.

Expectations put some people's backs up. "I don't care about flouting convention. My story, like my genius, is unique." Okay, but your aim in writing a book *that you intend to publish* should be to deliver a great reader experience. Are you entitled to write "the book that you want to write," and to hell with them if they don't want to read it? Of course you are. But writing is a method of communication. If you don't communicate your ideas and your story to your intended audience, then it can't be judged successful writing. If you truly don't care about communicating with an audience, then why are you worried about editing? In fact, a more fundamental question: if you don't care about communicating with an audience, why are you writing a book?

There is an unwritten contract between an author and a reader, one of expectation of entertainment (or education, for non-fiction). A reader who picks up your book and is led to expect, by means of blurb and cover and where the book is marketed on Amazon or in a bookshop, that they're getting a romance, is not going to be very happy if the book doesn't deliver the conventional Happily Ever After (HEA) ending that the romance convention demands. David Nicholls' publishers, when they published *One Day* in 2009, had to be very careful not to market his book as romance (even though the romance between Emma and Dexter forms a central part of the book) because it has a very unconventional ending.

A reader who picks up your crime novel is going to be disconcerted if the crime central to the story hasn't occurred within the first few chapters of the book. And if they get to the end of the book and a mystery character appears out of nowhere to solve the crime/catch the suspect using information that the reader hasn't been told about, they're going to feel aggrieved.

Understand the genre that your book falls into. Put your MS down a moment and go to a bookshop and imagine where in that bookshop a prospective reader will find your book. Look at other books on adjoining shelves. Hopefully you've read some of them, because you should be well-read in the genre you're writing in. If not, buy a few, or borrow them from the local library or reading club. Do they share common structural elements—are they all happy endings, for example—and if so, does your book share those same elements?

"But my book is a romance, set in a sci-fi fantasy world far in the future. Does that make it a romance, or sci-fi? How do I know which genre it fits into?" Look at your synopsis. In the first sentence or two, if you remember, you tried to come up with a summation of your story. What did you identify as the key theme? Think about the film *Blade Runner*. In one line, this film could be summed up as "Can Deckard and Rachael's love survive?" but I don't think that would really summarise the film adequately. It's a significant part of the plot, and Warner Bros struggled when they first released the film because audience feedback desperately wanted an HEA ending to fulfil the romance genre that they thought the film was directed to be, much to Ridley Scott's disgust. But truly the film (and especially the Director's Cut if you watch that version) is closer to the original book by Philip K. Dick (*Do Androids Dream of Electric Sheep?*), whose fundamental question is "What does it mean to be human?" This is sci-fi, not romance, no matter how significant a theme Deckard's infatuation with Rachael grows to be.

If you're satisfied that your book follows its genre conventions, then let's look at how well it fulfils them, particularly with respect to some common problems with plot.

Plot problems

Conflict

At the heart of all plot is conflict. Conflict doesn't have to mean bullets and bayonets. It can be internal or emotional, the main character tortured by some inner demon, some regret, some loss, that won't let them move on with their lives or alternatively, in a romance, being thwarted in love and relationships. Conflict can also be external, the main character thwarted in their ambitions to achieve some goal by an external force. That might be physical—a tsunami, or abstract—racial oppression.

In some of the most effective stories both internal and external conflict is present. In many crime stories, for example, the detective is thwarted from solving the crime by a number of external factors: lack of evidence, lack of witnesses, perhaps a lack of the body. But often the detective is fighting an internal battle as well: Robbie Coltrane in the TV series *Cracker* with his various bad habits, alcohol, smoking and gambling, Tony Shalhoub's *Monk* character, with his obsessive compulsive disorder, and even the original dysfunctional detective, Sherlock Holmes, with his opiate addiction.

Conflict is the driving force of story. It's what gives a narrative momentum, working towards the inevitable resolution of the conflict, whether that resolution is in the main character's favour or not. What kind of problems can arise with conflict?

Conflict is not sufficient to propel the story

Ali falls in love with Sasha, but Sasha lives in the next town. As it stands, insufficient conflict. Has Ali not got a car? Is it too far to cycle/walk? Is there no public transport? Can Ali's mum give him a lift? There are multiple simple solutions to his dilemma that seem to present themselves. Sasha living in the next town is just not a big enough problem.

But what if the next town is over an international border? Can Ali get a visa? Can he emigrate? Can he sneak over the border, or under, in a tunnel? Love will find a way, but there's definitely more conflict here, the obstructions to Ali's pining heart more tangible.

What if Ali is Palestinian and Sasha Israeli? Now we've suddenly upped the stakes dramatically. This is conflict. The more insurmountable the problems that Ali and Sasha's romance faces, the bigger the reader's payback when the characters achieve their HEA ending.

The conflict doesn't escalate

Even a cross-border love like Ali and Sasha's can't propel a narrative of 75,000 words without an escalation of that conflict. We see at the outset what Ali and Sasha's problem is—their eyes meet across a barbed wire fence, but any relationship between them would flout all nationalistic, religious and family/peer group beliefs. It's an impossible situation, and one that can only end badly. But we read on in the hope and belief (since this is a romance) that there is an HEA ending, and we are intrigued to see how the author manages this sleight of hand.

However, if there is just chapter after chapter of Ali sneaking across the border for trysts with Sasha, even this precarious situation will get dull, quite quickly. In what way could the conflict escalate? Perhaps Ali's uncle is in the Hezbollah, and they fire a few rockets over the border at nearby Israeli settlements. Sasha is part of an Israeli expeditionary force that storms over the border to find the perpetrators, and Sasha kills Ali's uncle in a shoot-out. Ali is arrested as a suspect and taken back for questioning. Now how is their incipient relationship going to survive? Does Ali forgive Sasha? Does Sasha believe Ali fired the rockets?

The initial premise has to be substantial and then, to be a gripping, really engrossing page-turner of a book, that conflict must escalate as the story progresses. Stagnation in a plot is boredom in a reader. How does the conflict grow in your book? Are the stakes ever-increasing, culminating in a climax where satisfactory resolution appears to be impossible, but is achieved against all the odds?

What to check in your book

What's the conflict at the beginning of your book? Do your main characters face external conflict, or internal, or both? Is it significant? Is the reader going to empathise with the character's ambitions, or are they going to think them unrealistic? Is the character empathetic enough that we care about their happiness and their hope to conquer whatever inner demons they face? If you're not sure, then perhaps you need to put some more significant hoops between the character and the realisation of their ambitions. In a romance, perhaps we need to be closer to the character to understand their worldview and why they, the school nerd, really think they have a chance with the prom queen or the captain of the football team.

Plausibility

You might think that I pushed the boundaries of plausibility with the Ali and Sasha story, but it isn't *impossible*. The plausibility of the HEA ending of that particular story will be key as to whether it makes a good book. But perhaps the author of this particular romance likes sci-fi, too? It seems that Sacha and Ali's relationship is doomed (the author hasn't worked out how they're going to resolve this plot problem realistically), so three chapters from the end, aliens invade Planet Earth and Sasha and Ali find themselves fighting the Martians side by side. The entire Middle East is vaporised and Sasha and Ali escape in a miniature submarine built by Ali's uncle to live out their days on a small tropical island in the Caribbean. That's implausible. It might deliver the HEA ending that the genre requires, but it relies on coincidence and acts of God to deliver that ending. The reader will feel cheated.

This concept, of avoiding acts of God or sheer coincidence to achieve resolution of the story, is a crucial one. If the core couple in a romance split up in what seem to be irreconcilable circumstances and go their separate ways, it's not going to be a satisfactory ending to have them happen to bump into each other in a café in another city half way round the world five years later, get back together (all differences magically resolved) and live happily ever after. Quite apart from the sheer coincidence of meeting someone by accident, your characters are going to be far more empathetic if they forge their own destinies, rather than being at the whim of chance. The rags to riches story of someone who starts their own business, fails, starts another and after many trials and tribulations eventually succeeds hugely, is going to be far more interesting than someone who works in a chicken processing plant for twenty-five years and then wins the lottery.

Sci-fi and fantasy writers have to manage the plausibility of their stories quite actively. Although in fiction anything is possible, if the story is implausible to the point of not being believable, or failing to follow the rules of logic and consistency within the imagined world, then readers are going to have problems. Sometimes authors can get away with it. There's a well-known criticism of Tolkien's Lord of the Rings epic; if the eagles could fly into Mordor to pick Frodo and Sam up from the crack of Mount Doom, how come they couldn't just drop him off there in the first place? Because most people like Tolkien's work so much, they tend to overlook that logical plot fallacy.

With plot devices like time travel, the inadvertent creation of plotting problems becomes much easier, unfortunately. In any plot where a main character can go back and change the course of future events to suit themselves, it's hard not to take the nuclear option. If a bad guy ends up nearly destroying the planet, why doesn't the hero go all the way back to the bad guy's birth and put an end to the problem then and there? It's interesting to watch writers wriggle out of time travel plot problems. Audrey Niffenegger, in *The Time Traveler's Wife*, avoided the issues of determinism and the manipulation of fate by making Henry's condition random. He cannot choose his destination in time.

In both Stephen King's book *11/22/63*, the 2013 film *About Time* and the 2004 movie *The Butterfly Effect*, the ability of main characters who have the ability to time travel to manipulate the future is constrained by the unexpected side effects that their manipulation causes. In King's book, the well-meaning attempts by Jake Epping to prevent the assassination of John F. Kennedy result in a far worse global catastrophe. In all of these works the possibilities of time-travel, seemingly an open-ended plotting device, is actually remarkably limited. If time travel features in your book, how do you restrain the use of what could otherwise be a plot-unravelling trope?

Since the days of Superman in 1938, some fantasy/sci-fi characters have had superpowers. The story of Superman's evolution over the decades reveals that Superman's actual powers have waxed and waned over time as different writers worked on the franchise. The problem with creating characters that are just too omnipotent is that they can essentially do what they want. Unless a character struggles, and actually faces the prospect of defeat, empathising with them becomes difficult.

Similarly with fantasy in which magic systems play a large part, how have you managed to constrain that magic as a plot device? If the puniest wizard can fireball the direst enemy into oblivion from a distance, what real challenge do they face? If a dragon does meet a dwarf and ends up skewered, how does the dwarf manage it, given the size difference?

What to check in your own book

Have a look at your plot. If it's sci-fi or fantasy, are your world rules (how the science or magic system works) believable and at least consistent within themselves? If some of your characters have superpowers, what's to stop them steamrollering the opposition from the outset?

If it's romance, is the climactic reconciliation a progression from earlier plotlines, or is there a feeling that it has been dropped in from on high?

If it's crime, has the answer to the puzzle been parachuted in right at the end, or are there sufficient details throughout the book for the reader to come to some "whodunit" conclusions on their own?

A good plot isn't just a sequence of events. The Coen brothers excel, in films like *Blood Simple* and *Miller's Crossing*, at creating story lines that are what you might call *consequential*, rather than just sequential. Each aspect of the plot not just follows, but derives from, the previous plot point. A character might make what seems like an inconsequential decision to skip a car service, but the next time they drive their car out of the garage, the brakes fail and they run over a child. They then make another more serious decision. They leave the car in a far-off rundown neighbourhood, to pretend that it was stolen. Someone does steal it, and the police, investigating the theft, discover that it was stolen from outside an apartment block where a man was murdered the previous night. The man has a connection with the car owner, and now the police are looking a little more closely at the car owner ... This isn't an actual plot from a Coen brothers movie (although they're welcome to get in touch!), but hopefully demonstrates that every plot point derives from a decision the character made at a previous juncture. It's not just a sequence of random, apparently unconnected events that happen to the character.

Too little plot

Books thrive on a little complexity. Only books for very young children have entirely linear narratives, where one story unfolds in consequential scenes. Most books, from middle-grade onwards, have more than one storyline, subplots that keep the narrative rolling even when there appears to be no progress in the main plot. The wonderful children's book *Skellig* by David Almond, for example, is ostensibly about the mysterious creature that Michael finds in the garden shed. Little by little, we begin to discover what the creature is, and what strange powers he might have.

Beneath all of this, however, is a more worrying and upsetting subplot. Michael's newborn sister is very ill and, we're given to believe, might even die. The multi-layered nature of the book adds richly to the narrative, and the climax of the book, when the eponymous Skellig saves Michael's sister's life as a reward for Michael being so kind, is doubly satisfying.

I mentioned earlier that having both internal and external conflict is a great way to add complexity to a plot. Many Marvel and DC comic characters are perfect examples of characters fighting both inner demons (Batman's loss of his parents, Superman's loneliness on a planet that isn't his, Iron Man's fatal heart condition, Hulk's rage) as well as the external sources of conflict, evil characters and their henchmen out to destroy and pillage. In addition to making the characters far more empathetic, it makes the story far more interesting and nuanced. These characters can't always be having fist fights with bad guys on the top of skyscrapers. What are they doing in their downtime, when the character, and the reader, is taking a bit of a breather?

What to check in your own book

What subplots are rumbling along in the background of your book? If there are subplots, how do they relate to the main story? In an ideal situation they are not merely minor contemporaneous plots, but actually serve to illuminate the main plot in some way, alter its trajectory and throw up alternative courses of action that, without the subplot, wouldn't be possible.

If the story is merely a linear progression of one scene after another, is there a way to shake it up a little? Can you build up a minor character to have their own character arc and subplot? Can you introduce a little more complexity to the main character, give them some quirk, some tic, that affects how they are perceived, or creates more problems for them achieving their ambition? A warrior-knight who is actually a haemophiliac? A submarine captain who is claustrophobic?

Too much plot

The opposite can also be true, where there are many subplots all jostling for the reader's attention. This isn't necessarily a problem, and occurs quite often in epic fantasy (George Martin's A Song of Ice and Fire series, for example), but unless the author keeps a firm grip of the many strands of plot that are running through the book, the central theme can get buried in complexity.

There are techniques to manage multi-stranded narratives, where it's not really subplots vying for attention, but plots of equal significance all happening at the same time. George Martin names each chapter by their main protagonist, priming the reader to delve back and pick up what they remember of the thread of that particular plot. This compartmentalisation of the narrative is the only way that such a multi-stranded epic could work and even so, Martin felt it necessary to put one group of characters (Tyrion Lannister, Daenerys Targaryen and, largely, Jon Snow) on hold for an entire book (*A Feast for Crows,* A Song of Ice and Fire: Book Four) while he told us the separate stories of the other group, the Lannisters at King's Landing, the surviving Stark siblings and Sam.

He then turns the structure round and tells us what was happening to Tyrion, Daenerys and Jon, at the same time as the events in *A Feast for Crows* were unfolding, in *A Dance with Dragons*, leaving Cersei, Jaime and the rest suspended in fictional limbo. This is an extreme measure, but it's a reflection of the fact that Martin recognised it was unrealistic to expect even the most dedicated of readers to hold in their head multiple plot strands of the complexity that he was weaving.

What to check in your own book

Does your book have multiple plot strands? Are they of equal story significance? How have you managed those strands so that the reader doesn't get lost between one strand and another? Are some genuinely subplots, clearly subservient in importance to one or two main plot threads? If they are truly subplots, how much page space do they take up? Even though they are a subplot, do they form a necessary part of the main plot or character development? If they don't, should they be included, or are they just an indulgence?

Chekhov's gun

One final point on plot: "Chekhov's Gun" and its opposite, call it "Chekhov's Missing Gun." Anton Chekhov—who, while renowned for his plays, was also a consummate short story writer—famously wrote that if your characters note a gun hanging on the wall of the cabin in the woods in Act One, they'd better use it in Act Two. His point was that readers will pick up the tiniest detail in your story. They will notice the mention of the gun and store that fact away for future reference. If the gun is never mentioned again they will be a little bewildered. "Why did they mention that gun on the wall? I thought someone was going to get shot." If this happens repeatedly throughout the book, the reader will lose faith in your ability to tell them a story. They're going to begin to wonder how much of anything you're telling them is actually relevant, and what they can just skip.

With description in general, Chekhov would say only include detail *relevant to the story*. He was writing short stories, in which every word counts, and in novels you do have a little more leeway, but this concept of relevance is crucial to eliminating unnecessary detail and bogging your reader down in facts they don't need to know.

But what about description, you might ask? "If I describe the house the character is living in, some of it might not be strictly *relevant*, but I still want to give the reader an idea of what the character is like from their living space." You've answered your own question. You're giving details about the house *so that we can get an idea of what your character is like.* You're showing us that they're a frazzled, stressed individual who's not looking after themselves properly by describing the bin heaving with pizza boxes and fast food wrappers, dirty dishes in the sink, a pile of empty beer cans by the back door, the half empty bottle of whisky on the stand beside the bed. You're showing us what your character is like, instead of blandly telling us "Robert was overweight and unkempt, with an alcohol problem and low self-esteem." The key point is that while you're describing the house, you're really shedding great insight into your character, which is far more important.

As with all things, it is genre dependent. Some literary fiction authors expend a great deal of creative energy and word count describing settings and landscapes that have no direct impact on the characters, but very much impact on the mood and tone of the book. That's all well and good in literary fiction, but it won't be so readily accepted in genre fiction.

The converse to "Chekhov's Gun" (I called it "Chekhov's Missing Gun" at the start) is also true.

> *If there is an item relevant to the story that the reader needs to know about, then you shouldn't introduce it just at the moment that a character turns to it as the solution (particularly the* only possible *solution) to the immediate plot problem.*

It's again to do with trust, and this important relationship between writer and reader that I keep mentioning. Let's go back to the cabin in the woods. Four over-sexed teenagers (teenagers are always over-sexed—horror story trope #299) are trapped in a cabin in the woods. They've barricaded the doors and windows, but these zombies are smart—they've climbed up on the roof and are pulling the tin sheeting off. The biggest and baddest zombie drops down in to the middle of the screaming teens. Are they done for? No, because Alice says, "Oh look, there's old Uncle Septimus's ancient blunderbuss hanging over the mantelpiece. Let's see if it's loaded? It is. Hurrah! Duck, everybody." And she blows the zombie's head off.

If the reader hadn't been made aware of the existence of this blunderbuss before this point, the author is cheating, trying to create a level of tension that doesn't exist. The reader, if they're immersed in the story, is going to be extremely concerned for the characters they've made an emotional investment in when the zombie drops through the ceiling, but then they're going to realise that their concern was entirely misplaced. Alice was always going to save the day and blow the zombie's brains out, just with a gun the reader knew nothing about. Instead of real tension, there was *apparent* tension. The author was trying to fool the reader. In the next crisis, the reader isn't going to believe in the tension the author is trying to create, because they will suspect that it too will turn out to be apparent tension, not real tension. You've lost the reader's trust.

Three more zombies drop from the roof. The reader thinks, "Ha, now they're done for. The old blunderbuss trick won't work with three of them. But ... hang on. I was tricked before. What is this author going to pull out of the bag to save the day this time?" And sure enough, Alice shouts out over the moaning and screaming, "It's lucky that Uncle Septimus was a gifted gunsmith, and actually converted this blunderbuss to a semi-automatic," and lo and behold, she totally wastes the oncoming undead with a barrage of hot lead. You're converting a climax to an anti-climax. Your reader isn't going to invest emotionally in the story any further because they know that they'll more than likely get the rug pulled from under their feet.

What to check in your own book

If there are critical points in the plot where some tool or some power or ability is used for the first time, did you make your readers aware of this special ability or weapon before that moment, or did you spring it on them? If you did, think about subtly foreshadowing that ability before that point. If your surprise is intentional (the geek saves the football captain from a gang of muggers by demonstrating her black belt aikido skills, which even her best friends didn't know she had), when in the past few chapters has she turned up breathless to chess matches or old film showings (or whatever geeky thing she does)? When in a previous scene has she turned up at school with a bruised cheek and laughed it off as having rolled off the sofa? If you've left little breadcrumbs like this throughout the text, it might still be a *surprise* that she's a black belt in martial arts, but it won't be unrealistic. Your reader is likely going to have a lightbulb moment and say to themselves "Oh, *that's* why ..." In addition, at all those little breadcrumb moments that are left unexplained earlier on, your reader is going to be intrigued. What *had* she been doing to arrive at the cinema all hot and sweaty? How did her cheek *really* get bruised? Your reader is going to be asking questions, and that's what you want in an immersive story.

Conversely, if you make a big deal about what a great car the main character has, and how he waxes it and polishes it every Sunday, tunes it and buys special parts for it so that it can "outrun any cop car in the county," how come it plays absolutely no part in the story, and he escapes from the climactic bank robbery on a bicycle?

Concluding with plots

That finishes our look at plots and plotting. Hopefully you can already see how that editing mindset that you cultivated before you started self-editing is critically important. When looking at plot problems such as conflict, plausibility and complexity, you need to be able to sit back from the book as you wrote it, and look instead at how it reads. This will have particular significance when it comes to cutting sections. As the author of all these subplots that you lovingly crafted, if you're still in your writing mindset you'll be appalled at even the suggestion that you should cull one or more of them. However, as a reader or editor you are trying to look dispassionately at each subplot and decide, "Does it actually add anything to the story?"

For example, in your teen romance, is the fact that Jim tries and tries and finally succeeds in getting the high score on the video machine in the arcade of any relevance to the plot? Maybe it is. Perhaps it shows us Jim's determination and perseverance in achieving his goals, which he will use to dramatic effect in his locker-room showdown with the school football team jock over who is taking Mary to the prom.

But perhaps it's just a happy and vivid recollection of your life at Jim's age, when you were indeed the

"Asteroids" champion in the local record shop for a brief but glorious interval in your early teens. If that's the case, and it doesn't really tell us anything about Jim and his story, then I'm afraid an objective editor (which is what you're trying to be) would recommend cutting this entire subplot, however well-written it is. However, a useful tip: don't delete it entirely. It might make a great short story for a magazine, or a "bonus material" teaser post on your author blog or book website for when you do finally publish.

There's an important message here to do with editing generally. The inclusion of a subplot or a scene or even an entire chapter in your final draft doesn't depend on how well-written it is. It depends on its relevance to the story. This is the origin of the expression "kill your darlings." However much you might like, and be rightly proud of, a well-written scene in a coffee shop where two characters have a funny conversation about their favourite films, if it's not relevant, if it doesn't push the story along or illuminate their characters, then I'm afraid it has no place in the book and should be cut.

Pacing

The pacing of a book has a lot to do with plot. Where in the story do the critical events happen that go to make up your plot? I was joking earlier about the critical "inciting incident," the event that starts the whole story rolling, *having* to occur on page two. However, it must happen early in your story. There are no rules, but best practice would imply that your core plot starts in chapter one (hopefully that's kind of obvious), and if it didn't start in the first few pages of chapter one, my concern would be that you're starting your story at the wrong point.

Where does your story start?

One of the most common problems I encounter on my work with authors on my TheOpeningLines.com website, where I critique novel openings for submission to agents (it's a free service—try it), is writers who don't start their book at the beginning of the story. They start writing at some earlier point before the real story starts and, almost always, the radical solution that I propose is to cut everything that occurs before the critical moment that gets the ball rolling.

Some genres are more relaxed about this than others. In a crime or thriller novel, it's most critical to start the story with a bang. Let's see; I'm revising this book in someone else's house and I'm going to pull books off their shelves at random. So, I see Robert Ludlum begins *The Bourne Ultimatum* with Jason cutting through a wire fence and shooting a Doberman guard dog. Dick Francis begins *Hot Money* with a phone call for the main character's estranged father saying he needs help. P. D. James begins *Devices and Desires* with the line "The Whistler's fourth victim was his youngest, Valerie Mitchell, aged fifteen years, eight months and four days, and she died because she missed the nine-forty bus ..."

However, further along the shelf, Jenny Eclair begins *Moving* with a several-thousand-word chapter about a woman lying in the bath, reflecting on her life. It's not until the first line of chapter two that the plot actually starts developing. *Moving* could be described as commercial literary fiction, sometimes referred to as "women's fiction," a term that some people are comfortable with and others detest (I'll refer to it as "commercial lit fic" throughout the rest of this book).

Quite often a submission to TheOpeningLines.com will begin: "I woke up, yawned, and stretched. It looked like a fine day outside." The author gives us five pages of this character getting up, having breakfast, showering (I kid you not), discussing details of no importance with other family members and going to work. Once the character is at work they get a message saying that the boss wants to see them in their office right away, and only then do we find out, ten pages into the narrative, that they're being sent to troubleshoot some mysterious goings-on in the company's mining operations in Darkest Peru.

When do you think that story might start? In the meeting with the boss? Possibly. Saying tearful goodbyes to concerned family? Perhaps. I think my advice to that author would be to start the story when the plane touches down in Jorge Chávez International Airport. Everything that happens before that point is prosaic and a bit dull. We've all woken up (some of us with rather boring jobs possibly more than once a day). We've all had a shower, gone to work, been told our boss wants to see us. Most of us have gone to an airport and got on a plane. There could be minor drama in the meeting with the boss. Perhaps the boss hates the main character and is sending him out there on a suicide mission in the hope that he disappears too, something that the main character is well aware of and tries to resist. There's conflict right there, but I suspect that any drama in that confrontation, instead of being related in a full transcript of the meeting, could well be portrayed much more efficiently in passing, in dialogue, with whoever meets the character at the airport in Lima.

Frequently, unedited fantasy or sci-fi novels start with a long passage of exposition, "world-building," explaining who exactly the main character is, what kind of world they're inhabiting, what religion or creed or magic system the world operates under and where the character stands in it. I'll go into this more in the section on exposition in Part III but the truth is that, in spite of what you might think, readers *couldn't care less* about the setting for your novel in the first few pages (and they care a good deal less than you might think throughout the book). Any words you use to describe the world you've lovingly and painstakingly crafted in such detail in the first few pages of your book are almost entirely wasted, if the reader hasn't got a character to hang on to while navigating that world. And even that character must be doing something interesting, not showering, or getting a taxi to the airport.

This truth can be demonstrated visually using film. The camera opens on a magnificent mountainous valley, lakes at the foot of steep rocky slopes, a twisting road clinging to one side of the precipice. Driving along the road is a rather dilapidated Volkswagen Beetle. Our eye is drawn to the car, and in the two or three minutes that this title sequence rolls (the opening to the film adaptation of Stephen King's *The Shining*, with Jack Nicholson and Shelley Duvall) we rarely take our eyes off the car to gaze at the spectacular scenery, even though the car is doing something pretty banal, just rolling along the road. The car is character, the mountain valley and twisting road are purely backdrop, a pretty scene. Where is the car going, we wonder? Is it going to crash, miss a bend and tumble down the mountainside? Who's in the car? Why is the car the only vehicle on the road?

In a book's opening, we watch for the equivalent of movement. We want something to follow, to concentrate on. There's no point in giving us pages and pages of description of a beautiful elven city, all spires and minarets high in the treetops, if there's no one in it. Give us a character walking along one of the rope bridges, or on the forest floor, pulling back a bowstring with a flaming arrow aimed at the heart of one of the wooden elven houses, and we've suddenly got a reference point, some context.

However, as I stated, this requirement that the story starts almost immediately isn't fundamental to character-driven novels, that is, most literary fiction and much commercial lit fic that focuses mostly on personal growth and development. Some literary fiction doesn't really contain a plot. In Kafka's *The Castle*, "K," the protagonist, arrives in the first few pages at an inn on his way up to see the castellan. He never goes on to reach the castle, or even move far from the inn—no car chases, no shoot-outs.

In literary fiction the nature of the main character is what is important to bring to the fore as quickly as possible. In a sense, that is the plot of the book—how that character develops and changes in the course of the book. The quicker we understand that character, and from what point they're starting off, the sooner we can join them on their journey of self-discovery.

Where does your story end?

Think about where the climax of your book occurs. Obviously it should be close to the end of your book—the story presumably ends with the resolution of the climax, so anything after that event is tying up loose ends. A reader wants time for this, like a cool-down period after a bout of exercise, to resolve all the subplots if there are any, understand the lesson learned, reflect on the drama and emotion that the book stirred. However, five chapters of loose ends means there were probably too many loose ends in the first place.

Spacing of other critical moments

And what of other critical moments in the book? Where do they occur? As I said in the section on story structure, I don't subscribe to the theory that there are rules that can determine where exactly in the book the resolution of subplots or minor climaxes can be placed, although there are many well-argued books on narrative structure that suggest just that. There's a general agreement that the pace of the book should increase towards the final climax and therefore, bearing in mind our thoughts about *escalation of conflict* earlier, that escalation of conflict should happen at a more and more rapid pace towards the final chapters. You've probably seen those saw-tooth graphs that attempt to plot the dramatic moments of a story in writing-theory classes and books. They all share a couple of common characteristics. They're not symmetrical. Tension rises from left (beginning) to right (end of the book), and although tension might drop periodically, the moment of highest drama is in the climax at the end.

We've already analysed the Star Wars story from a structural point of view, with the dramatic arc. How does it stack up when graphing tension? There are some clear rises and falls in tension during the course of the story. There's an initial growing tension as Luke finds the droid, discovers the message to Princess Leia, tracks the droid to Obi-Wan Kenobi and learns of his true heritage. He turns his back on this future though and tries to recover the status quo, only to find Empire stormtroopers have destroyed the farm and killed his step-parents. He barely escapes (end of mini-climax one) and on Han Solo's ship there's a lull in tension. We take a breather as Luke trains to use the Force; we meet the other characters; there are comic interludes with C-3PO and Chewbacca playing a version of chess.

The next crisis is Solo's ship being caught by the tractor beam of the Death Star. The stakes have now been raised. The Rebel planet has been destroyed and they must escape the Death Star (and execution) to get the data to the Rebel leadership.

They manage to escape, and there is another short lull as they find the hidden Rebel base and learn how to defeat the Death Star. This lull is much shorter, however. The Death Star has tracked them and now emerges from hyperspace to destroy the Rebel base and all hopes of victory against the Empire. This is the climax. The stakes are at their highest, kill or be killed, victory or utter defeat. (After the resolution of this climax, Luke destroying the Death Star, there is a "winding down" section of the story, where the heroes get their medals in a long, drawn-out victory celebration.) It should be fairly clear that the "shape" of the Star Wars story is this steadily building tension throughout, with mini-crises, lulls in tension, more dramatic crises, their at least partial resolution, and then the final climax where the stakes are at their highest. Most successful stories share this basic format, although the spacing of the crises, their relative intensity, and the length of the dramatic lulls after them can all vary.

Pacing within scenes

Perhaps the final thing to consider with regard to pacing are the almost mechanical effects a writer can create by use of language, and chapter and scene length.

> *Long words slow a reader down. Short words make for fast and snappy lines. A plethora of languidly described adverbial and adjectival flourishes illuminate and entertain. But verbs and nouns get the job done.*

Every writer has an innate writing style; some styles are languid, and some are extremely curt. Too much tinkering with that style (which can happen in heavy-handed editing or over-reliance on writing apps) and you run the risk of losing your writer's "voice," but an accomplished writer will use all these tricks to speed up or slow down the narrative where it's most appropriate.

If chapter and scene breaks are few and far between (very long chapters, or long scenes within the chapter), the slower the pace of the book will appear to be, regardless of word count. This can be used to great effect in slowing down the pace of the narrative for dramatic purposes. The opposite also holds true. Short chapters, short scenes, and fast, punchy writing speeds up the narrative, but note that it's not the absolute length of the scenes/chapters that matters, but their length relative to each other. Don't assume that your chapters must all be around the same length, or that there are a "correct" number of pages per scene.

What to check in your own book

Where does your story start? Mindful of the genre you're writing in, is your opening scene a pacy, rapid-fire, heart-stopping roller coaster? Sounds great for a thriller, but not so appropriate for a romance. On the other hand, is your ex-SAS, sociopathic hitman baking fairy-cakes for the first ten pages? Some of your thriller readers might find that approach a little off-putting.

How close to the end of the book is your climax? If there are a lot of post-climactic chapters could they be brought forwards ahead of the climax? Could they be cut, or could they be used in the opening to the next book of the series instead?

Consider the other critical plot moments in your book. How are they spaced out? Is the reader given breathing space between one crisis and another, or is the pace relentless? The outright speed of pacing will matter more in some genres (crime, thriller, some horror) than others (literary fiction, historical fiction, romance)—people talk about a pacy thriller, but rarely about a pacy romance. How quickly do your significant plot points follow each other? Is there revelation after revelation in quick succession? No sooner has the mysterious stranger moved in next door to the heroine than they've met, shared a pizza, had sex, had their first row and the heroine has discovered he's actually her half-brother—and that's just chapter one? This type of rapid-fire pacing might suit some genres, but even in a thriller we generally appreciate a crisis and growing tension more if we've been able to wind down a little since the last crisis.

Have a look at those critical scenes—the climactic moments—and have a look at their length. Are they short and punchy, or long and drawn out? What effect do you want to create in those scenes? Are they dramatic and full of action? If they are, the action should resolve itself quickly. Everyone reading epic fantasy probably likes a swordfight, but a swordfight that goes on for twenty pages? That would be both exhausting and boring at the same time. How many ducks and weaves and slashes and cuts do you really want to describe? Even if the point is that the fight goes on for hours, your average reader won't want to read every moment of it. Instead, I'd suggest cutting some of the hacking and bashing and stunt work and deal in abstracts. Rather than describe every twist and leap of the fight, describe their surroundings, how the sun that had been so hot at the start of the battle was now setting, and cooler, but also lower, and dazzling the person facing it.

Monologuing is a trope. As the bad guy looms over the prostrate hero with a rusty knife in the climactic scene, he then proceeds to moan on for ten pages about what a traumatic childhood he had and how no-one ever listened? Anti-climax, much?

However, in a romance, in an intimate scene, you may want to draw out the pace. Here's a situation where lots of long, languid descriptive words might suit the scene, a lot of caressing and whispering and silk sheets shimmering may get your reader very precisely into the mood you're looking to bring to life.

As a writer gains experience, they begin to intuitively alter their language and scene length to suit the pace and tension in the scene. If you're not positive you're at that level of ability, having a read through your book with this specific focus might be a good idea.

Characters

If you're writing non-fiction, this next section is not as relevant to you, although you might still want to read through, particularly the sections on "Too many characters" and "Consistency," which can affect non-fiction genres such as memoir.

In the same way that there are many books on story structure, there are even more on creating characters: how to create believable characters; what makes a character empathetic; how to write characters that people will remember. Again, read as many or as few of these books as you feel you need to but, even more than plotting, characters are often the most personal aspect of your writing, and as such the creation of them is extremely difficult to "teach."

Often our characters are based on facets of our own personality, or those of family or friends (or enemies). We might build a character around a life experience that we, or someone close to us, has had. Sometimes a character will drop, almost fully formed, into our imagination, and that character is the inspiration for the entire book. This genesis might be inspired by a piece of clothing, or a song, or a picture in a gallery.

We grow to love our characters, even (and sometimes especially) the villains. We put them through all sorts of trials and tribulations and they hopefully come out of the book at the other end richer in experience and knowledge. Sometimes, in magical moments, our own characters surprise us. We are writing dialogue and think we have a good idea of how the conversation in a scene is going to unfold, but the character says something completely unexpected and the conversation, and even plot, might go off in an entirely different direction than we'd planned.

This book doesn't pretend to teach you how to create great characters, but great characters do share some common traits that we'll be looking for when we self-edit.

Character arcs

As we did with plot, before you form an opinion on whether the characters in your book perform their functions fully, you must understand first what kind of book you have written. If it's a character-driven novel (in which the development and change in a character or group of characters forms the main thrust of the story), *character arcs* are extremely important, and replace an overriding plot structure in forming the narrative of the book.

In Jeanette Winterson's *Oranges are Not the Only Fruit*, the plot, such as there is, plays a secondary role to the development of the main character, Jeanette, from seven-year-old would-be missionary in a fundamentalist Christian household to young "fallen woman" living alone in the city as a lesbian.

How Jeanette obeys, rebels, confronts and eventually comes to a form of reconciliation with her evangelical, harsh and loveless adoptive mother, and finds her own way in life, is the story. We call this a character arc. The plot consists of relationships forming and unravelling, being a member of or being excluded from social groups and how that affects personality and behaviour, and so on.

What if your book isn't particularly character-driven, however? What if you've written in a plot-driven genre like a thriller, or crime? Some of the significance of the character arc diminishes, but not all. It's still important to have complex and empathetic characters, but the book isn't carried solely by the development in their character. For a crime thriller, for example, the detective's mission, for the purposes of the book, is the solution to the crime. It might be that in the course of the case the detective learns new skills and abilities and therefore develops professionally or personally, but their *character* hasn't really changed all that much. The solution to the crime and apprehension of the villain are the main elements driving the story. (Bear in mind, however, that often the most successful crime series *do* also develop a significant character arc in their main protagonist—*The Girl with the Dragon Tattoo* trilogy by Stieg Larsson is a good example.)

In order for a character arc to successfully carry a character-driven novel, it needs to fulfil a few basic functions:

Change must be substantial

Growing up is not a character arc. Growing up is just a function of maturity that everyone goes through—okay, not everyone, but let's leave that very immature adult you happen to know out of it, will we? Our needs, desires and wants change as we go from child (a new toy, parental affection, school friends) to adult (a new car, sexual partners, career satisfaction). These are all fundamental and important changes, but there's nothing really remarkable about that evolution. They are largely changes that happen *to* us, rather than are made *by* us (see the section about achieving change, in a moment). A substantial character arc revolves around a significant problem that the character has, internal or external—perhaps isolation/loneliness, physical or mental disability, lack of direction or focus in life—that, in the course of the book, they confront and overcome. This might be an amputee who wants to be a mountaineer, and eventually conquers Everest. It might be a less literal challenge, such as someone in mid-life, recently divorced and reconciled to a future without a partner, finding a significant relationship, in an unlikely place.

The character must actually change

With the resolution of the problem, the character must be changed. If the character arc is a substantial one, then the character undergoes real change, not just superficial satisfaction. Consider the film *As Good As It Gets*, in which Jack Nicholson plays a misanthropic, OCD-suffering but bestselling writer. At the beginning of the film he is virtually friendless, prone to crippling superstition and fear. He can barely function in the modern world, and only can do so cocooned by wealth. By the end of the film he has conquered his obsessions. He can walk on the cracks in the pavement with equanimity. He can bear bodily contact with someone. It looks as if he might even have the beginnings of a real relationship. He has learned some significant lessons, and this heralds a life-altering change in direction for his character.

Change should be achieved, rather than imposed

The character needs to achieve the resolution, rather than have it imposed upon them. This is what is called "having agency." If a character drifts along through the book, reacting to the things that happen to them, then it won't make for a very interesting character. Perhaps a character starts their story on the wrong side of the tracks, in and out of juvenile detention centres, a life of petty crime and ever-lengthening custodial sentences looming in front of them. It isn't going to be enough that the character meets a wonderful therapist who "cures" them. There might be a therapist in the story, but they can only be a *catalyst* for the character's change, not the prime mover. The need to change, the realisation that the character's life will not be complete or fulfilled without that change, must come from within. Perhaps they recognise the truth in the therapist's advice. Perhaps they receive valuable insight from a friend, or an ex, but they must accept and recognise that changes are needed and realise that they can implement those changes. It might mean sacrifices. It might mean betraying previously fiercely held opinions but the key decision, that they will make those sacrifices and that they are now prepared to compromise those opinions (like Jack Nicholson in *As Good As It Gets*), has to come from within.

It's important to note that the most fulfilling character arcs concentrate not on what the character *wants*, but what they *need*, which might be something else entirely (this is sometimes described as *conscious* versus *subconscious* motivation). Going back to Melvin Udall, what Jack Nicholson's character *wants* is for everything to carry on just as before, each day the same, allowing him to wallow in his self-imposed isolation. What his character *needs*, though, is for this isolation to be broken down and for him to start to properly connect with people. The revelation that a satisfying climax brings is that the right story outcome for a character might not have been what they started out looking for.

It's also important to note that the characters don't need to make the "correct" decisions, only those that are true to their character. A great way of infusing tension in a narrative is to have the characters mess up. You'd love to have a situation where a reader is pulling their hair out, shouting in frustration at the character: "Why did you give *her* the only gun? Can't you *see* she isn't right in the head?" They will read on now, desperate to find out if their conclusions were right. But characters can't behave randomly. If the reader feels that the character is making odd and unrealistic decisions, they'll be asking you the writer the same questions in their review: "Why did you have him give *her* the gun? It made no sense. He had already said she was too unstable to be trusted."

Character arcs in series

I mentioned the Stieg Larsson trilogy earlier, which brings up another issue. Some series are truly episodic; the books are largely substitutable—they can be read in any order. This has an important implication for character arcs. In an episodic series the main character must begin each story from roughly the same starting point. In such a series the main character can't have a significant character arc. They can't develop significantly in terms of personality (or even skill set) because if they did, reading books out of order would throw up all sorts of plotting anachronisms. If a reader picks up book four, in which the lead character learns to drive, but the reader then reads book three, they'll be confused as to why the character is taking buses everywhere.

This is another reason why you need to know your genre and the expectations of that genre when writing and, subsequently, when marketing. A cosy mystery reader of a series of five or ten books or more might rely on the main character being much the same in each book. There's a comfort in the familiar which is part of the appeal of the cosy mystery genre. The character might be complex and empathetic, have their good and bad qualities, but they don't change materially from one book to the next.

Other series, however, are not episodic. While it's possible to read the Stieg Larsson trilogy in any order (the books do stand alone as cohesive stories), the reader will get far more out of the trilogy if they are read in the order in which they were written. Thrillers like the *Bourne* series by Robert Ludlum would actually make little sense if read out of order. The *Harry Potter* books follow a definite sequential order. Not only does the MC grow older in each book, but he grows in skills, in self-knowledge, and in the complexity of relationships with those around him in each volume. This kind of series is sequential. Both plot and main character arc, while forming satisfying trajectories within each volume, also follow a larger design across the whole series. A largely unsung part of J.K.Rowling's talent was the ability, with the Harry Potter books, to create separate satisfying novels within a grander design that developed a much broader plot and character growth arc over the entire series.

The question comes back to what kind of book you've written, which is again where your synopsis/summary should help. The questions you need to ask yourself are, "Is my book primarily character-driven or plot-driven, and will it be part of a series or is it a stand-alone novel?" If it is character-driven and stand-alone, does the character arc satisfy the attributes we mentioned earlier about being *substantial* and instigating *real change*, and are those changes *self-determined* or merely *imposed* by a higher authority?

If it's character-driven and part of a series, is it the first of a series? If it is, does the character change significantly in personal circumstances by the end of the book? If they do, you're writing a sequential series in which the character will be expected to grow and develop over the entire series (not much good if they develop over the course of the first book and then remain rigidly the same for the next six volumes).

If they don't, then the option (which could also be called a constraint) of an episodic series is open to you. Here, the MC can't change materially from one book to another (if they do, you will undermine the episodic nature of the series and make reading the books in any order a problem). In terms of plotting that means, for example, that they can't move house (or city or country). In terms of character development they can't have any kind of relationship or, if they do, it must remain on an entirely static emotional and material plane (they can't have a massive row and her husband move out, or, if he does, he has to be reconciled with her and move back in by the end of the book).

The character's advertised skills and abilities can't change from one book to another, which is more of a drawback than you might think at first. If, for example, they have to learn conversational French to solve one mystery, that talent should stay with them. One doesn't forget how to speak a language, so in subsequent books they might use that ability, perhaps have a conversation with someone in French. For a reader coming to the series out of order, it would be peculiar for your character to have a conversation in French in one book, and to start learning the language in a "later" book.

These issues are more closely inspected in the chapter "Consistency."

What to check in your own book

Decide who your main characters are. This should be fairly simple, even if yours is a plot-driven book. There will be one or two characters who figure in most scenes and through whose eyes the tale is told (the concept of a "point-of-view character," which we'll explore in depth later).

See if you can write down, for each main character, their character arc—*how they change* in the book. Are they different at the end of the book to how they were at the start, and is that difference relatively substantial? How does this change come about? Does the change happen to them, or are they the agents of their own change? Are there critical points in the book where the direction of the plot development changes because of a decision that the character made? Would that character really make that decision at this point in the book, or did they have to make that decision because you wanted the plot to develop in a particular direction?

If you can't answer those questions easily, then there are some things to think about. Focusing on each character that you consider a main character:

Is this character really a main character? If they remain a constant presence throughout the story but they don't really develop as a character, it's likely that they are a significant character, but not a main character that you want the reader to really empathise with. If so, that's all right, you can relax about comprehensive character arcs, but then, is there a bit too much of them in the book? After all, if you've made that mistake, a reader might make the same one, trying to empathise with a character who will never be fleshed out fully and therefore likely to be a bit of a disappointment.

Is the change in your character just down to circumstances, rather than choices made? If the character does change in the story, did their change in direction affect the plot in any tangible way, or did things just happen and they reacted to those events?

Did your character really make that decision, or did you? How well do you know your own character? If they have gone against type (the tone-deaf introvert suddenly up on stage and belting out *My Way* on the karaoke at the Christmas party, thus winning the girl), is that a realistic development? If you feel it was, have you flagged the change in mindset of the character adequately to the reader, to allow them to believe this change?

Can you make the change in character more substantial? If you're worried that the final version of the character isn't so very different from their beginning state, one option, instead of altering the ending of the book, is to alter the beginning; change where they came from rather than where they get to. This might be easier than rewriting the entire ending of a complicated plot.

How many characters?

The specific question we're really asking here is how many main characters, or *point-of-view characters*, do you have in your book? (I'll cover the subject of point of view in depth in the next section.) A point-of-view character is someone with whom we travel at least part of the way through the book—we see some of the story through their eyes. This is a character who, although they might not be the main protagonist, is someone that you wish us to empathise with, whose perspective you want us to share.

The acceptable number of such characters varies wildly from genre to genre, so here again is where your synopsis will help you—what genre have you written in? Some genres, epic sci-fi or fantasy in particular, support a large cast. I've already mentioned the Game of Thrones series and the fact that the cast list in this epic saga is so large, George Martin had to mothball half of them for the duration of an entire book, because there were too many plot threads and character perspectives happening at once to reasonably expect a reader to keep track of.

But for a romance to have a large cast list wouldn't make any sense. The plot of a romance depends on the couple meeting, falling in love, falling out, reconciling and achieving their HEA ending. The PoV throughout the book is likely to be of a single character (although quite often romances have two PoVs—they switch back and forth between each party in the relationship to give us both sides of the story, usually in alternate chapters). The idea that the reader's focus on this central theme should be distracted at intervals by other characters' PoVs who have no relevance to the central romance would be very odd, and quite unwelcomed by a romance genre reader.

In other genres the guidance is less clear. What about historical fiction, for example? There might be a huge cast of characters in a period drama, kings and queens of different houses, courtiers, courtesans. If you've written them well, they're all interesting characters champing at the bit to get their story heard. The key question is—do they need to be a PoV character?

There's a critical point to think about when you're looking at your PoV characters and wondering if there are too many, and that's *the reason for having a PoV character in the first place*. A PoV character is someone you want the reader to empathise with. You want the reader to be eager to find out more about this character, to root for them, to care if their dreams and ambitions are thwarted or achieved. But that's a double-edged sword. If that's the case, you have to deliver on that promise. The reader has to be able to see those characters through to whether their dreams are realised. The reason a book or a film that kills off a main PoV character (with whom we have become emotionally involved) before the end is so deeply jarring is because it breaks this unwritten "rule." We are left deeply unsettled by not being able to see this character's desires through to a "satisfactory" conclusion. Of course, sometimes that's the entire point—the film *Love Story*, for example!

But if you remember what we said about subplots, you can probably see a problem arising here. Those ambitions (think back to the section on plot) have to be relevant to the story, not some side issue. Having too many rather inconsequential subplots—minor characters finally being able to get the high score on the video arcade machine was the example I gave earlier—is going to bog down your book in trivia.

So, whether you're looking at your book from the perspective of plot, or character, you must make a similar judgement. Do you have too many subplots distracting us from the main thrust of the story, or do you have too many PoV characters clamouring for attention, drowning out the main character/s? Quite often, these two problems will be closely related.

This kind of issue is where an objective third party, be it a beta reader or a professional editor, will find it much easier to come to a decision than the author. Remember that phrase from earlier, "killing your darlings"? It refers to the heartache that comes from trying to cut out, sometimes in their entirety, characters that you have spent many hours crafting, often because they're actually too good. They're too compelling, too interesting, too smart or sadistic or funny—they detract from the characters that the reader should be rooting for. Going back to the first Star Wars film, many cinema-goers felt that the Harrison Ford character Han Solo was far more interesting and engaging than the rather wimpy, by comparison, Luke Skywalker who was really the hero of the story. There was an ensemble cast, so Han Solo remained in the movie, in spite of upstaging Luke in almost every scene. But if it came to a choice between one character and the other? I think most people would rather lose Luke than lose Han Solo, which is probably not what Spielberg intended. The time you take off between writing the MS and sitting down to self-edit, which I mentioned at the very outset, will help you get close, at least, to the objectivity that is necessary to have a real cold, hard look at all your characters and decide whether they should be kept or discarded.

The good news is that, having been created, those extra characters shouldn't be just thrown on the scrap heap. There are many books or TV series (the NBC shows *Cheers* and the subsequent *Frasier* spring to mind) where one character out of an ensemble cast has proven too interesting to relegate to a bit-part character, and an entirely new story or series grows up around them. So instead of thinking of this exercise as a cutting or excising of characters, in which you actually "lose" work, think of it as a potential repurposing. The inspiration and creative energies you drew upon to create these characters aren't wasted—it's just that these characters haven't found the right book yet.

What to check in your own book

Look again at that list of main characters you drew up for the previous section. How many are there? Is it vital that all of them are main PoV characters? Is the number of PoV characters suitable for your genre? Are their character arcs complementary to the main plot, or a diversion from it? If a diversion, do they over-shadow the "main" main character? How much time do we spend following their story rather than the main story? If, on reflection, you think you do have too many PoV characters, instead of cutting them completely can you dial back on our engagement with them, be a little less detailed in letting us know what they're thinking and feeling—effectively distance us from them a little more? If you do think you probably need to cut them completely, how practical is that? Are they in every scene? Are their fortunes tied in with the main characters too much? It would be very easy to make a mess of self-editing the book, leaving references in that won't make any sense, if you have to cut a significant character out. It might be better to try and cut their involvement down, rather than cut them out entirely.

And, as I said, don't delete all that text. Cut it out and stick it in a separate folder, marked "Characters," or something. They might come in very useful in another book, or even be the main character they so clearly want to be, in their own book.

Consistency

To have believable, empathetic characters, they must be consistent in all things. They must have a consistent worldview (they are happy people, or outgoing, or short-tempered). They should speak with the same speech patterns throughout (if they speak formally at the beginning of the book, they shouldn't flip to using contractions and ghetto slang midway through the book). If they have phobias or obsessions those shouldn't just disappear. In every scene where that character appears, you should ensure that they're behaving, and speaking, true to type.

It can help to draw up character profiles if you have too many characters to keep track of in your head. These profiles can be as basic or as detailed as you like. In addition to describing the character's physical appearance and attributes, and basic details like name, birthdate, birthplace, schooling and career, immediate family and relationships with them, a character profile might also include other more abstract traits. What is the character's favourite drink? Where is the character on the optimistic/pessimistic scale? How self-confident is the character? What significant psychological issues coloured the character's early life, if any? How does the character deal with conflict, or with change? There are numerous templates available online if you can't be bothered to draw one up of your own design, some of which go into microscopic detail about a character's past.

However, caution is required. I mentioned the "iceberg principle" early on. This idea is that, just because you know all this information about a character and write it down in a profile, it doesn't mean that you have to share all of it with your readers. This is your personal information bank. In the same way that a large proportion of an iceberg floats beneath the surface, much of the information you know about your character doesn't need to be detailed to the reader. Everything you've listed about the character is there for you to make your character rich and complex, to help make the character real to *you*, to ensure the character reacts to things that happen in the story in a consistent and natural way. (Bear in mind it's not the details of what their first car was, whether they can swim or if they have a sweet tooth, that are important. That's just exposition, unless it's of importance in the story.)

With this consistency in mind, having drawn up character profiles, have a read through the book ensuring that both any *factual* references agree to the details in the profile (if he gets a call from his sister, she has the right name. If she's his favourite sister, he's pleased to hear from her), and that the character's *behaviour* is consistent with their *psychological* profile. If the character is a bit of an introvert, in the situations of conflict that they encounter in the story it should take a lot for them to get aggressive. It's very unlikely that the introvert is going to be the first to swing a punch, for example. If there's a scene at a party, they should not be the first one up on the kitchen table dancing the can-can while swigging from a bottle of vodka.

How does this consistency reconcile with character development and what we said about substantial change? Well, the character *will* change in the course of the book, but they will change in response to stimuli and events you put in front of them, not at random. For example, a cripplingly introverted character at the beginning of the story might find self-expression and self-belief through acting in the school play, and by the end of the story has come to realise their full potential, helped by an inspiring teacher (roughly the plot of *Dead Poets Society*). This is the character arc of that character. If it's written well, the reader shares that journey and the catharsis at the end. This isn't being inconsistent. This is the character reacting to conflict, making decisions within the story, and developing as a person. Hopefully you've grounded the character so well in the reader's mind at the start of the story that they will appreciate all the more deeply when and why that character changes their attitude to something, or someone. If you've worked that magic, then you will have a truly compelling book on your hands.

When you realise that you need to make sure all PoV characters (i.e. those whom you draw in some depth), are behaving consistently with where they are in their character arc, in every scene, it's easier to see that having lots of PoV characters is not necessarily a great idea!

Consistent characters in a series

I mentioned earlier that, if you're writing an episodic series (one in which the books can be read in any order), not only must you keep the character consistent within each book, but you must keep them consistent across the entire series. Here a character profile is invaluable. It would be too easy to forget minor details about a character that were revealed in book one (his first car was a Volkswagen Beetle) and contradict yourself in book seven ("Oh, I had a Golf GTI; it was my first car," he said), but, readers being readers, they will point these issues out.

Even in a normal series, a character profile is valuable but, since the character will evolve over a normal series, you might need to make the entries longer and have more of them. For example, a detective character in a long series of crime thrillers might have an affair in book two, and their lover turn up again in book six. If you have a handy sub-profile on the main character's main data sheet, detailing where they met, how often they got together, any particular events in the course of their affair, and, crucially, why they split up, that will save you going back to book two and trying to pull out all the scenes in which they appear together, to ensure that book six is consistent.

Some series writers construct what they term "series bibles." (They are used extensively in TV series, where guest writers may propose an episode to an existing soap opera or long-running sitcom, precisely for the reason of ensuring continuity across characters.) In this, the author will collate all the character templates they've drawn up, for not only the main characters, but also those secondary characters who are likely to reappear in later books. It will include timelines of significant events and also include descriptions of recurring settings (it's a cedar that stands in the middle of the lawn outside the family home, for example, and the kitchen is to the left of the sitting room). If you're writing fantasy, tough luck, because instead of being able to refer constantly to reality in terms of geography and locations (the city of Bath is about thirteen and a half miles from Bristol), you will have made it all up, and therefore the onus is on you to be consistent with it. (One of the great positives about this is that a beautifully drawn map can be a pictorial reminder of exactly how many leagues it is between the castle and the desert to the south. I'd imagine that Tolkien found his maps of Middle Earth useful, in the first instance, before someone pointed out they were also very decorative.)

Minor characters

Minor characters are individuals who might be mentioned by name, but who are never explored in any great psychological depth and from whose PoV we never (or at least very rarely and if so for very short periods) see the story. These are characters who perform a supporting role. Although we might meet them on quite a few occasions throughout the book, we don't need to know their hopes and dreams and we are unlikely to be party to their inner thoughts. We usually only see them from the PoV of one of our main characters, who might love them (parent figure), hate them (horrible boss), or depend upon them (trusty sidekick).

There's a practical reason that we don't get to empathise with these characters. Quite often they're cannon fodder, getting shot or eaten or blown up or lost in the snow or blasted out of the airlock. In movie parlance they're bit-part players, actors with a speaking role, but not too many lines. They might have a critical role to play in the plot. Think of the greedy technician,

Dennis Nedry, in the first *Jurassic Park* movie. Without him, none of the ensuing chaos would have happened—there would literally be no movie—but he only has about twenty speaking lines in the whole film. Quite often in post-apocalyptic stories there's a Patient Zero, someone who is the first infected with the plague or the zombie virus or whatever lays waste to civilisation. Who they are is rarely important, although without them there wouldn't be a story.

So how many non-PoV characters should a book have? There's no right answer. Genre will play a huge part again (do you see how critical it is knowing even roughly which genre your book falls into? I keep having to mention it). Historical fiction or epic fantasy might have a huge cast list, romance a cast in the low teens. Bear in mind that as far as the reader is concerned they don't have your knowledge of the roles characters they meet in the story are going to play. When they meet a non-PoV character in the book for the first time, they don't know how significant that character will eventually turn out to be, so they will try and remember more details about the character, if you give them out, than they really need to.

For example, if the second spearman from the left is named as Nigel, and he's described as having a wart the size of a golf-ball on his nose, they're going to remember Nigel as a potentially significant character whose wart is possibly going to play a major part in the story. When they never meet Nigel again, or his wart, they'll wonder why they bothered. There are two details here that we might not need to know at all. Firstly, that the second spearman from the left is called Nigel, and secondly, that he has a huge wart. Do you need to name him? Do you need to describe him in quite such vivid detail? (Of course, if Nigel is drawn from life—a particularly odious junior manager at work that you wanted to humiliate—then ignore everything I've just said. They do say you should never be mean to a writer ...)

Of course, on the other hand, giving minor characters some detail will lend your book more depth. If you do, make sure it's worth the inclusion, and isn't just bland personal description. There might be a myriad of supporting characters in your book—ticket collectors, taxi drivers, charioteers, blacksmiths, parking attendants—who play a very minor role in the story, but they don't need to be clichés. Blacksmiths will probably be heavily muscled, but that doesn't preclude them from being female, or loving opera. Not all taxi drivers are middle-aged men with right wing political proclivities. Some, instead of telling you about the "real problem with the unemployed," will be able to carry a monologue on the deities of Ancient Egypt. A parking attendant might be a "resting" actor who deflects criticism while carrying out his job by quoting Shakespeare ("Oi, You can't be serious? I've only been here a minute!" "Alas. Better three hours too soon than a minute too late, as the Bard sayeth." "You what?" "*The Merry Wives of Windsor*, son. Pay up. Address is on the back").

But sometimes a surly bouncer who lets the girls in but looks askance at any male, however well-dressed, is just a shaven-headed stock figure who creates the impediment to the desired boy-meets-girl situation that the hero needs to achieve.

Names themselves are problematic. If you've deluged your reader with too many names they won't be able to keep track of them, and worse, they'll start losing their grip on the characters who *do* matter. There are rather laborious sections in the Game of Thrones books (sorry, George), where everyone sitting round a campfire, or standing around in a crowded throne-room at a coronation, is named in turn. Most of the people we never hear of again, and one wonders whether the exercise was just to display the author's vast imagination in coming up with vivid names. As a reader though, one's eyes glaze over and you find yourself skipping through the lists of who comes from what castle and who wears what emblem on their shield, to get to some action or dialogue where *something happens*. When looking at minor characters you need to assess whether their named inclusion is necessary. Think of yourself as the director of a film. If you have a named character, with lines, they are paid bit-part actor rates that, while insignificant compared to the stars' fees, are a hell of a lot more than you pay extras (who just hang around and get wordlessly trampled by elephants or eviscerated by chariots).

> *Think of your book as having a casting budget. Everyone you name and give some page space and lines to, you're going to have to pay, out of your own pocket.*

One aside on names. Try not to name characters too similarly. They may be very different to you, but they will tend to blur into one another in a reader's eyes. You may have hidden biases as an author when coming up with character names that you won't even be aware of. I once edited a book in which the names of every single character apart from one began with the letter *m* and were one or two syllables. It wasn't quite "Milly, Molly, Mandy," but close. The funny thing was that the author was completely unaware of it. In your role as your own self-editor, now is the time to look closely at your choice of names and make sure they are quite distinct and unlikely to be confused.

What to check in your own book

How many characters do you actually name? Do you need to name them? Think about whether your main characters would know their names, or, even having been told, remember them. Isn't the king more likely to say "Hey, you there!" to the second spearman from the left, not "Hey, Nigel!" (He might of course say, "Hey, wartface! You first into the cave. Find out what's roaring and stamping around in there making the ground shake. No need to take your spear, it'll only slow you down," but you're just being self-indulgent ... that junior manager again.)

Make sure you only include such details as you need to, that are relevant to the main plot, especially at the beginning of the book when readers will be working hard trying to absorb all the details they can find in order to immerse themselves in the story. If you have them trying to memorise a whole heap of trivia about every single child in the classroom from the first page, it's quite possible that they'll be frazzled by the end of chapter one, and won't have even taken in the vital information about your main characters that they should have.

Is the detail you have included about minor characters worth the inclusion? Does it lend colour and interest to the book generally, or is it just endless descriptions of hair and eye colour?

Villains

I thought it worthwhile to have a brief note specifically on villains. While the main heroic characters are often well-drawn and nuanced, because they are generally the PoV characters, often villain characters can be rather flat and stereotypical, with thick necks, bruised knuckles and cold, staring eyes (and that's just the women). Your bad guys should be just as complex and intriguing as your heroines (I'm thinking of Hannibal Lecter, or the Joker) if you want your story to be truly engrossing.

What to check in your own book

How much thought have you put in to the motivation of exactly why your serial killer is driven to do what he does? What weird twisted logic (and there must be some kind of logic) is it that drives your pet psychopath? Your book might not ever describe a scene from the PoV of the villain, so it would be easy to neglect them as a secondary character. But if you pay attention to their background and motivations, to the extent that you might want to draw up a character sheet for them too, even though we never read from their PoV, you'll have a more enthralling and believable antagonist for your main character.

Point of view

Point of view (PoV) is one of the fundamental tools with which to tell your story. It's one of the most complex issues in writing a novel, one of the easiest to get wrong and one about which there is the most confusion.

Discussions on PoV can get very technical, for no good reason. We can micro-analyse PoV and decide exactly where in the continuum of *first person close* to *omniscient* a book's perspective lies, but there seems little point. There are four main PoVs and your book will fall into one of those categories (hopefully no more than one, of which more later).

I don't want to bog the aspiring self-editor down with information they already know, so if you're confident you know the basics of PoV and are really just looking for things to check in your own book, then read on. If you'd like a more comprehensive analysis of PoV from a writing perspective, please take a detour and read Appendix II, which goes in to the subject in some depth, and explains thoroughly the terms that I'll use in the next sections.

In this chapter we'll talk about common problems arising with each type of PoV, and what you might do about them.

If you haven't ever considered the concept of PoV in isolation before, then it should be an interesting exercise to have a look at your MS. It will almost certainly be written in the PoV that you find most natural to tell stories in. There's probably no reason to change that, unless, by the time you've finished this section, you feel certain that the story would be better told in another PoV. That's not something to be undertaken lightly—

altering the PoV would be a major rewrite—so don't jump to any sudden conclusions.

The chances are that the PoV you write in naturally will be the one that comes easiest and flows the best. PoV has a huge impact on a writer's voice and personal style, and vice versa, and trying to force your book into a particular PoV that your imagination hasn't already suggested might lead to very awkward and uncomfortable prose and headaches as a writer. (Having said that, a writer shouldn't be afraid to experiment with other PoVs—it's all part of learning the craft, like a painter in oils choosing to do a few landscapes in watercolour for a change. However, perhaps experiment with short stories, so that you can get a feel for how the different PoVs work without committing to a novel-length project.)

PoV can shift within a story, of course. Although it's common practice to have a single type of PoV dominate a book, to give the reader some continuity, in some genres it's quite usual to have PoV manipulated similarly to how a film director uses his cameras on a film set, a bird's-eye view (in our language an omniscient narrator, looking down on the scene from on high) zooming in to a close-up of a character on, say, a battlefield (our equivalent of a close first or third person PoV thrown into the heat of immersive action). This kind of shift is normally from omniscient PoV into a closer third person, or vice versa, attempting to give an epic story a more personal human touch. I go into this in some more detail in the summary—things to check.

Common problems in first person PoV

If your book is written in first person PoV, there are a number of common problems to look out for.

Your PoV character, and therefore your reader, *cannot know anything out of that character's direct experience.* The character cannot know what's round the corner, or what other people are thinking (although they might try and guess), or what happens "offstage." This impacts the story in ways that you might not consider. A character, unless remarkably self-obsessed, will not comment on their own appearance—"my cornflower-blue eyes were fixed on the distant hills" would just sound weird. (Avoid the temptation to get round this problem with the "reflective surface" trope. Authors determined to describe their main character resort to their protagonist looking in a mirror or the surface of a lake and describing to themselves what they see—"I looked in the mirror and my cornflower-blue eyes stared back at me" is a writing cliché to be avoided at all costs.)

If the PoV is that of *a child*, it might be difficult to fully realise the world you need to describe because children, especially young ones, don't have the life experience or vocabulary to appreciate or describe why things happen, or the cause and effect of events. This naivety can work very well for voice, but can be restrictive when plotting. If you have a child as a main character, how appropriately limited is their understanding of their immediate world and what's going on in it, particularly adult motivations and emotions. Adults can be angry when they're afraid, upset when they're happy, aloof when they're trying to be supportive. Is your child suitably confused, or do they seem presciently aware of things they won't be mature enough to understand until they're older?

It's easy to fall into the trap of too many *pronouns*. Too many sentences beginning with "I" will get quickly repetitive. Make sure that the narrative is mixed up to avoid too many "I," "me" and "my" pronouns.

Another related pitfall is to narrate too much through *filters*. Filter words are those words describing the senses, to hear, to see, to feel, and also to think, to realise and to wonder. Filter words distance us from the character. They reduce the experience the character is having from being direct, to one of narration. Given that the prime reasons for having a first person PoV are depth of perception and empathy with the character, it makes sense to avoid filtering those sensations, thoughts and feelings as much as possible, and have the reader experience them directly. I'll touch more on this in its own section in "Show, don't tell," but for now consider this passage.

> I thought I heard a noise upstairs. It sounded like a footstep. I wondered if someone was up there. I could feel a cold draft. I rounded the corner. At first glance the kitchen window looked strange, and then I realised, there was no glass in the lower pane. It has been removed, I thought. Now I knew someone was upstairs.

That's flush with plenty of filter words and a lot of "I" pronouns. Although it's a scene with potentially a lot of tension, it seems flat and uninteresting, almost boring, and those "I"s get plain irritating. A much more terse and direct rendition would eliminate all of the filters, chop three-quarters of the pronouns, and bring us far closer in to the character's actual experience.

> Was that a noise upstairs? A footstep? Was someone up there? Cold air moved in the hall. I rounded the corner. Something about the kitchen window ... A chill settled around me. There was no glass in the lower pane. *Removed.* I looked up again at the ceiling.

It's a subjective issue, as so much of writing is, but I think most people would find the second passage much more immersive. It's slightly different, not just because of the lack of filter words, but also because without them, as a writer, you're forced to think about what the character in that situation would *really do*. They wouldn't stand there and think to themselves "Now I knew there was someone upstairs." Their concern that there was an intruder would evidence itself by an appropriate action, by looking up at the ceiling. As a reader you completely understand that. You *would* look up. Instinctively you would want to listen for more footsteps, trying to work out where the intruder was.

There is a danger that the first person PoV can get claustrophobic. Without the regular injection of other perspectives on the story, the reader is stuck solely in one PoV. If your protagonist is a rounded, interesting, empathetic character, that might not be a problem, but still take the time to break up the narrative. First person PoV doesn't mean that the character needs to constantly jabber away in your reader's ear, telling them every inner thought and fantasy. If your main character is a psychopath, it might get exhausting very quickly. However, everything has its uses. Bret Easton Ellis used that claustrophobia (of being stuck in the mind of a lunatic) to positive effect (if that's the right term) in his intensely claustrophobic novel *American Psycho*.

In a similar vein, "quirky" PoVs often materialise in YA fiction. That's okay, and almost a trope of the genre, but how confident are you that your quirky PoV isn't just plain irritating by chapter three? As with everything, less is more.

Common problems in third person PoV

The usual problem that occurs with third person PoVs of any variety is a failure to hold a specific character viewpoint. A scene might lapse either into an omniscient PoV and drop out of the character PoV entirely, or skip from one character PoV to another without sufficient warning or "cool-down" for the reader to accommodate the leap (head-hopping, which is such a common problem that I give it its own section, in a moment).

A typical scenario would be a thriller, told in a fairly close third person PoV, that suddenly zooms out to a default omniscient narrator.

> Jack squinted along the barrel of the rifle, sweat smearing the vision in his left eye. *I've got you. Just pop your head above that wall one more time.* The pain in his knee ballooned with each pump of his heart. He couldn't stay like this for much longer. *If it's gonna be a waiting game, I might lose.*
>
> The tribesman hadn't seen Jack, but knew that there had been soldiers in the area the previous day. He was from the

> mountains, generations of goat herders clinging to the precipitous ledges of the Khyber region, famed for the eponymous Pass, the legendary Silk Route from China to Spain. He had come to fight against the invaders, for the glory of himself and his village.
>
> He saw a turbaned head cautiously peering through a window. Bang! The head disappeared.

Although one might assume that Jack shot the tribesman, we cannot be sure without further explanation. We have lost the direct link with the character PoV of Jack because of the interlude describing, from no particular PoV at all, who the tribesman was and what he was doing there. It might have been Jack shooting the tribesman, but he was waiting for the head to stick up over a wall, not through a window. Inasmuch as we were in any PoV, we were with the tribesman when the "turbaned head" peered through the window, but why would Jack be wearing a turban? Is he a Muslim? Was he wearing a disguise?

In addition to the confusion over who shot whom, the interlude about the Pashtun tribesman steals all the tension from the scene. One minute we are looking down the barrel of a gun, sweat in our eyes, pain from our wounded knee growing more intense by the moment, and the next we are away in the mountainous region on the border with Pakistan, having a little history lesson about medieval trade routes.

In a similar way to first person PoV, third person PoVs can be littered with pronouns; "he did this," "he said that," and filter words. If it's a close third PoV, you can break up the third person pronouns by zooming in to internal monologue, like we did in the first paragraph of the example above, and use the first person pronouns to indicate we're now close in to the character's experience: "*I've got you.*"

The example we used in first person PoV could be rewritten from a third person PoV perspective quite easily, and look equally awkward.

> He thought he heard a noise upstairs. It sounded like a footstep. He wondered if someone was up there. He could feel a cold draft. He rounded the corner.

We can apply the same techniques to strip out most of the pronouns and bring the reader closer into the action.

> Was that a noise upstairs? A footstep? Was someone up there? Cold air moved in the hall. He rounded the corner.

Another common issue in third person PoV is having too many PoV characters. We discussed this at length in the section on characters, so I won't repeat myself. Briefly, if you write a scene from the PoV of a character, that character should be an important one, one in which the reader is going to make some emotional investment. Otherwise, why would the reader care about that character's perspective? It's difficult for a reader to empathise with a great number of characters, and it's particularly difficult to get a reader to empathise with a lot of PoV characters in quick succession. If you're writing epic fantasy, and you do have a large ensemble cast of PoV characters whose individual narratives the reader needs to follow, best to split those out into fairly lengthy sections, or even give them whole chapters to themselves.

Common problems in omniscient PoV

Because omniscient PoV is a more general, distant perspective, there are fewer technical errors that can arise with it. It's the most flexible PoV. An author can narrate from a "God view," and then dip down into any character's head at any time at will. The narrator of the story knows everything about everyone.

The problems arising with the use of an omniscient PoV are generally a tendency to rely too much on exposition. I'll be going into some depth on "Show, don't tell" in the next section, because it's a common problem that spans all PoVs and writing styles, so I won't belabour the point here. It's easy to get carried away, particularly in the sci-fi or fantasy genres, with describing the world you've lovingly created at great length. You can't do that in a close third or first person PoV because the character can't be standing around tapping their feet while you give all this description—you are automatically brought to heel by your character, who needs to be told what to do next. With an omniscient PoV, there's no such constraint. Can you see areas where you're describing scenes or landscapes at great length, or talking about people in generalities without moving either plot or characterisation on a great deal? If there are too many of these static scenes the pacing of your book will slow to a crawl, so if you've already identified a problem with pacing, this is one of the things to look for.

An omniscient PoV by its nature distances the reader from the characters. We can't know everything there is to know about a story and then realistically assume the close PoV of a particular character. We know too much about what's going on elsewhere. This means that it's going to be a struggle to develop really profound characters that resonate with readers in an omniscient PoV.

As a result of this distancing effect, omniscient can feel quite remote and unengaging, more a history textbook than a novel.

Regardless of the omniscient narrator's ability to dip into the heads of any of the characters in a scene, it's still a bad idea to jump from one character to another within a scene. A scene should generally be told with respect to one character, the character with the most at stake, who will be changed most by its outcome. Jumping from one character to another, as well as giving the reader a kind of mental whiplash, is going to undermine the impact of the scene on that critical character. If you come across scenes where you do jump from one character to another, think about retelling the scene from just one character's PoV, and see if that makes the scene more powerful.

Common problems in second person PoV

Potential problems in second person PoV largely stem from its unusual nature. It will be unfamiliar to most readers, so they will be more aware that they're reading a book, probably regarding it as quite an experimental book. The PoV will draw attention to itself as a literary device, so it's not going to be as immersive an experience as a "normal" PoV.

While all deep PoVs seek to place the reader in the heart and mind of the character, there's something quite pointed and aggressive about the second person PoV. The PoV tells your reader that "you do this" and "you say that." If your main character is a kind of Everyman, someone with whom a lot of your readers will feel a commonality, whose opinions aren't going to rock the boat, then this can work. If, however, your character has some radical perspectives on certain issues, then it's unlikely that a reader is going to feel that they *are* the character, so its use may be questionable.

Second person PoV can also get very claustrophobic very quickly, which is why it's more often used for short stories than novels. If you've written a book in second person PoV, congratulations. You're one of the few who have.

Common problems in free indirect style

I mentioned that there were four main classifications of PoV. That's true, but there is a hybrid style called free indirect style (also called free indirect speech, or free indirect discourse). If you're unfamiliar with the term and would like to know more about this style of writing, I go in to a bit of depth about it and the differences between it and normal first person and third person PoVs in Appendix II. Put briefly, it's a hybrid style of writing in which the third person narrator sometimes becomes a first person character in relating their direct thought. In normal third person, direct thought would be "reported," either using the italics convention in a close PoV, or using thought tags ("he wondered"). In free indirect style the thoughts of the character are related seamlessly in roman script as if they were the thoughts of the narrator.

The problems that can arise in this subtle and advanced style are largely to do with consistency and clarity. In a conversation between two characters, where the narrator can assume the thoughts of any character at will, how do you make it clear who is thinking what without any kind of tag? How do you avoid head-hopping (which I'm coming on to in a moment) when you are dipping in and out of character's heads at whim and quite possibly within a scene or even paragraph? Doing so takes a lot of skill and writing dexterity. It's an advanced style, and perhaps isn't suitable for novice writers with their first book. *Wolf Hall*, by Hilary Mantel, won the Booker Prize and is written in a hybrid omniscient free indirect style. Mantel gives any information she wants, from a character perspective or from a narrated perspective, dips into any character's thought process at whim, sometimes in alternate lines so that it *is* quite hard to work out whose thoughts you're actually reading. It works for Mantel—she won the Booker—but it's not going to work for everyone.

Head-hopping

The problem of head-hopping has risen in significance over the last couple of decades with the increasing prevalence of immersive close PoV characters. It is normally defined as an author jumping from one character's PoV to another, without an adequate transition such as a new chapter, new scene or even line space to give the reader adequate notice.

Let's go back to why we have "close" PoVs in the first place. The whole point of an intimate PoV is that the reader can be absorbed in the character, living their life as they lead it, experiencing their triumphs and disasters, forming a deep emotional connection. In head-hopping, the reader has successfully formed this emotional connection to a character and is closely following their version of events when suddenly they are wrenched out of it and thrown in to the close PoV of another character. This abrupt dislocation in the reader's profound engagement with the character (which is, after all, what you've been striving to achieve) creates a couple of problems.

Firstly that primary PoV character is left stranded in limbo—whatever was happening in that scene for them is unresolved. Secondly we readers now have a decision to make. Do we immerse ourselves in this new PoV that we've been offered? Perhaps we're unsure if we want to make a deep emotional commitment to another close PoV character in case we're abruptly wrenched out of that, too. We will therefore have a fundamental problem engaging with the book going forwards.

Jumping from one character to another *in an omniscient PoV* is not head-hopping, under the commonly accepted definition. With an omniscient narrator, the author is at liberty to take any PoV at any time. The transition between one character and another still needs to be managed well, just to avoid any possible confusion in the reader, but the intensity of the dislocation in the reader's mind is muted because the deep emotional connection is just not there in an omniscient PoV.

Head-hopping generally occurs in third person PoV narratives, and it's only a real problem in *close* third person, where the reader is encouraged to empathise deeply with a character. Quite frequently, the dislocation in PoV only extends to one or two lines within a scene, which makes it all the harder to spot.

> "I think you should do it. I think you'd make a great leader." He looked pensive, as if he was undecided. She put a hand on his arm. "You've got all the qualities we need, bravery, weapons handling, tech smarts. Why don't you put yourself forwards?"
>
> She gazed at him with her pale blue eyes.
>
> "I don't know," he said. "I think I'm just better off being a mechanic."
>
> *Modest too. He just doesn't know what he's really capable of.* "You should go for it," she said. "I'd vote for you, any day. You can still work on your beloved engines."

Quite often a PoV slip is not this easy to recognise, but there it is, in the middle of the dialogue. The PoV of this scene is the girl. It's her inner thoughts we hear when she thinks he's not confident enough. So if we are her, looking at him, how can we be aware of our own eye colour?

That's a minor slip, subtle but not too intrusive. How about this exchange?

> "I'd like to think you didn't mean it," he said.
>
> "I didn't mean it," she said. *I bloody did.*

> *I know she didn't mean it.*
>
> *He knows I did.*
>
> "I know you didn't, but it came over as if you did."

Confused? I am. We shouldn't be, really, because, paying attention to our paragraphing, it's quite clear who is thinking and saying what. But it's very unclear what we should be *feeling*, as readers. Should we be siding with the girl, who says she didn't mean it but did, or the boy, who believes he knows she didn't mean it, but quite possibly thinks she did? What's the point of this scene? Are we supposed to be feeling the girl's frustration, where she's clearly wanted to express something but held back for some reason? Or are we supposed to be empathising with him, slightly but not wholly reassured by the girl's emphatic denial? Because we're bouncing around between both protagonists, we end up not really getting a good handle on either emotion, so the exchange is wasted.

There's no real failsafe method of identifying head-hopping, but if you've written in a close third person PoV you should be aware that it might have happened and, when reading through scenes, be on the lookout for scenes that don't seem to quite "work." It could well be, as in the example above, that head-hopping is the problem.

Of course there's nothing straightforward about rules in writing, and you may well come across examples of head-hopping in published, even traditionally published books. Don't write in to the publisher or author pointing this out and expecting a medal, however. Some authors can manage to get away with head-hopping without too much damage to their narrative, but until you're confident (or successful enough) to flout any rule about writing with impunity, it's definitely not recommended.

If you do need to shift PoV within a scene, one of the simplest techniques is simply to use a line space as a break. Finish with one PoV, insert a line space, and then start the new PoV as a new paragraph.

> Harriet toyed with her hair in the hall mirror.
>
> "I made a mistake," he said, "a silly mistake. Can you ever forgive me?"
>
> "The thing is," she said, "you're not the only one who's been unfaithful. I've been shagging Barry behind your back for months. Sorry. Let's just leave it at that." She put the phone down and looked at herself in the mirror, twirled. *Not too bad.* She pouted. *Good riddance.*
>
> John stared at the handset. A dial tone. Did she really just say that? And then hang up on him? Barry? For God's sake ... Barry? Whose knuckles dragged on the ground when he walked? Who she said she hated being around because he stared at her cleavage all the time?

In this scene, the author makes use of a line space to split the PoV between the two participants of a phone call. The space serves to notify the reader that we're making a jump in scene or PoV, or in this case both.

With the above example, it's clear that the author wants to capture both participants' reactions to this perhaps crucial phone call. If you find yourself splitting a lot of scenes this way, however, you should be asking yourself if it's appropriate to jump from one PoV to another within that scene. It's usually good writing advice to always write a scene from the PoV of the character who is most involved in it, who is going to be changed most by events that take place in that scene. It would be unusual for two characters to share that definition, and if it's necessary to switch PoV merely to accommodate a plot point, then that might indicate plotting problems generally.

Summary: PoV issues to check

We'll finish this complex section with a checklist of things to look out for in your own MS. Because PoV is such a fundamental building block of story, it's probably worth going through your MS one full pass just looking at PoV issues.

Is your book in the right PoV?

First and most important, is your book in the right PoV? As we discussed at the beginning, there's no right and wrong, and most authors gravitate to the PoV that they feel most comfortable in. However, write an intensive character-driven story in an omniscient PoV, or a complex epic thriller on a global scale in a close first person PoV, and you will probably run into technical problems that will be visible in the story.

Character-driven stories are best written from the close perspective of the character (or characters) whose story you want the reader to follow. This wasn't always the case, but is the style of fiction to which we've grown accustomed over the last half a century. If you've written a character-driven story from an omniscient perspective, you will probably have needed to use lots of filter words (words describing thoughts or feelings like "he realised" or "she understood" or "he felt") in order to tell us what emotions the character is experiencing, or what the character is truly thinking about an event. Because we are in an omniscient PoV looking down on the character, it's impossible for us to tell exactly what is going on in a character's mind merely by observing their actions, and "showing" us these details would necessitate lengthy and contrived passages to avoid the use of filters (I go into "showing and telling" at some length in the next section). If you find yourself frequently having to explain what your characters are really thinking, or spelling out their motivations for doing or saying something, then you're struggling with a character-driven story in an omniscient, or at least distant, PoV. You *can* tell us all of this, of course, but *telling* us the story is less immersive and less compelling than allowing the reader to *be* the character and experience those emotions first-hand.

If you've written a complex thriller in a single close PoV, have you managed to ensure that the character doesn't know things they cannot be aware of knowing, or have you relied on plot contrivances that may feel a little awkward now that you're looking at them again? If you've chosen to convey a complex plot through the close PoVs of many characters, how many PoVs have you used? Bear in mind that beyond five or six close PoVs, readers might struggle to keep characters distinct, which could impact on their appreciation of the finer details of the plot.

There is a lesser distinction between close first and third person PoVs when telling a character-driven story. Either PoV is equally valid, but rendering the story from a third person perspective does make it slightly more impersonal. If the narrative contains very harrowing scenes, you may even find it necessary to *create* a little distance; otherwise the emotion of the story you are telling could overwhelm the plot.

Consider the PoV of other books in your genre. Are they consistently written in a particular PoV? Is there a good reason why, and if so, is your book written in the same PoV, and if not, is there a good reason why not?

Although it's a major task to rewrite the PoV of a finished draft, don't be put off doing so if it's really the right thing to do. It might be that you started with a third person narrative because that's what you're used to reading. But in the course of the book, your main character blossomed in so many unexpectedly engaging and quirky directions that if the book were rewritten from a first person PoV they would be an intriguing and compelling narrator in their own right, someone that readers would really bond with. If that's the happy turn of events, then the only thing to do is to respect your character, and give them free rein to tell their story in their own voice.

Do you establish the PoV early?

Have you established your chosen PoV early in the book? It's usually a good idea in most genre fiction to start a book *in medias res*, literally *in the middle of things*. Instead of lengthy preambles about your main character, what they look like, what their name is, where they live etc., start with an incident, some dialogue, something that can ground your reader immediately in the PoV that you are going to use to tell the story. We mentioned this earlier in the section book structure, "Where does your story start?" If you're narrating a lot of exposition about the character at the start of the book, then you can't be in a close PoV until you start telling the reader what's going on inside the character's head. If that's a chapter later, you're having to hope that readers who were expecting an engaging and immersive story in a genre that usually gives them that experience are still reading, and haven't left your book on the bookshop shelf.

If you are going to have more than one PoV character, introduce them sooner rather than later. It is going to be disconcerting for a reader to "meet" another PoV character for the first time half way through the book.

Do you change PoV?

Within a close PoV story, shifting PoV from omniscient to close in (at, say, the beginning of a chapter) can be a valid device for scene-setting. If you do use this narrative tool, have you avoided the temptation to "dump" a lot of exposition on the reader? One or two lines of "bird's eye" description might help the reader immerse themselves in the detail of a scene that then plays out from a close PoV, but two or three pages of elaborate description might tip the balance between scene-setting and losing the pace and focus of the narrative. Every time you stop narrating the story from a close PoV, the reader is effectively taking a break from immersion in your characters. If you do that too often, or for too long, you run the risk that they may not regain that immersion.

More difficult to justify would be a shift within a chapter from a close PoV "out" to an omniscient perspective. The whole point of a close PoV is to allow the reader to live the story vicariously. If you suddenly zoom out to accommodate an omniscient overview, then the reader will naturally lose their connection to the character. They will suddenly know or see things that the character they are meant to be cannot know, or that are beyond the character's field of vision. This negates the whole point of having a close PoV in the first place, and subsequent immersion in that character's PoV is going to be compromised because, in the reader's mind, they are aware of the knowledge that the character doesn't know.

However, when using a story with multiple PoVs, sometimes authors will zoom out from a particular character, spend a small amount in an omniscient viewpoint, and then zoom back in to a different character from whose PoV they want to continue with the scene. This sophisticated juggling of PoV needs to be adeptly managed if it's to be successful, and should probably be avoided by less experienced authors.

Shifting PoVs from distant to close, or in the other direction, is not breaking any rules, but you should be aware that each time you do this you are requiring your reader to recalibrate their involvement in the characters and the story. Too much, and that might well prove tiring, or just tiresome, to many readers.

Do you manage transitions from one PoV to another successfully?

In a book where the story is told from a multitude of PoVs, how well have you managed the transitions from one PoV to another? Are the transitions clear, at logical places like scene changes or chapter breaks? If you have used the technique of zooming out and zooming back in to manage transitions from one PoV to another, have you been successful, or are you likely to lose the reader's immersion in the scene?

Have you avoided head-hopping?

If your story is in a close PoV, poorly managed transitions from one PoV character to another constitute head-hopping. Generally, jumping from the close PoV of one character to that of another, without any kind of break in the narrative, is likely to disorient and confuse your readers. If you start a scene in one PoV, it's probably best to continue in that PoV until the end of the scene. Think about why you've written that scene in the first place. One character, above all, is going to be changed by the events in that scene, and that is probably your PoV character. To enable the reader to fully engage with the change in that character, they are going to need to be in that character's head for the duration of the scene.

In a multiple PoV story, this might just involve poorly managed transitions from one character to another that could be fixed by either creating scene breaks, or engineering a transition by means of switching to a temporary omniscient PoV.

Is your single character PoV consistent?

In a close single PoV narrative, have you managed to keep a solid grip on the PoV, and not be distracted into providing information that is beyond the character's experience of the story for the sake of plot or description? You might not have actually moved so far from your character's PoV that you are in another, but you might have included information that only an observer might see, and sometimes this can be very subtle.

> James panted. *I'm losing this fight.* He ducked a swinging haymaker but sweat dripped in his eyes and, blinking to clear his vision, he was caught full in the face by Barry's next punch, which raised a purple lump the size of a walnut on his cheek.

Doesn't this scene feel a bit flat? It seems an okay description of a punch-up, but if you look closely, we're mixing a close PoV *and* an omniscient narrator when narrating this passage, which is probably why it fails to sparkle. James pants, and we hear his internal thoughts as he realises he's losing the fight. A few stage directions later and he is caught by a punch that raises "a purple lump the size of a walnut" on his cheek. But it can't be James telling us this, because he has no means of knowing there is a lump the size of a walnut on his cheek, or its colour, unless he halts the fist fight and calls for a mirror, which seems unlikely in the circumstances. It might not be a glaring error, but it's enough of one to alert our subconscious to the fact that something is not quite right with the telling of the scene.

A problem happens sometimes in crime thrillers where the PoV character is set upon, beaten up in a dark alley perhaps, and left unconscious. At the point the character blacks out, the scene should end as far as the reader is concerned. Many authors make the mistake of continuing the scene (the hoodlums staging their getaway, or discussing how the victim deserved their beating) while the PoV character lies unconscious at their feet. If the author is aware of the fact that they can't really be narrating the continuation of the scene while their PoV character is out cold, they sometimes switch PoVs to one of the gang, or pull back to look down on the victim from an omniscient PoV. In a close PoV story, neither solution is particularly elegant, and both do a lot to destroy the immersion of the reader in the PoV character. If the reader feels they are "immortal," and not subject to the character's problems, they are aloof from that character, and not wholly involved.

In a PoV with a distinct voice, are all the passages of that PoV in the same voice? To make the PoV believable, the voice of the character must be consistent, their attitudes and responses to events and conversations "in character" at all times. Of course, in the course of the story those attitudes might have genuinely changed. If they have, then the reader needs to be made aware of when and why they changed. In an adventure story, if a character is terrified of snakes at the beginning of the book, how is it that they manage to steel themselves to explore an underground tomb full of them by the end of the story? Did they undergo therapy? Were they convinced by someone that snakes only bite in self-defence? Are they just generally braver, and this subterranean ordeal is a good example of their newfound courage?

Show, don't tell

"Show, don't tell" is an enormous subject and impacts on many different facets of writing. Some of the topics will have already come up, and some may be covered more than once in later sections, for which, no apology. This is a wide-ranging issue.

Where do we start? Let's talk first about the fact that a preference for showing over telling is relatively modern advice, although the argument is ancient. Plato and Aristotle sat around after double physics on a Friday afternoon discussing whether diegesis (telling and narration) or mimesis (showing and enacting) were the better form of story-telling. I don't think it's coincidence that the obsession with showing over telling has occurred in perfect step with the ever greater exposure we have to video and moving images in media. A filmmaker can't resort to voiceover all the time. If every time a director needed a character to communicate something to the audience he cut to a headshot and let the character literally tell us what they are thinking it would be a very strange film indeed. Instead, the filmmaker tries to literally *show* us what their characters are thinking, by juxtaposing images and letting us work out the connection.

For example, Mary is mourning her dead son, who died in a tragic accident. Mary doesn't face the camera and tell us blandly that she's missing her son. Instead, the camera follows her into his bedroom. Her hand trails over his shirt hanging on the door; she picks up his old teddy bear sitting on the pillow; zoom in to a headshot and her tear-filled eyes gazing out of the window; cross-fade to her view, of the old swing hanging from the bough of the wych elm moving slowly in the breeze and ... cut. Viewers like to work out that association by themselves, and the mental process they go through (asking a question—what is she thinking about?—and deducing the answer themselves—she's thinking about her dead son, poor woman) encourages their immersion and empathy with the character ("If I'd lost my child, that's exactly how I'd feel," they think).

Here's another psychological perspective on "show, don't tell." Have you ever heard it said of someone that they need to think an idea is theirs before they'll act on it? That they can't be told to do something but, gently manipulated in the right direction, might come to the "correct" decision in their own time? Standard modern corporate psychology is designed to get employees to "buy into" an idea. Instead of telling staff what to do and threatening them if they don't comply, employers spell out the situation and cajole/persuade their staff to come to the right conclusion. If the staff suggest a problem's solution to management (which might involve working longer hours to fulfil a tight contract schedule, or giving up a bank holiday to keep a shop open), they are much more likely to accept the circumstances willingly, rather than resent management "putting their foot down."

It's the same with showing and telling in writing. Don't *tell* the reader that a character is bossy and didactic (which the reader might or might not believe depending on their own assessment of that character so far in the story). If you *show* the reader that character constantly telling everyone what to do and exactly how to do it, the reader will come to their own conclusion and believe in it far more strongly as a result. This is absolutely key to generating empathetic characters.

Telling and showing are also directly related to point of view and narrative distance, and it's the dominance of close PoV fiction in late twentieth and early twenty-first century fiction, again, probably influenced by film, that has helped create the issue. Put simply, telling is narration, the giving of information, and in a close PoV, narration stands out because it isn't immersive. (In an omniscient PoV it's impossible not to include a large amount of narration, obviously.) Let's look at an example of a scene that is "told," and then rewritten as "shown," to clarify what we mean by the terms. In the first paragraph the passage is narrated.

> It was a steep climb, and towards the summit the path disappeared into a scree-filled slope that was loose underfoot. He was unfit, and tired, and he regretted wearing flip-flops—they had no grip and he kept stumbling, cutting his hands. It was much colder up here than it had been down in the valley. He should have been wearing more than a T-shirt.

In this second example, the PoV is a lot closer and much more is shown.

> He panted heavily, head down, the loose stone stretching up away from him, filling his vision. His thighs burned. He slipped again, and where his hand slammed down on the rock he felt a sudden sharp stab of pain. *Bloody flip-flops. Stupid bravado that was, down in the valley.* He shivered, the sweat he

> had built up lower down the mountain
> now cooling and sticking to his T-shirt.

There's nothing technically wrong with either version, but you should be able to see a clear difference in how you *feel* about the climber.

In the first version his physical state is described (unfit and tired) rather than shown (his panting and his thighs burning). The steepness of the climb, while specified in the first example, is only alluded to indirectly in the second passage, by the physical effort he is needing to put into the climb and the fact that all he can see is the stone in front of him. His regret at wearing flip-flops is expressed directly in the first passage but implied by his inner monologue in the second. The temperature gradient on the mountain, while explicit in the first example ("it was much colder up here"), is shown by the cooling of his sweat, implying, with his shiver, that he is wearing inappropriate clothing as well as footwear.

Telling is often described as being more economical with words, and the second passage here is slightly longer than the first, but the truth is that efficient showing can often multi-task. The information conveyed in the last two sentences of the first version is also conveyed, in four less words, in the last sentence of the second version.

Which version is more "correct" depends on the voice of the book in general. Is this a close third person PoV novel, written from this character's perspective? If it is, then the first version has lost its grip on the close PoV and has retreated to a narrator perspective, to the detriment of the reader's engagement with the character's struggle up the mountain. However, if this is a passage from a more distant third person or even an omniscient PoV, or if the book is a close third person PoV but this isn't the main character, then it's perfectly adequate.

Is telling ever okay in a close PoV?

There are certain circumstances where showing could be laborious and over-complicated.

Repetition. If a character performs an action or sequence of actions repeatedly then showing each incidence of this action, rather than telling us, is unnecessary. In a story about a racing driver, for example, it is not necessary to show the character turning into every bend and flooring it on the straight, on every lap. It's not even necessary to describe every race in the season. Doing so would be utterly boring for the reader, and also detract from the description of the crucial race, the race where he crashes into the trees at one corner and breaks every bone in his body. Summarise the racing season in a short piece of narration, then pick up the close first person PoV as soon as you've finished.

> In every race he was getting faster, more confident, more aggressive. Imola, Hockenheim, Singapore. In Adelaide the race took place in a deluge and he was one of only five cars to finish. Schnabel's challenge had faded. Honda kept having trouble with their engines overheating. It was Silverstone where he could clinch the title, and everybody knew it.

> "Welcome home," Melanie said, standing by his Audi as he emerged from the arrivals hall into a bright blue London sky.
>
> "Good to be back," he said, grinning. She looked delicious.

The first paragraph of this passage is pure exposition, but the author has taken the decision that all those races in Europe and Asia and the woes of the other drivers and racing teams are not necessary to be related in great detail. Instead, the move from distant narration to zooming in to the close PoV of the last few lines gives the reader a focus. We can anticipate, almost by the change in narrative distance alone, that something important in the story is about to happen.

History. If something has occurred outside the span of the main PoV character's experience, you have little option but to tell it. It doesn't have to be something vital to the plot or the story, just an historical fact or a geographical detail about the location that adds vital colour.

> By the time Frankie had finished writing her first draft that spring, the first swallows were arriving. There were storms all the way from North Africa, and the tiny birds, exhausted, shivered their little blue-black wings outside her window.

We're not in close PoV here. Frankie may or may well not know that storms dogged the swallows' annual migration. She may not even know that they fly up from North Africa. What the passage does do is add local colour and a more subtle indication of time and season than a rather blunt "Frankie finished writing her first draft in early April." It is perfectly possible to show this information, but it's a little contrived.

> Frankie typed "The End" and slumped back in her chair. She looked over at the calendar. April the fourth.

While that's perfectly adequate and conveys the same information, it places an undue emphasis on the actual date that may be inappropriate. Written like that, I immediately assume, as a reader, that the date holds some significance for her. Is it an anniversary? Was it the date her husband left, or a parent died, or the birthdate of her eldest child?

Passing of time. Similarly to the first example, of repetition, if a period of time passes in your novel without much going on, there's no need to work out some laborious method of showing this. It's quite adequate to begin a new chapter with "It was October before he'd saved enough for a new car ..." (You could, of course, *show* that it was October, by having your character turning up to the car dealership in a scarf and woolly hat, with Halloween decorations festooning the salesman's office, but you might feel—and I think you'd be right—that that's taking the showing mantra a little too seriously.)

There's a notable scene in the film *Notting Hill* where Hugh Grant takes a walk through Portobello market as the seasons change all around him, implying the passage of time after he first met Julia Roberts' character. We can't digress like that in writing. For us, every scene needs to have a purpose, needs to have conflict at its core, or it has no place in the story. The film sequence is a lovely segue but Roger Michell, the director, could have saved quite a few thousand pounds of his production budget by fading in to the next scene with "A year later" stencilled across the middle of the screen.

Variation. I mentioned while discussing close PoV (third or first person) that one of the drawbacks of such a PoV can be their rather claustrophobic nature, and also the problem of drawing in anything other than the character's personal experience into the narrative. One way to combat both problems is short passages of narration. Used sparingly and appropriately, they can break up the intensity of the close PoV and subtly introduce information that the reader needs to know but would have to be laboriously shown (the detailed progress of the racing season in the passage about the driver above, for example). That way, when you do want to dive in and give the reader a really intense experience as the main character, they won't already be exhausted with following every look and glance and thought of that character.

What to check in your own book

If you realise that a passage is "telling" and narration, rather than immersive character-led showing, is there a good reason for it? Does it fulfil one of the situations above, where you're using telling as shorthand to describe the passage of time, or something repetitious, or something outside your close PoV character's experience? If not, could you show the scene from the character's PoV instead, and make it more immersive?

And, to have a balanced narrative, are there situations where you find the close PoV a bit awkward or claustrophobic? Are there long stretches of dialogue that probably need a break?

Filtering

I mentioned filtering in the "Point of view" section, but here's another chance to look at the issue from a "show, don't tell" perspective. As we discussed, filtering is a problem primarily for close PoV narratives and involves the use of sensory words like "saw" and "heard," and mental awareness words like "thought," "felt" and "knew." They are insidious and they do weaken prose. There are two issues. One is that by saying "He knew that ..." you are essentially telling, rather than showing. You are interposing a narrator's voice between us and the character's experience, which is anathema to close PoV prose. The other issue is that by avoiding using a filtering phrase, you are forced to adopt a much closer and intimate narrative style.

> He saw a yellow taxi turn in to the street and drive slowly towards him. He thought it was probably Susan. He felt nervous, but excited.
>
> A yellow taxi came round the corner and drove slowly towards him. *It's Susan, must be.* He took a few quick breaths, bouncing on the balls of his feet.

Instead of telling us that he saw something, the second version shows us what he is seeing. Instead of telling us what he is thinking, the second version gives us his thoughts. Instead of telling us how he is feeling, the second version shows his emotions.

One thing that filtering also tends to generate is a lot of pronouns. If you see many examples of "I" in the text, or in third person "he" and "she," then there's a good chance you're filtering. In the examples above there are three instances of "he" in the first and only one in the second.

Common filter words to look for are, saw, heard, felt, knew, thought, wondered, and realised, but any word that interprets how a character is reacting to their environment, rather than just demonstrating how they are reacting, is a filter word.

Should all such filter words be excised in all circumstances? There are very few absolutes in writing. If your narrative is not written in a close PoV, you will need to filter much more (that's one of the weaknesses of the more distant PoVs), because, since the reader isn't close to the character, you'll need to tell them what's going on and what's going through the character's mind a lot more frequently. But even if your book is written in a close PoV, sometimes a filter word is just the best way of expressing what you want to say. In a situation where the filter word is linked to some other action, it can be difficult to avoid.

> As I arrived at the party I saw Josephine, arms round the neck of some Indian guy, laughing her head off.
>
> As I arrived at the party, Josephine, her arms round the neck of some Indian guy, was laughing her head off.

The second example avoids the filter "I saw" but ends up (I think) being a more clunky sentence which also has a different emphasis. In the first sentence the narrator remains the subject throughout and Josephine and the Indian guy are what that person sees. We get the distinct feeling that this isn't what they want to be seeing.

In the second sentence Josephine takes over as the subject, and instead of relating to the narrator throughout, instead we are more likely to be wondering what Josephine is laughing about. It's a subtle distinction, but demonstrates that removing all filter words from a narrative isn't necessarily ideal.

> *Quite often the best way of expressing an idea is the first way you write the sentence, and subsequently changing that sentence to conform to a grammar rule that may not even be a rule may make it not as effective, or as good.*

Emotions

In a close PoV, one area you really don't want to be telling if you want an immersive story is when describing emotion. Your characters' emotions are key to engagement in the story. You really need your readers to empathise, otherwise they're not going to be engaged, and when writing-class advice covers "show, don't tell," this is usually what they're referring to.

> She looked at him. He was angry again—she could see from his face.
>
> "I'm really sorry," she said, but she wasn't, really. She was tired of all his drama. She carried on with the washing up.

Not only are there significant problems with *telling* emotions here, but there are better ways to present this whole confrontation.

> She looked at him. He was frowning—that familiar, bilious, mottled look to his face.
>
> "I'm really sorry," she said. *But I'm not, am I? Just bored with all his drama.* She carried on with the washing up.

Here his face is described, his expression is familiar to her, letting us know this is not an isolated incident. She conveys her private thoughts in interior monologue. I think it could still be improved upon, though.

> She looked over her shoulder at him. He was frowning—that familiar, bilious, mottled look to his face.
>
> "I'm really sorry," she said. Turning back to the sink, she sighed. She opened the drawer, and began sorting the coffee spoons.

There are more subtle indications here as to her mood and her reaction to his anger. She doesn't turn to fully face him, which would indicate engagement and taking him seriously, but merely looks over her shoulder at him. Although she says she's sorry, it doesn't sound as if she is because she doesn't qualify her statement with any word or gesture, and stated so blankly, the "really" could even be ironic. She displays her equanimity at and boredom with his anger by turning away and sighing and doing something mundane and trivial.

Note also that since this is her PoV, we as reader don't even get told he "is angry." That would be too close to engaging with his mood, which the PoV character certainly doesn't seem to be keen to do. In that sense we are drawn even closer to her perspective. The choice of adjectives that the author, and therefore the character in her PoV, uses to describe his face, "mottled" and "bilious," doesn't make his anger sound something to be fearful of, which might be the case if his face were described as "red" or "at boiling point," but more to be somewhat pitied and possibly concerned for his health.

Many writing classes insist that *telling* the reader a character "is sad" is bad, but *showing* that he is by describing the "tears rolling down his cheeks" is fine. The truth is that good writing avoids those clichés too, and when showing your characters' emotions, you have a lot more tools at your disposal than mere facial expression.

What to check in your own book

Look out for all those emotive adjectives—sad, angry, miserable, bored. There's almost always a more immersive way to show that emotion instead of tell it, and, by doing so, you will be bringing us closer in to your characters. But, avoid those ghastly clichéd descriptions of character emoting—all those heavy sighs and flushed cheeks and flooding, rolling tears. What do *you* do when you're upset? Children cry and bawl and wail when they're upset, and, conversely, they don't bawl and wail and cry when they're not upset. Adults are far more complicated. We adults express our emotions in a whole range of different ways, and many times those expressions are coded and concealed. We learn from a relatively young age that expressing emotions openly is not necessarily a great tactic for social acceptance, so we smile when we might actually be angry or insulted, and we laugh when we're trying to deflect criticism. Conversely, we sometimes don't have as great a control over our emotions as we might think, so we cry when we're happy, or we laugh at totally inappropriate moments when we're trying to process shock.

Try not to have tears rolling down the face of everyone who gets a bit upset in your book. It gets very dull. Have them break some crockery or something—much more exciting.

Description

When you think about it, all description is telling. It's not possible to *show* a reader that a character's dress is red, without making elaborate comparisons to other things that are red ("the colour of her dress matched the fire engine that drove past just at that moment") in which case, on the grounds of efficiency, you're probably better off just saying that the dress is red.

Extending that idea further, in a close PoV, strictly speaking all description is out of place. Why? The PoV character is experiencing the story as it unfolds. If we are meant to be empathising with them, to be immersed in their story, they can't be constantly making asides along the lines of, "Oh look, that car is green." Who are they talking to, the voices in their head? Every time you describe something, you are narrating, although it might not feel like it. Any genre where you feel you need to explain or describe unfamiliar things to the reader, be it epic sci-fi, or complex thrillers involving a huge global cast of different people and organisations, is not going to be easy to narrate in a close PoV.

"Oh, he's one of those militant 'no adjectives and no adverbs' types," you're saying to the person next to you. No, not at all. They're both vital tools in a writer's arsenal, but they have to be used sparingly and appropriately, otherwise you will drown your story in a thick treacle of exposition. There's leeway in some genres to be a little more descriptive than in others. In epic fantasy you might feel you *need* to be able to stop the action for a moment and let loose your imagination with wild sweeps of fancy. Otherwise, what's the point of writing in that genre?

> The roughly hewn black granite stairs led up to an imposing monumental portico, thick white pillars symmetrically flanking an enormous studded door emblazoned with brilliant red intertwining serpents. On the massive stone roof, the chiselled, iconic statues of two golden unicorns pranced energetically, endlessly locked in mortal combat.

What's wrong with that, someone said at the back? Well, you might get away with "purple prose" like this in an epic fantasy, where very noun has an adjective, most adjectives have other adjectives, and if you can't put an adjective in front of it, put an adverb instead.

Personally, I think there are better ways than this to bring a scene to life. This is a hugely indigestible slice of exposition, all served up at once. Better, I would have thought, to break it up a little and drip-feed it, if you really think it's all needed. Writers going overboard with endlessly detailed description are worried that, if they leave anything out, the reader will not "get" the scene with the required clarity. Authors want the reader to be able to imagine the scene *exactly* as they see it. This isn't necessary; in fact, it's a fool's errand.

> *By trying to describe a scene precisely in every detail, all you're doing is overloading the reader's imagination, making the prose flat and dull—visually precise, but emotionally tedious.*

It's okay to have gone overboard in your first draft—you were rushing to get to the end, remember?—but this is the stage at which you begin paring back these descriptive passages. What's actually necessary for readers to get the importance of the scene? In this scene above, who's doing the looking? The description is flat. It doesn't relate to any character. It reads like a travel brochure. Although the doorway is described as imposing, we don't get any feeling for whether the character gazing at it is feeling *imposed upon*. And they *are* gazing at it. In order to describe all this detail, the character has come to a complete stop on the way up towards the doorway, remarking on all the fine stone and carving, before resuming their journey. Is that what the character would do? When the war is over and they hang up their halberd are they going to retrain as a stonemason, or an architect? The danger is that you're describing things that are important to you as an author, but that are rather unimportant to your characters. You're interposing yourself as author between your reader and your story.

So how much description can you include in a close PoV story? If we come across a passage like the one above should we cut it completely, pare it down or rewrite it? Well, we have, for its duration of nearly fifty words, slipped entirely out of PoV and into that of a narrator. But before we get out the red pen, or start hitting the delete button, it's not *necessarily* a problem. Such a passage might be fine in context, or even necessary if we've been immersed for a long time in character. Perhaps the author is giving us a bit of a "step back and have a look round" kind of break, before our character goes into the building and has a massive confrontation (presumably) with whoever lives there.

What about the odd descriptive phrase, here and there? Of course, fine. But just remember, in moderation. Prose without any description at all is flat and dull. If your character is describing something to someone else, they can be as florid as they like, if that's their voice, but if you describe something as narrator, just remember you are compromising your close PoV.

WHAT TO CHECK IN YOUR OWN BOOK

Look at the adjective and adverb use in your descriptive passages. Is there a lot of description? Is it really necessary for the plot? Are there places where there are a lot of sequential adjectives ("he ran up the grey steps to the green door and hammered on the brass doorknocker") that overpower the action beat? Do you describe things from a narrator's perspective, or from your character's PoV? If from a narrator, is there any way you can bring that into a character's PoV? For example, in a middle-grade book (aimed at nine- to twelve-year-old readers), you might have a scene where a child is standing at the top of the cellar stairs.

> Jimmy stood at the open door. The stairs led down into an impenetrable, Stygian darkness.

That's fine, but you could tell this from closer to Jimmy's perspective.

> Jimmy gulped, and shook his head. *I can't go down there.* In his pocket, his trembling fingers clutched his lucky Pokémon. *I can't even see the floor.*

In the context of the book we would probably know that Jimmy is a child, but if you read the first version in isolation, you have no idea how old Jimmy is. The adjectives don't sound as if they're coming from a child's perspective; they sound like an adult interpreting the scene—it would be a well-read nine-year-old who understood the Greek myth reference. In the second version, it's much more apparent that Jimmy is a child. It's told in a mixture of action and interior monologue and references a toy, and the thoughts are simple, not complicated or abstract. He doesn't want to go down the stairs because he can't see where they end, and in his child's imagination, that means they might go on for ever.

For adverbs, are they needed, or would a better choice of verb work instead? Instead of "ran quickly," might "sprinted" work better? If you have made an effort to use more interesting verbs, have you doubled down with adverbial description straight after ("he yawned, wearily," "he shouted, angrily"). This is a very common problem where the author isn't too sure that, having used a verb with a particular nuance, they're not confident that the reader has picked up on the meaning the author wants to convey. To this I'd just say, readers are smart. They'll get it.

Personal appearance

In some genres, like romance, it's quite common to see a description of the main characters' appearance in detail ("She was blonde, 5'4," petite with a slim but curvy figure, blue eyes and a pert button nose that wrinkled endearingly when she laughed" or "He was ruggedly good-looking, with a strong jaw, piercing dark eyes, and a slightly dishevelled air that indicated an entire absence of vanity"). Apart from the fact that those types of description are almost always horribly clichéd, be aware that once again you're suspending your close PoV (given that you're writing a romance in a close PoV, right?) while you're doing the describing.

As your love interests' eyes meet across a crowded coffee shop, listing a hair-down-to-toes description of each character might sound like a good idea—"so the readers know exactly what they look like"—but do ask yourself if it's necessary. While you might be titillating some readers, who will enjoy the experience of getting down and dirty by proxy with some "rebel without a cause" who is rugged and brutal but kind to animals, you might also be putting some readers off. After all, not all of your readers are going to be blonde, 5'4," petite with a slim but curvy figure, have blue eyes and a pert button nose. The more specifically you describe your love interests, the less chance that a reader is going to think, "Oh, that could be me."

And if you think it's really necessary for the love interests in your book to be gorgeous examples of human pulchritude, have a think about how Jane Austen describes the two main characters in one of the most famous romances in the English language.

Pride and Prejudice is written in the omniscient narrator style that was very much the vogue at the time, but Austen still spent very few lines describing Mr Darcy, and in no greater detail than "fine, tall, handsome features." When she describes Elizabeth Bennet, her major female love interest in one of the great romances of English literature, it is through the eyes of a rival.

> "Her face is too thin; her complexion has no brilliancy; and her features are not at all handsome. Her nose wants character; there is nothing marked in its lines. Her teeth are tolerable, but not out of the common way; and as for her eyes, which have sometimes been called so fine, I never could perceive anything extraordinary in them. They have a sharp, shrewish look, which I do not like at all; and in her air altogether, there is a self-sufficiency without fashion which is intolerable"

Of *course* describe physical characteristics if they are important to the plot. If your main character happens to be a red-head and your psycho serial killer happens to have a penchant for ginger, then that particular aspect of their appearance is important to the story. But their hip-to-waist ratio? Really? It's the twenty-first century, and we can all move on from there.

Thinking further about expectations, have you ever watched the film of a book you adore and been put off the minute the main character makes an appearance—the actor cast in the lead role really doesn't fit your private, imagined perception of the character? By defining the appearance of your characters too closely you are doing exactly the same thing—an overbearing casting agent trampling over your readers' expectations.

There will always be novels, often romances, written about characters who are the most stunning physical specimens. It's a trope, just as it is to have some bare-chested hunk with a six-pack and abs carved from stone on the cover. We are generally pathetic, shallow creatures. We want to watch a romance between Bradley Cooper and Jennifer Lawrence, rather than between some middle manager with a beer belly and a florist with bingo-wings. Why is that? Because it's easy to imagine falling in love with Jennifer Lawrence, hard to refuse Bradley when he pulls up at the kerb to whisk you off to some fancy restaurant. But the whole point of books is that you can throw off the manacles of physicality and let your imagination run wild, both as author and reader. Think very hard about defining your characters' appearance too closely. You may actually be alienating readers, rather than engaging them.

WHAT TO CHECK IN YOUR OWN BOOK

How much time do you spend describing each of your main characters' appearance? Have you avoided that temptation to list all the main physical attributes of each character as we meet them?

> Jon, tall, with dark hair and blue-grey
> eyes, met Susan, blonde and petite with

> brown eyes, in the restaurant owned by Flavio, black hair and very dark brown eyes.

The passage above seems ludicrous when condensed into a single line, but many novice authors write exactly like this, introducing a new character, pausing while their hair and eye colour are duly noted, and then carrying on with the story, as if it's at all necessary to know these details about someone's appearance.

If you have described a character's appearance, is that description original and interesting, or clichéd? Does it reveal anything about the character and their personal journey to where they are in their life, like a particular tattoo, or a missing limb, or a particular nervous tic they might have when stressed? These are potentially interesting details about a character's appearance that might intrigue us, that might make us want to find out more about the character. Their eye colour is almost certainly not intriguing, even if their eyes are different colours (momentarily interesting, but still a mere fluke of genetics), or a very odd colour. There are a lot of albinos with pink eyes in fiction, and they are almost always baddies because, of course, anything unusual in physical appearance is clearly an outward sign of inner corruption and evil—yawn.

Even if your book is in a genre which traditionally focuses quite heavily on appearance (romance, for example), is your book improved or weighed down with physical descriptions that really don't add much to the story? Isn't your book about the characters in it, and not what they look like? There are genre expectations and you should pay heed to them, but clever romance writers work out ways to avoid the worst excesses of "telling" descriptions.

Names

Here's another contentious subject that not everyone is going to agree with, but I think is worth considering if you want polished and professional prose. It's a relatively tiny detail, but why introduce every character by their full name when we first meet them, as if calling out a roll-call at school? Does your novel start something like this?

> John Williams strode into work where his secretary, Stephanie Parker, was buffing her nails at her desk outside his office. The phone rang before he'd even sat down at his desk.
>
> "Hullo," he barked, still standing.

If the PoV of this book is one of omniscient narration, then you might consider it necessary to give factual details like this. It is "telling" rather than "showing," but, you might ask, how could you possibly "show" someone's name? Well, quite easily, given a little thought.

> He strode into work where his secretary was buffing her nails at her desk outside his office.
>
> "Hi Mr. Williams," she said, putting down her nail file.
>
> "Steph," he muttered. The phone rang before he'd even sat down at his desk.

> "John here," he barked, still standing.

Once again, the *showing* version is a little lengthier than the *telling* version, but apart from her surname, we are made aware of what their names are, and we haven't even noticed the information we've been given because it occurs naturally, in the course of normal day-to-day conversation. As another positive, in the snippet of dialogue between them before he answers the phone we get a little information about their relationship (she addresses him formally, but he is familiar with her) which we don't get at all in the first version. So even with an omniscient narrator it's possible to organically divulge factual information rather than laboriously spell it out and, if we're clever, we can do that smart thing of doing two things at once, give the reader information, *and* give them some colour about the characters. The sooner and more frequently you fill in the reader's mind about the characters they're reading about, their thoughts, feelings and relationships with other characters, the quicker your readers will become immersed in your story.

When writing in the more personal and close third person PoV we've been talking about in previous sections, listing names of characters becomes even more awkward. In that split second of "telling" the reader the name of the character, we are not in character. We can't begin, "John Williams strode into work ..." because we're not in a close PoV in that sentence, we're in narrator mode. In a close PoV we have to begin, "He strode into work ..." Neither can we continue, "... where Stephanie Parker was buffing her nails ..." He knows her name, so in a close PoV he wouldn't *think* it. So how would we phrase this if we were in close PoV?

> He strode into work. *I bet he rings first thing about that bloody contract.*
>
> "Hi Mr. Williams."
>
> "Steph," he muttered. "Any calls?"
>
> She shook her head and went back to buffing her nails. The phone rang before he'd even walked round his desk. *Here we go.*
>
> "John here," he barked, still standing.

This version is slightly longer again; we've got all the information that we were told in the very first example, but we're also given much more information about his state of mind, the anticipation of this problem phone call. It illuminates why he doesn't have any "Good morning; how was your weekend?" banter with his secretary and gives us a heads-up as to the likely tone of the phone conversation. We're already dreading the call slightly. We pick up from his "*bloody contract*" and "*here we go*" interior monologue that there's going to be conflict.

Note also that there's some information, the fact that Stephanie is his secretary (which we are told explicitly in the first example), that's left for the reader to deduce in this last example. That's encouraging reader immersion in the passage. If the reader has to deduce something, if they have to work something out from unspoken subtext, they're more likely to take it on board, and that deduction process draws them into the story naturally.

In Hilary Mantel's book *Wolf Hall*, it's not until the third page that we discover that the young man being beaten within an inch of his life by his own father in the stable-yard in the opening scene is Thomas Cromwell. Why is that? Because Mantel wanted to drop you in to the middle of the scene without hindrance, without even the slightest pause to namecheck the victim, which would have thrown you out of the close PoV that the scene is written in.

WHAT TO CHECK IN YOUR OWN BOOK

Have you spelled out names in an authorial narrative style? If your book is written in a close PoV you should be aware that you've suspended that PoV as you introduce each character. You may think it doesn't matter, it's only a name after all, but every time you create a diversion away from the reader's immersion in the story and characters, you run the risk of their not being able to re-engage, not being able to find the right path back to your story.

Even if the book is not in a close PoV, there are better, more organic ways to introduce names than just blandly stating them. You will find many examples of books by prestigious authors whose first two words are their main character's name (Stephen King's *The Shining*, for example). You can do better.

Brand names

What about using brand names? There is a breed of genre fiction that has every article of clothing, drink, watch and car name-checked.

> Tiny Z checked his Rolex. It was gone five. He shrugged on his new Gucci loafers and his Chanel camel coat and

> jumped in the Ferrari 488. It was time to meet Cynthia and the others at the Chateau Marmont for a glass of Cristal.

This type of fiction is an acquired taste, which I haven't acquired, so if that's your thing, then good luck with it. My personal view would be that unless the conspicuous consumption tags are necessary for us to understand your character, they completely overpower the story. We are so busy either relishing (or trying to ignore, according to taste) the labels that are scattered across the text like rabbit droppings, that we've forgotten we are reading a piece of fiction.

There are a few dangers too, with name-dropping real brands. Fashions and trends change, and what was cool and hip in your day might have been superseded a long time ago by people who are the current cool and hip, who love brands you've yet to hear of. Use of a particular brand name will date your book. That might be a useful tool to give your reader some context for your story but it might also backfire if that brand goes out of business (the Pan Am airline in the US, or Triumph cars in the UK).

There are also some legal challenges with using brand names that are registered trademarks. We need to put our serious head on for a moment. They revolve around three issues, **trademark infringement**, **defamation** and **dilution**.

Trademark infringement shouldn't be an issue in fiction. Even though you might mention the name of a brand of car, or even a particular model of that brand, you are not setting yourself up in business selling cars. You are neither in competition with the trademark holder, nor holding yourself out to be an expert on their product.

Defamation could be a considerable problem in fiction. Reasonably, a registered trademark holder is not going to want their product directly associated with immoral, dangerous or illegal behaviour.

> *Don't describe someone dying from alcohol poisoning after a night spent drinking one particular named brand of whisky, and it's probably best not to mention a real make of car habitually breaking down and leaving its owner stranded in great danger, otherwise letters from company lawyers might start thudding on to your doormat.*

If trademarked items are credited with altering the course of your story (by poisoning the drinker, or leaving the motorist stranded) you are crediting that item with "agency" in your story. The trademark holder would have to be comfortable that their product is being used in that way, which would require, to make the situation legally watertight, written permission from the company/trademark holder's lawyers. That process could be time-consuming and possibly expensive, and permission is not going to be forthcoming if it's to the detriment of the holder's business or brand reputation.

If in doubt, make up a brand of car or whisky or, going back to the principle of naming people or things generally, avoid the use of proper nouns at all where possible. Use generic terms instead (but note the concept of dilution, next).

Dilution is a little more complex to identify, but involves the use of a trademark name in another context other than that to which the trademark relates. A character might be wearing Chrysler shoes, or driving a Boeing car. As far as I'm aware Chrysler don't make shoes, nor Boeing cars, so using the trademarks in this way dilutes, in the public's mind, the association of the trademark with the holder's real product. (In order for this to be actionable, it must be a brand known on a national or international scale. This is reasonable, if you think about it. A writer can't be expected to know every possible brand, their trademarks and associated products.)

WHAT TO CHECK IN YOUR OWN BOOK

If you've used brand names, have you correctly capitalised them where they are recognised trademarks? Have you used them in a situation where the trademark holder could claim a loss of reputation or value to the brand? In such circumstances, would you be better off inventing a "brand" of your own (after all, you are a writer, in the business of invention). If you believe that the trademark name is generic, can you point to its listing in a major dictionary as a generic noun (*Merriam-Webster* or *Collins* or *Oxford* dictionaries) as support for your claim?

Also, check the facts. If you don't, some reviewer on Amazon will.

> *If you're absolutely determined to drop brand names all over your text, like dead flies in a bakery window, you*

need to be quite sure that you've got your facts correct.

Going back to our Tiny Z example, the people who care about these things will take great delight in pointing out that Chanel has never made a camel coat (please don't tell me they have—I couldn't care less!) They'll write in their review of your book that the Chateau Marmont doesn't serve Cristal, and that it would be a physical impossibility to get four adults into a Ferrari 488, so how come Tiny Z picks up Cynthia and her two friends and whisks them off to LAX for a weekend in Vegas?

If you do choose to use lots of brand names, you should be aware that the whole conspicuous consumption thing was parodied mercilessly in *American Psycho*, by Bret Easton Ellis, way back in 1991. Patrick Bateman, the main character in the cut-throat world of investment banking, is intensely aware of the slightest nuance of success or failure unconsciously expressed by any of his peers wearing the wrong kind of shoe, or a cheap tie. Whole scenes are given over to discussions about trivia like the design of business cards: card stock, embossing, font and whether a square or bevelled edge gives the correct impression. In his world, brand and associated cachet is everything, and acceptance or exclusion from the inner circle can depend on whether your tiepin is silver or platinum. The irony is exposed when it turns out that Bateman, underneath all that beautifully curated debonair charm, is a sadistic murdering psychopath. Ellis got away with this brand association on a defence of satire—the consumerist obsession Bateman has with labels can only be satirical, the outfits he describes totally over the top, the "different" business cards actually identical.

Finally on this subject, some erstwhile brand names have lost their trademark protection because they have become, in the general public's mind, genericised; in other words, the trademark is synonymous with the article it is most closely associated with. Examples of such brands include some surprising items, like chapstick, bubble wrap, dumpster, aspirin, cat eyes and kerosene. Even here though, be careful. In the US aspirin is a generic term, so your character could legally say, "Gimme a couple of aspirin" after a heavy night out. In Canada the trademark is still recognised.

It may be that you could get away with mentioning trademark names in your book without any thought as to how you've used them. I'm quite sure that there are many self-published books out there (that have not been professionally edited, in which case this kind of issue should have been picked up) littered with brand names, and whose authors are oblivious to trademark law. Good luck to them, but what I've stated above is generally accepted to be best and prudent practice.

WHAT TO CHECK IN YOUR OWN BOOK

Check the usage of any brand names. Could you use a generic name instead? Is there a reason it has to be that make? Could the owner of the brand interpret your mention as anything other than entirely complimentary to their brand? If you have to include trademarked names (in non-fiction, for example), you *don't* need to include the trademark symbol, unless you're the trademark owner and want to establish it as a mark.

Song titles and lyrics

It's a nice idea to be able to quote a few song lyrics to illustrate a plot point or character mood somewhere in your novel. Unfortunately, that's a hard no. Unless those lyrics are in the public domain (which generally means published before a certain date—in the US it's 1st January, 1923, or after the death of the artist plus 70 years elsewhere) then someone, somewhere, can and usually will require at the very least that you have asked permission to quote them. It may not be the original artist, who may be long since gone to that concert hall in the sky. It's more likely, in fact, to be a record company or music publishing operation who has bought the rights, and bear in mind *their only raison d'être* is to exploit their library of rights for money. If they hear about your quote and you haven't asked permission, they are entitled to come after you by law. They can insist you retract the usage, pay fines and pulp existing paper copies, or they can grant you permission, but set the terms and charge what they like.

There are a number of loopholes.

Song titles are not copyright. You can quote a song title any time you like within the text, but you'd be unwise to use it as your book title in case it infringes any trademark issues.

There is a defence of **fair use**, where you can claim that the extent of the song you quote is so insignificant that it doesn't constitute copyright infringement. However, there are limits, and in many songs there really aren't a great number of lyrics so even a single line might be 5 or 10% of a song. It's important to note that "fair use" is a **defence** against a legal action. You would already have had all the hassle and stress of hostile lawyer's letters, hiring your own defence team, attending a preliminary court hearing and waiting on tenterhooks to find out if the case is going to proceed to a full trial to even *get* to the point of making a claim of fair use. Is it worth it? (It's easier to defend a claim of fair use in specific circumstances: criticism, where a reviewer quotes some part of the song to illustrate a point of critique, news reporting, research and scholarship and general non-profit work, or parody.)

If you think this is harsh on writers and that you'll just quote a musician's lyrics and be damned ("they should be grateful for the plug I'm giving their song"), have a thought for your fellow artist, the musician. They are constantly asked to play for free, "for the publicity." Between a choice of getting even more publicity and getting some cold hard cash, I'd bet that most musicians would take the cash. After all, most writers would be absolutely incensed if they found an entire 5,000-word chapter of their 75,000-word book reproduced somewhere else without their permission. Relatively speaking, in terms of percentage of the work, it would be much the same thing. Having said that, you are much more likely to find that a small up-and-coming band, or a band that's launching a reissue album or a comeback tour, might be grateful for some timely publicity. The only problem with small bands is the universality of the quote you're using. How many of your readers will know the quote, or the band? If it's a particular niche they share with your characters, they might.

In conclusion, it's generally much easier to invent your own lyrics than it is to track down the copyright holders of a particular song (across all jurisdictions that you are going to sell your book into), ask for permission and be granted it. The penalties for not going down the official route can be onerous. You might think that you can get away with it because, realistically, hardly anyone is going to read your book anyway. Well, that's a bit of a defeatist attitude, and wouldn't it be a royal pain if you had actually written a book that, by word of mouth, becomes a huge bestseller, only to be confronted with a massive lawsuit from a rapacious firm of intellectual property rights lawyers?

WHAT TO CHECK IN YOUR OWN BOOK

I really recommend that, if you've used any lyrics in your book, you take them out. If you decide to include them without getting the rights owners' permission then don't say I didn't warn you. Substitute your own made-up lyrics (you're a writer, aren't you?), or just reference the title if it's a cultural reference that you can't do without.

Facts

If you've done a whole heap of in-depth research on a particular subject, era or event, it might be tempting to use all that research in the course of your novel. That's what you did it for, after all—to create a feeling of truth, of authenticity. However, I mentioned the "iceberg principle" before, in relation to facts about your characters. The same principle applies to facts you've researched about the background to your story. Less is more. Although readers might be interested in the odd startling nugget of information (like the fact that some eighteenth-century pirates had same-sex marriages, for example) they do want a *story*, primarily, not a history lesson or a very long Wikipedia entry.

Relevant information is fascinating. Dropping some small detail that you as author couldn't possibly know if you hadn't researched the subject thoroughly can give an unrivalled air of authenticity to the story. A writer client who specialises in Sherlock Holmes stories made reference to a "tantalus" in one of his books, when Dr Watson needed a bit of "liquid fortification" after some unnerving development. I had to look it up, the first time I came across it, but when I did I realised that this author had gone to some trouble to research the minutiae of Victorian domesticity.

However, readers will quickly detect an air of artificiality if you drown the narrative in facts, however interesting, especially if those facts have nothing to do with the characters, and only tangential relevance to the story.

All that research isn't wasted. The few choice and relevant details you do include will add that valuable authenticity you're looking for, and the rest of the research you've uncovered but don't include can go to making interesting blog posts about the background to your book, marketing material, titbits of information to divulge in radio and television interviews once interest in your book goes global, as of course it will.

Of course, non-fiction may be heavily laced with facts, so this concern really doesn't apply to that genre.

WHAT TO CHECK IN YOUR OWN BOOK

You have two opportunities, in the process of self-editing, to check all those facts you've included: now and in the detailed level pass I describe in Part III. At this stage, rather than their accuracy, you're really more interested in whether there are too many facts (or, unusually, too few). It's hard to give guidelines, and much depends on the book and genre, but try to assess whether you've overdone it. More than one startling or unusual fact that readers probably won't know per chapter and there's a risk that your book starts to come across as less fiction and more like a Wikipedia entry.

Stage management

What I call stage management is the habit of some novice writers to mention every move that their character makes in a scene.

> Turning the handle, he opened the door. He walked inside the house, and then closed the door behind him. Standing at the sink, he poured himself some water and drank it all, then left the glass upside down on the drainer.

There might be a scene where you want to slow the action right down to the tiniest detail—perhaps a pause after a breathless action scene, or the "calm before the storm" ahead of the climax of the book—but this kind of move-by-move narration can get very tedious if overdone.

Consider, when you come across the description of a prosaic action like turning the handle of the door, if it really adds to the reader's sense of the scene or of the state of mind of the character. If it doesn't then consider cutting it, or at least abbreviating it such that it doesn't assume a significance in the reader's mind out of all proportion to its importance.

> He went inside and, standing at the kitchen sink, poured himself a glass of water.

This might suffice instead of the first example. We can infer that he enters the house by a door. Having assumed that, we can certainly infer that he opens the door and walks inside, rather than crashes through it. We might not infer that he closes the door behind him, but do we need to know that anyway? We might, of course. If the inhabitants of the house are subsequently robbed with no signs of forced entry, a significant plot point might be whether he remembers closing the door behind him when he came in. You do need to be careful, when editing, that you don't cut vital pieces of information that you will need later on in the book.

If you remember the principle of "Chekhov's Gun" that I mentioned in the section on plot, Chekhov advised that, "If in the first act you have hung a pistol on the wall, then in the following one it should be fired." In our first example, the reader might be waiting a long time before realising that the character's act of leaving the glass on the drainer in chapter two was actually of no importance whatsoever. When you include an action, readers are apt to infer a significance to that action that might not be warranted. That's a good reason to leave out any action that's *not* significant.

WHAT TO CHECK IN YOUR OWN BOOK

When reading through and coming across action beats, consider whether they are incidental to the story, or really important. Are you going in to too much detail describing what your characters are physically doing? If they're traveling, for example, it's not usually that important to actually describe the journey, unless something happens on the trip. This might be an event, or it might just be a conversation between characters en route, but there's still no reason to describe every stop at a petrol station, unless they rob the place, of course.

Transitioning

Closely related to stage management is "transitioning," the process whereby the reader follows characters from one scene to the next. Many novice authors make the mistake of thinking that readers need to be led along that path almost literally.

> She drove home, picking up some couscous from the deli on the corner. When she arrived at her parking space in the garage under the building, she killed the engine and opened the car door. She stepped out and closed the door, and clicked on the remote locking fob. The car locked itself with a satisfying thud. Then she remembered that she'd left the couscous on the passenger seat. She clicked on the unlock button on the remote fob, and the driver's door unlocked. She opened it and tried to reach over without actually getting back into the car, but the couscous had slid all the way to the far side of the passenger seat. She sighed. She shut the driver's door and went round to the other side of the car.

> She pressed the remote again. This time the other doors unlocked, the passenger door among them. She opened the passenger door and retrieved the couscous.

If you're happy and engaged reading that, cool, but if you're the slightest bit, "Dear God, when is something interesting going to happen in this bloody scene? This woman took 157 words to get out of a car with some couscous" then you are my tribe. The only reason to include any of this lengthy preamble is if the next sentence is:

> The first bullet shattered the driver's side window. The second plucked the tub of couscous from her hand and mashed it against the open passenger door just to the left of her shoulder. She dropped to the cement, fumbling in her handbag for her Glock.

Now we're off and running. There's an immediate acceleration of pace. The author wasn't being utterly dull; they were actually lulling us into a false sense of banal routine so that when the crisis hit, it was doubly surprising and electric in its impact.

Sadly, that's not usually what happens. The next sentences following on from "She opened the passenger door and retrieved the couscous" are usually something along the lines of:

> She locked the car and walked to the elevator. She pressed the "Call" button. The doors opened, she stepped inside

> and pressed "Four." When she got inside her apartment, she checked her answering machine. There were no messages, so then she walked in to the kitchen, put the couscous in the fridge and went into the bathroom to run a bath.

At this point the reader has either put down your book or committed hara-kiri with the butter knife, or both.

The short version of this entire passage could be simply:

> She drove home, picking up some couscous from the deli. There were no messages on the answering machine, so she threw the couscous in the fridge and ran a bath.

That's 29 words instead of 217 and tells us everything we need to know. You don't need to tell the reader how long the journey took, where she parked, whether she locked the car (unless the car is subsequently stolen), her walk to the elevator (unless she gets mugged in the dark garage) and all round the rooms of her apartment. After all, we know instinctively that the bath is not in the kitchen. This is the same as the "Inverse Chekhov" I mentioned earlier. There's no need to mention such things as the elevator and pressing button four, unless pressing the button for floor four doesn't work, or unless it does work but the elevator stops on floor three, the doors open, and all the lights are out in the corridor. By mentioning pressing the button, you should be foreshadowing that something untoward happens when she does, or as a result of doing it later on.

WHAT TO CHECK IN YOUR OWN BOOK

How have you managed moving from scene to scene? Have you over-explained those transitions, giving more information than we strictly need? If there are passages where nothing really happens apart from a character moving from one place or state of mind to another, then can they be cut, or is their journey both literal and metaphorical—the journey having an effect on their character?

Tense

After the major section on "Show, don't tell" it will probably come as a relief to discuss the issue of tense, which, although it has a big impact on the feel of a story, is fairly straightforward. Most books are written in a simple past tense, but there are other options to be aware of.

Present tense

Present tense is an alternative option, good for imbuing narrative with an immediacy and urgency. There's a compelling sense of immersion in a present tense narrative, really encouraging the reader to see themselves as the character in the scene.

> Jack looks up at the old house. "Back here again," he mutters to himself.

Similarly, description can be added with the present perfect, although it is not quite as seamless.

> Jack looks up at the old house. Someone has stuck an old Guinness sign in one of the upstairs windows. "Back here again," he mutters, under his breath.

Present tense can be used with the second person PoV to create a "choose your own adventure" type narrative.

> You look down at the floor. You notice a large iron ring set in a wooden trapdoor. Do you a) ignore it and walk past, taking care not to step on the

> trapdoor, b) pull on the ring, c) cast a Hold Door spell on the trapdoor?

Present tense can meld very efficiently with a close first person PoV, as Suzanne Collins did with Katniss Everdeen in her Hunger Games trilogy. Using present tense and close first person PoV together maximise the immediacy and reader engagement with the character.

But present tense with a more distant PoV, or even a narrated PoV like omniscient, can come across as contrived. It should be obvious that a narrator can't be *in the moment* of the narrative and at the same time *telling us* the story.

Because of its relative rarity, readers might notice you've written in present tense. If they do, they will probably want to know why you challenged them in this way—hopefully you have a good reason! Done poorly, present tense can be a bit breathless and exhausting, and inappropriate. How could it be inappropriate? Present tense is great for thrillers and suspense/mystery stories, because of that immediacy factor, but if your novel is character-driven, and deals with more personal development issues, then present tense may be a wasted effort and could even be intrusive. People don't change overnight, generally.

As an aside, synopses are often written in the present tense, even if the story they describe is written in the past tense, and most film scripts are written in present tense because, of course, film can only describe what is happening *in the moment.* Film, unlike books, can't relate what happened in the past without recourse to contrivances like voice-overs and fades to sepia-tinged cut-scenes

Past tense

Simple past tense is most commonly used to tell stories. It's effective, flexible, utilitarian and tonally neutral, and because it's so naturally the tense used for telling stories, almost invisible to the reader.

> Jack looked up at the old house. "Back here again," he muttered, under his breath.

It can be combined easily with other tenses such as the past perfect (sometimes called the pluperfect) to add colour.

> Jack looked up at the old house. Someone had stuck an old Guinness sign in one of the upstairs windows. "Back here again," he muttered, under his breath.

You can vary the pace of past tense much more easily than you can vary the pace of present tense because there are so many varieties of past tense and you don't need to rely on contrivances like "flashbacks" to relate something that happened prior to the current moment of the story. As a result, it's much easier to develop profound characters because they are able to evolve over time, rather than only being able to react to immediate stimulation.

Mixing tenses

An interesting tool for adding some complexity to a book is mixing tenses. It's not a good idea to mix tenses within a sentence—that's usually just an error—but mixing tenses to make a particular scene more effective can work well.

Many crime thrillers start with the murder/robbery in the opening chapter or prologue. Rather than relate this all in past tense, like the rest of the book, it's quite commonly written in present tense, putting the reader in the shoes of the criminal, or even the victim. The breathlessness of present tense renders a gripping scene of tension very well.

> He opens the door slowly. Across the room, broken glass sparkles on the carpet, beneath the smashed window. Too late, he realises that he can hear heavy panting from behind the door, and before he can turn and flee, a black-gloved hand grips the door and wrenches it from his hand.

For the rest of the book to continue in this breathless tone could be quite exhausting, while leaving just this scene in the present tense emphasises the immediacy of the events leading up to what will, presumably, be a murder.

This device, known in rhetoric as anthypallage, can be used to great effect in dialogue when a character is telling an anecdote. In the same way as the example above, it brings an immediacy to the narrative that is lacking if told in conventional past tense. Imagine a World War Two veteran describing landing on Omaha beach:

> "So I'm standing at the very back of the boat when the ramp goes down. The

> machine guns take out everyone ahead of me and I realise I've got to get off the boat. I try to climb up ... but the bastards get me in the leg, shattering the femur. That's why I walk with a limp."

The present tense ("I'm standing") brings us right into the landing craft with him, even though he's clearly narrating an historic event. There's an immediacy to the memory that wouldn't be the case if it were merely "I was standing." However, the same caveats apply. It would be exhausting to read this first person present tense narrative for very long, and it could be difficult to blend that style of conversational dialogue in with a more normal past tense for longer passages, so use with caution.

What to check in your own book

What tense have you written your book in? Is it all consistently in the same tense? If you've mixed your tenses up a little, is there a reason for that, or is it a mistake? Similarly to PoV, rewriting the book in a different tense would be a major undertaking, so it's unlikely to be a recommended course of action if you're self-editing—certainly not to be undertaken lightly. But, could individual scenes be made more immediate and engaging by means of playing with present tense in a past tense narrative, as with the war veteran's story above?

Similarly, in some dialects past tense events are often told in a present tense narrative, so would using the present tense add to the characters' voices?

> So, I'm walking into the pub when this huge bloke steps in front of me. "Are you Charlie's son?" he says. "Depends who's asking," I say.

If writing in the present tense, have you found yourself using lots of flashbacks to explain previous events that impact on the current narrative? If so, you might have been better off writing in a past tense, where it's much easier to manipulate the timeline of your story without making artificial leaps.

Passive voice

Passive voice is beloved by guilty politicians and business owners the world over. “Mistakes were made.” “Poor instructions were given.” “Shots were fired.” Passive voice removes from the *owner* of the action the *responsibility* for it. In news reporting and non-fiction text generally, passive phrasing is a real problem, because it fails to credit responsibility for an event to a particular person or agency. That might be because of legal problems (the details of the case are unclear, or not able to be proven) but it also might be the result of corruption (bribes) or undue influence (“Print I did that and you’ll never get another interview in this town again”).

As a result, many writing and editing software packages, which are generally designed to correct business writing, will highlight any occurrence of passive voice as an error. In fiction it’s less of a heinous crime, but it can still be a problem if you want your work to be the most immersive and engaging.

The reason I dedicate a small section to passive voice here is that people with little understanding of writing rules often latch on to the idea of passive voice as a grave writing sin. Novice writers can then be intimidated into trying to avoid using the words “was” and “were” when they’re not even using passive voice, and also take to heart the idea that passive voice is a mortal sin which they’re never to use. It’s silly advice.

What is passive voice?

Passive voice is the creation of sentences whose normal order (in the English language, at any rate) is reversed, where the subject of the sentence is not the subject of the verb in the sentence, but the object. In linguistic terms an SVO sentence (subject-verb-object) becomes an OVS sentence.

> The soldiers were trampled by the cavalry.

In active writing the subject of the verb performs the action.

> The cavalry trampled the soldiers.

Authors generally construct passive sentences by using a form of the verb *to be* ("the soldiers were trampled," "the ball was thrown") which has led to that rather daft writing advice about eliminating the word "was" in your writing. This is quite clearly bonkers. "The day was dull and overcast" is not a passive construction, and trying to eliminate the word "was" in that sentence is as pointless as it is challenging.

Can passive voice ever be the right choice?

Active writing is generally more dynamic and impactful (your characters should do things, rather than have things happen to them). In certain phrases, passive voice would read very awkwardly.

> The wall was crashed into by Nigel's car.

That sentence really illuminates the absurdity of making the object of the verb the focus. But not all passive voice is incorrect. Are there any circumstances where passive voice might actually be preferred?

If there is some doubt as to who performed an action, having a character describe a scene or an event is going to naturally fall into passive voice.

> "It's a mystery," Dean said. "The vault was blown open, but none of the gold was stolen."

Avoiding the use of passive voice in that situation would require artificially creating a subject.

> "It's a mystery," Dean said. "Someone blew the vault open, but they didn't steal any of the gold."

There's nothing wrong with that, even if it is slightly more wordy.

In certain circumstances the subject of the verb is a generalisation and unimportant, and it's actually the object and verb that rightfully demand our attention.

> Women are often paid less, for doing the same or more work.

In this particular sentence it's not that important precisely *who* is paying women less. What's important is that it's a general state of affairs.

What to check in your own book

Can you identify sentences in your book written in passive voice? Are there many of them? Would it be better to rewrite them in an active voice, or rephrase the sentence, or does the passivity serve a purpose (as in the example about women being paid less)?

In non-fiction it's sometimes difficult to describe a set of circumstances or events without using passive voice, because the protagonist is unknown or undefined. In that situation it might be less awkward to use passive voice than to artificially create a subject for each sentence.

Memoir

Many self-publishers want to write a memoir. If it's about their life generally, it's properly called an autobiography. A memoir has a narrower focus, about specific events in their life. The structural editing we've done up to this point has seemingly focused on fiction, but I thought that it would be a useful exercise to demonstrate how similar the structural concerns of a memoir are to fiction.

Why write a memoir?

We live in a fast-changing world, and the older generation could be forgiven for thinking that young people don't really understand what things were like before the trappings of modern life, in which the internet and social media play such a huge part. Some writers simply want to record how things used to be, a small memento of their lives and experiences to be handed down in a written record to younger generations as a (hopefully) fascinating insight into family, and social, history. These authors have to be realistic. Unless their life experiences were particularly strange or unique or exciting, the readership for this kind of autobiography is probably not going to extend beyond close friends and immediate family.

That doesn't mean that such books shouldn't be written, and in fact, those in their sixties and seventies now are among the last generations who won't have had every last detail of their lives recorded and filmed ad nauseam. They are the last generation whose memories could well be lost unless they are written down, and personal histories of the twentieth century, which contained such momentous upheaval, war and conflict, will likely be of enormous interest to future historians.

The reasons for writing a memoir may be more specific. A memoir is often about a particular challenge, be it illness, bereavement, overcoming a disability, or achieving a goal against the odds. There are perhaps two main reasons for writing such a memoir.

For the author it's considered cathartic by some to write about traumatic events. Writing things down can allow people to process thoughts and feelings more objectively, to work out why things happened, or to try and come to terms with the apparent randomness of fate.

Other authors hope to be able to help readers confronting similar situations, such as bereavement or illness, by relating their experiences, their coping strategies, their treatments—how they overcame the challenge that they were faced with. If in no other respect than telling a reader that they are not alone, and the challenges they are facing have been faced by others and overcome, a memoir can be an inspiring and potentially life-saving work.

Structure of a memoir

An autobiography is constrained by the subject matter. It's a chronological record of the author's life, from birth (or at least, early childhood) to the present. There's not much room for manoeuvre in that sequence, but the author can redirect focus away from the pure chronology by concentrating on particular themes, be it career achievements, relationships, geographical moves—

whatever the author thinks are the most significant events in their life.

The overriding importance for an autobiography must be to be honest. There's nothing stopping an autobiographer from painting themselves in the most rosy light; it is their story, their point of view, after all. But to be dishonest in an autobiography is a pretty shameful act. It might sometimes require a bit of introspection, or even pain or embarrassment, to put down in words how you failed at something, or let someone down, but a genuine autobiography will include moments of failure as well as those of success, and be the far richer for it.

A memoir has a much more specific focus on a particular event or sequence of events. It might be a tour of duty in a foreign war zone. It might be about founding a start-up business in a cutting–edge technology. Because of this "event focus," the structural issues for fiction we have looked at up to this point do have some relevance.

Tense is clearly going to be past tense, and **PoV** is going to be first person, so those two issues are easily dealt with. The challenge or ordeal that the memoir is about has a beginning, a middle and an end, so the structure of the memoir should follow that pattern, essentially a three- or five-act structure. Depending on the story of the memoir, it could be plot-based, driven by events, or character-based, charting a development of character in order to deal with the problem or (probably the most likely in a memoir), a mixture of both. This leaves a rich vein of material with which to write a memoir, very naturally and conveniently structured. Let's examine the structure of a typical memoir that deals with an illness. I'll use the five-act structural template that we used when looking at book structure earlier.

Act One: A call to action. We meet you, the protagonist, going about your daily life. After a routine check-up and tests at your doctor, you receive a phone call. There is something showing up in one of the tests that doesn't look right. You are told that it's a little known or talked about condition that is degenerative, and ultimately fatal. Worried and fearful, you are comforted by the doctors who say that it should be eminently treatable, caught this early.

Act Two: Complications. You are following a course of treatment and for a while all seems well. However, complications emerge. This particular condition is a rare type, and isn't responding well to the conventional treatment. Consultants are consulted, specialists from abroad contacted with late night phone calls. You begin to confront the possibility that you may not recover. Talks with family begin to revolve around what will happen "after."

Act Three: Apparent success. A new and radical treatment is suggested. It is unproven, but has performed well in clinical trials. Although a harsh regime, and leaving you very weak, early signs are that the treatment is successful. Although weaker, you are re-energised to fight for life, especially that your daughter is now pregnant.

Act Four: Reversal. After months of tough treatment, awful news at the hospital. The condition has returned, and is no longer responding to treatment. The doctors begin to talk about palliative care.

Act Five: Climax. Inspired by talking to a survivor of your particular condition, you carry on treatment, but also adopt an entirely new diet and lifestyle that they suggest. Determined to see your grandchild, you stick with the tough regime and, after a year, the condition has abated and you get the all clear.

That's a typical memoir structure—an inspirational and possibly even useful account of a fight against illness. It goes through ups and downs—at times the future looks very bleak—but you triumph in the end. The success of the memoir is not only how doctors intervened and treatments were delivered—the plot side of the story—but also how you developed as a person, and found a new appetite for survival and a determination to do whatever it takes to see your granddaughter born. It was that determination that formed a major contribution to your recovery.

What's been left out of this memoir? You'll note that there's hardly any detail about you or your life prior to the illness. It might be very tempting to fill a few chapters with how you met your partner, what a wonderful life you had, with so many friends and so many accomplishments. I'm afraid *you* are not the subject of this memoir, and that's sometimes a little difficult to comprehend. "But it's my story!" It's not actually. It's the story of the progress, treatment and defeat of a disease, and it's likely that the people who want to read this book are struggling with the same disease, or know someone/have a loved one who is. They are not really interested in reading your autobiography.

The other subjects we have covered here in the structural part of this book are all relevant. Don't bog your memoir down with too many characters. You don't need a potted life-history of every medical professional you come in to contact with.

A memoir is probably a good example of where a first person PoV shouldn't be too close and claustrophobic.

While you want readers to empathise with you, you don't want them personally reliving the lonely hours in the middle of the night as you worried over what was going to happen to you and your family if things didn't go as you hoped.

A memoir can be quite a short book. The message is the disease and its defeat. Don't try and pad it out with endless descriptions of the same visits to the clinic, waiting in the grubby waiting room with the wilting aspidistra, the ridiculously long nails of the nursing assistant who could never find a vein. Mention these details once if you feel they give a context, make the memoir a personal recounting and provide relief from the otherwise possibly relentless medical terminology, but not repeatedly.

If the book isn't intended just for friends and family, have a think about what audience it *is* intended for. Thinking about your prospective audience will focus you on what language you need to use, what details and explanations you need to include, and what your audience is likely to already know. If it's a military memoir, for example, a lot of military terminology and procedural detail is going to be relevant. However, if your audience is likely to be other vets, then you won't need to include too much detail—you talk the same language. If you believe your audience could extend to non-military types, they will need a bit more hand-holding with the jargon. You will need to explain terminology, explain standard procedures that someone with military training would understand intuitively. All this will colour your writing.

Other cautions. Unless you are a medical professional, you are not in a position to give out medical advice. All you can do, in an illness memoir like this, is say what worked for you and give links to as much independent information as you can, so that your readers can go away and do their own research. I'm not sure it could be made to stick, but you might be inviting legal action from distraught family members if, for example, you recommended stopping taking medication against medical advice, some other sufferer reading your book did the same, quoting you as an authority, and then died.

Cross-check your memories with other family members and friends before committing pen to paper or fingers to keyboard. You might be absolutely convinced that it was Uncle Albert that drove his car into the lake to escape from a bear, but if you're wrong, and it was actually Aunt Jessica behind the wheel, your memoir is going to be flawed irreparably.

Don't defame people, however much you might like to. It might turn out that one clinician was completely misguided about your condition and, if you had followed their advice, you "wouldn't be sitting here writing this memoir." You are living proof that they were wrong. In the course of your treatment, medical knowledge has been advanced. It's extremely unlikely, even if they were the most blinkered and obstinate individual, that they won't have learned from your experience, and will be extremely reluctant to be made to look foolish again. If they were actually negligent, and you have a legal case against them, then pursue them through the courts, not through your memoir! Even if you win before the book is released, I'd mention the case, but not the individual.

Think long and hard about writing an autobiography that deals out criticism of individuals within your family. If the autobiography is destined just for friends and family anyway, you're essentially having a big public argument, and since it's your voice that is shouting the loudest, you might be surprised how many family members turn to support the "underdog"—families are kind of frustratingly self-levelling that way. You know that person treated you badly, everyone else in the family knows they treated you badly, but write a book about it and everyone starts saying, "Oh well, you survived, didn't you? And she had a very difficult upbringing herself, you know. And she's so kind to animals."

If you're writing such a book as a catharsis of frustrations and anger you've held about that particular family member or group, you know what a psychotherapist would say? Go and talk to them. You might even have real closure, not just a vent. If you're determined to get your bitterly critical autobiography on the Oprah Winfrey show, then start putting money aside for lawyers.

With any kind of memoir or autobiography, defamation can be an issue. If a real person can recognise themselves described in a critical light in your book, they may sue. In many jurisdictions it's not sufficient to merely change names. If the subject is readily recognisable by people of their acquaintance, then changing their name is not an adequate defence. I have seen advice that suggests changing name, gender, time and place of the person and event about whom you are making the allegation (and it is only an allegation, unless proven in a court of law) is normally sufficient to disguise the person beyond reasonable doubt. That may be so, but how then does the memoir hold up as a record of your life? Altering all those facts might change the narrative of your story beyond all recognition.

For a long time it has been a universally held truth that the dead cannot be defamed, so writers, particularly journalists, have been at liberty to say what they like about dead people. This has led to some powerful investigative journalism on icons whose darker sides were never explored in their lifetime. However, there have been a few marginal decisions in cases in Europe in the last decade that appear to extend the principle of defamation to surviving members of the deceased's family, so it's still probably a good idea to get legal advice if you really have to say some bad things about people you regard as bad people.

***

That concludes this section of the book. It contains a wide variety of structural issues that are difficult to take in all at once, and certainly difficult, particularly for an inexperienced writer, to apply to your MS all at once. The only way to make sure you've caught everything that you should have is to go through the book several times, concentrating each time on a specific topic, plot or character, or PoV, for example.

However, don't be disheartened if this sounds like an awful lot of work. It's unlikely that your MS suffers from every single problem I've discussed in this section. Only some of them are going to apply to your writing and the other issues you can zip past, perhaps drawing comfort from the knowledge that your writing has avoided at least some of the pitfalls that have caught others.

The two big issues were character and plot. If those sections helped you to look analytically at your own story and really assess whether your plot hangs together and your characters are working, and if not to make some corrective changes, then you'll have achieved a huge amount.

The next part of the book is getting down to the small details, and is much more a reference section. If you have a question about a particular type of punctuation, for example, you can look it up. I've called the section "A style guide for fiction." Editors and publishers talk about "style guides" when they're producing books. They will have come to a decision, for example, as to whether to use the serial (or "Oxford") comma, whether to use double or single quotation marks around speech, how to treat numbers or contractions. Those individual decisions are often compiled in a document called a style sheet. That style sheet is then used as a reference for all editors who work for that publisher to adhere to, so that a publisher's catalogue of books is consistently edited.

If you're self-publishing, you don't have a style sheet imposed upon you, and you can make your own decisions about issues where there is more than one way to present your work. That's part of the joy of freedom of creative control. You need to be aware of the options available to you, however, the arguments for and against each one, where necessary, and you need to apply those decisions consistently in your MS.

This next section, then, is a template for a style sheet for the self-publishing author.

PART III: THE DETAILED LEVEL

A style guide for fiction

In this last part of the three-stage self-editing process, you are performing what a professional editor would call a copyedit. Your book is largely complete. You are happy with the underlying structure, the skeleton of the MS. The plot has rising and falling tension, ending with a satisfying climax. The number of characters is appropriate for plot and genre; the main character arcs are satisfying and believable. The three fundamental tools of point of view, narrative distance and tense are correct for the kind of story you're trying to tell, and consistent throughout.

Unless you're familiar with the process of self-editing, it may be the case that again with this stage you will want to go through the MS several times looking for certain types of problem in isolation. If you are familiar with self-editing, and also have a shrewd idea of your own writing weaknesses, then it might be possible to go through the text in one pass drawing everything that follows together, but there's a lot to get through!

I intend that you use this section of the book as more of a reference guide—lying open face down on the desk beside your keyboard, or festooned with hand-made bookmarks. It's not a truly comprehensive guide to grammar and punctuation. As I mentioned before, the *Chicago Manual of Style* that most American editors use as their primary guidebook is over 1000 pages of very small print, most of which covers things you'll never need to use. I'm going to focus instead on the subjects that authors commonly struggle most with. The idea is that this guide is short enough not to be intimidating, but long enough to be pretty comprehensive.

Is this next section a rulebook, then? It's not being pretentious to say that writing is an art, and as an art, there can be no rules. Any book that professes to tell you the rules of writing is myopic in the extreme. However, there are best practices which, like everyone who wants to learn a craft, you would be well-advised to understand before you go forging ahead with your bid for literary glory with your all-in-one-sentence, stream-of-consciousness, my-life-as-a-banana, three-volume road-trip masterpiece. Picasso learned to draw (he could draw almost perfect circles freehand) before he started painting blue women with both eyes on the same side of their face.

Style sheets

Part of the workflow of most copyeditors is the drawing up of what is called a style sheet. It's not compulsory, but many editors and authors find it a great aid to being consistent with their approach to copyediting issues like punctuation throughout a long novel. You'll see as you work through this section that, as I mentioned above, many of the so-called rules are in fact guidelines, and an element of choice pertains. This could be something simple. Are you going to use double quotes for dialogue, or single? When using an ellipsis, are you going to use the ellipsis glyph …, or three spaced points . . .? Which version of English spelling are you going to use on certain words, like traveling, or travelling? Either is fine, but you should be consistent, and keeping the result of all of these different style decisions in your head can quickly become cumbersome, killing off creativity. Far better to have them written down in a cheat sheet that you can then refer to, and that also, if you *are* going to hire a professional editor for a final polish, you can hand over so that they know immediately what decisions you have consciously made, and therefore what remains in your MS that they need to correct.

Many of these decisions will be made for you because you'll want to adhere to either US or UK English rules and guidelines, depending on where you're from, what is natural to you, and also what you see as the market for your book. If you're a US writer writing a book set in the US for the American market, then it would be unwise to vary from the US style of punctuation and spelling. If you're a UK writer writing a book set in the UK for a UK audience, you would naturally write in a UK English style. However, what about if you're a UK writer writing a book set in the US, for what you think could be a transatlantic audience? Major publishers can print US versions of UK books (*Harry Potter and the Philosopher's Stone* versus the *Harry Potter and the Sorcerer's Stone* of the US market) but that's beyond the means of most self-publishers. This question occurs a lot.

> *"If I'm writing a book that I expect to be read both in the US and in the UK, should I go with US or UK style rules?"*

As a general rule, always write, and edit, for your prospective audience. If your book is set in the US and has a largely American cast, then it would make sense, regardless of whether you're a US or UK writer, to write using US conventions. If you're a UK writer and you're writing for a predominantly UK audience, with characters and story set in the UK, then there's no reason to use American rules. If you're a UK writer and you're writing for a global audience, then you have to make a decision. The truth is that, because of the wide assimilation of US culture globally, UK readers will not generally stumble over US rules of punctuation (and spelling) even if they are aware of the differences, but the inverse is not always true. Some US readers, brought up on a diet of almost exclusively US written media, do make remarks in reviews on Amazon about "incorrect" punctuation, when all they've really identified is a foreign *style* of punctuation. To avoid this, there's a growing tendency to use a hybrid of styles that, while not completely applying US or UK rules, avoids conspicuous differences from the US standard. Some writers may complain about the homogenisation of culture that this implies. Personally, editorially speaking, it's not a hill I want to die on. This book is written, by an English-born author living in Ireland, in a hybrid of styles. You might have noticed that I use double quotes, but I don't use the "Oxford comma" unless clarity demands it (more on these subjects later), and I generally use UK spellings. As long as I'm consistent within the book, I don't think it matters a great deal.

In format, a style sheet is really nothing more than a list. Head it up "Style sheet for *name of book*" and if you think you need it, a version number. The headings you use can be the same as I use in the next sections, or whatever you feel you need.

Possibly the first thing to mention in your style sheet is your dictionary of choice, usually either the Oxford English Dictionary, or Merriam Webster. This will govern your spelling choices (and many other issues, such as capitalisation, and the hyphenation or not of compound words). Adopting a particular dictionary is not to say you can't choose a different spelling, but that alternative should be noted in your style sheet. If you do have an editor go over your book subsequently, that will alert them to the fact that you have chosen that spelling, rather than missed a typo when self-editing. Of course, readers won't get to see your style sheet, so if they see an "alternative" spelling they might just believe it's a typo anyway!

As we go through the next sections, I'll remind you to update your style sheet with the choices you've made so that, when coming back to revise your book, you'll be able to refer to a consistent authority—your own!

You might find it helpful to attach on separate pages the character sheets that you drew up for each of your main characters, if you prepared them. In that way, you have all of your notes for the book in one place and, if you do decide to get your book professionally edited, that information will save your editor time, and therefore you, money.

Dialogue

Dialogue is often the main driving force behind an immersive novel. There are many reasons for this. Good dialogue conveys character concisely, unobtrusively but vividly. It can move plot along at a rapid rate, but can also describe slow, emotional scenes with great profundity. It is also one of the novelist's principle tools against mountains of exposition and dull narration creeping into the book.

However, there's a drawback. Because dialogue has such a great clarity (something will either read like dialogue or it really won't—there's not much in between), it can be hard to do well, and if done badly, can flag mediocre writing much more visibly. How do you make sure that your dialogue passes muster and doesn't let your book down?

As part of your self-editing process, it can be a great idea to actually read your dialogue lines aloud, or get one of the automated text-to-speech applications to read them aloud to you. What you're listening for is dialogue that doesn't flow, that doesn't sound in character or, even if it does, doesn't sound consistently in the same character per speaker. People all talk at different speeds, using a different set of words. Some speak more formally, others use contractions ("I didn't," "I won't"). Some speak in dialect (of which more later); some speak in what used to be called "Received Pronunciation" (RP) which, while once accepted as "standard" pronunciation, is now deemed to be a "posh" accent (listen to the main characters speaking in almost any 1950s British film).

Let's first deal with the thorny issue of how dialogue is actually punctuated.

Dialogue punctuation

Dialogue punctuation often forms a significant part of copyediting an MS. The problem is, of course, that there's often a lot of dialogue in a novel, and if you've got something consistently wrong in your punctuation of dialogue throughout the book, you can be paying good money to an editor to correct the same thing over and over again. It really does literally pay you to get your MS as clean as possible before you hand it over, otherwise you're wasting your money or, at least, not getting the best value from your editor.

Simple dialogue

Spoken dialogue is generally enclosed in quotes, either double in the US, or single in the UK.

> "Hi," Jack said.
>
> 'Hello,' Charles said.

The actual spoken words are separated from the dialogue tag, *Jack said*, by a comma. There is a European literary convention that introduces dialogue with an em dash and omits the closing mark, but this is very rarely seen in English fiction.

> —Hi, Juan said.

There's an even rarer convention that omits dialogue punctuation completely. Cormac McCarthy, who writes incredibly sparse prose, quite often with fragmentary sentences, usually omits any punctuation or dialogue tags unless they're absolutely needed for clarity.

> I'm on it. The deputy hung up and put his feet on the table.

If you're an experienced author, extremely confident about the voice of your characters and the clarity of your prose, and you have an aesthetic issue with quote marks littering your pages, then have at it, but I wouldn't advise it for a novice—it's a very stylistic choice. Not using quotes is *more work*. Do you really want to be giving yourself more work when you're finding it hard enough to edit your book as it is?

If you're using quotes, and I recommend you do, always use "intelligent" quotes, that curve in towards the text to be enclosed, and not *prime* and *double prime* marks, which are the "straight" quotes that you can see on your computer keyboard. There is a setting in most word-processor packages to use intelligent quotes by default. Unless you've good reason not to, I'd recommend you use it.

Overall, which quotes you use, and indeed whether you use any quotes at all, is a personal style choice for a self-publishing author. If you've written your 150,000-word magnum opus and have just realised you *should* have used the *other* quotes, don't panic. When you hand the book over to your editor you can either claim that's your natural writing preference and tell them to keep it as is, or ask them to fix it. Professional editors have a number of tools to take the sting out of such mechanical tasks, and can do it much more efficiently and comprehensively than you are likely to be able to. It's not ideal, but it's no biggie.

In the normal course of dialogue writing, each speaker begins a new paragraph. This helps break up conversation visually on the page, so that we can see who is talking. Note, though, that this isn't a rule, contrary to popular opinion (you're well into this book now, so you should have realised that this is often the situation with "rules"). There are certain circumstances where you might want to run several different speakers into one paragraph to save space, if there are a lot of monosyllabic responses to a question from a crowd of characters, for example.

> "Who'll come and explore the dungeon with me?" said Nigel.
>
> "Me," said Roger. "I'll come," said Sarah. "S'pose so," said Hilary. "With you as leader?" said Charlie. "You've got to be kidding."

It's quite clear who is saying what, and it's all part of the group's response to Nigel's question, so there's no real need for separate paragraphs.

NOTE ON YOUR STYLE SHEET:

Which method of punctuating dialogue have you decided on?

More complex dialogue

Let's look at some more complex dialogue examples.

> "There's going to be trouble," Jack said, "bad trouble."

Notice the two commas. The one after *trouble* is merely to separate the dialogue from the dialogue tag. The one after *said* is the punctuation mark to consider. An important concept is to understand the separate components of the sentence. If you take out the tag, the sentence should remain perfectly punctuated. In this case,

> There's going to be trouble, bad trouble.

In this case the speech is all one sentence. Sometimes the dialogue tag can separate two sentences.

> "I'm thirsty," said Charles. "I'm getting a beer."

If we take out the tag, with its introductory comma before it, we are left with the two real sentences.

> "I'm thirsty. I'm getting a beer."

A common mistake is to have a comma in place of the full stop.

> "I'm thirsty," said Charles, "I'm getting a beer."

Do you see the comma after Charles, instead of the full stop? If we take out the tag and the comma before it, we now have,

> "I'm thirsty, I'm getting a beer."

That's an example of an error called a *comma splice*, which is fully explained under the comma section of **punctuation**, but let's just say that it's a situation where two full sentences are joined only by a comma, and not a conjunction like "and" or "so," or a stronger punctuation mark like a colon or semicolon.

Before we leave this example, there's one more fly in the ointment that writers following UK English rules might want to consider. UK English rules state that while points should be inside the quotes, commas should be outside *if they don't belong in the underlying dialogue*. While technically true, it's a distinction that seems to be slowly fading in observance. In the following sentence, traditional UK style would have single quotes and the comma outside them, because the underlying sentence ('I'm absolutely dying for a pint') would have no internal punctuation.

> 'I'm absolutely dying', said Charles, 'for a pint.'

However, in a lot of modern UK fiction you will see it presented in the US fashion, even though the author is still using the UK single quotes.

> 'I'm absolutely dying,' said Charles, 'for a pint.'

It's very unlikely that anyone will complain if you put the punctuation inside the quotes in the US style but, as with everything, be consistent. In this book, because I'm using double quotes (except in specifically UK English examples like the one above), I've adopted the US standard of including punctuation within the quotes, whether or not it "technically" belongs there.

Questions and exclamations

What about question marks and exclamation marks?

> "Is this right?" he asked.

Like the point, they will always be relevant to the dialogue, so inside the quotes.

NOTE ON YOUR STYLE SHEET:

Are you putting internal punctuation inside the quotes at all times, or outside on a discretionary basis?

Multiple paragraphs

When writing speech over multiple paragraphs, the convention is to start each new paragraph with another quote mark (single or double according to which you're using for dialogue), but only include the final closing quote at the end of the whole speech.

The reasons for this are twofold. It's obviously important to indicate to the reader that the character is continuing to talk, and that this new paragraph is still speech. However, if there were closing quotes at the end of the previous paragraph, the reader might jump to the conclusion that this is a new speaker. Leaving the closing quotes off is the obvious answer, the character's speech continues, but that lack of closing quotes at the end of that previous paragraph is easy to overlook. The new opening quotes without a previous closing quote make it obvious that the same character is continuing to speak.

> "I carried on up and up over the mountain," he said wearily, "until I reached the top of the pass and could see the ground descending ahead of me, to the vast plains in the far distance. It was such a relief!
>
> "I had no idea that the seasons had moved on so far here, and it is time for the harvest already."

Very short speech

As an exception to the general rule, very short lines of dialogue don't need the introductory comma before the opening quotes—in fact it's optional to include the quotes at all—and nor do fragments of reported speech that fit into the syntax of the surrounding sentence. All of the three following examples are reasonable style choices. Note that if you do enclose the speech in quotes, then it should have a capital to start.

> She said "Yes."
>
> She said yes.
>
> She said that we were "bound to fail."

NOTE ON YOUR STYLE SHEET:

What style will you use for short lines of dialogue?

Interrupted dialogue

What happens when a character is saying something and they are interrupted, either by a thought or action of their own, or an action by someone or something else?

In UK English *spaced en dashes* can be used in instances of interrupted dialogue (an en dash is a double length hyphen, typed by holding down the Alt key and the numerals 0150 on a Windows machine, or the Option key and the minus sign on a Mac). Whether the en dashes go inside or outside the single quotes depends on whether the dialogue is being interrupted, or whether the writer is merely introducing an action beat in the middle of the dialogue.

> 'In this next photo' – she clicked the remote – 'you can see the lion approaching the tent.'

In this case the dialogue is not being interrupted—the speaker is doing something while speaking, so the phrase is what is called an *action beat* (we'll come to action beats in a minute). In the next example someone else is interrupting the speaker.

> 'In this next slide –'
>
> 'Does this presentation go on much longer?' a voice shouted from the back of the hall.

In this case the en dash belongs to the dialogue, so goes inside the quotes. Note that while there is a space between the text and the dash, there is no space between the dash and the quote marks in this example.

There are slightly different rules in the US, in that US publishers (and the Oxford University Press in the UK) choose to use closed up em dashes (em dashes without any spaces) where other UK publishers might use spaced en dashes. The em dash is generally twice as long again as the en dash. The sure-fire way of creating an em dash is to use Alt and 0151 on the numeric keypad (Option + Shift and the minus sign on a Mac). So the examples given above would read as follows.

> "In this next photo"—she clicked the remote—"you can see the lion approaching the tent."

This is an action beat, so the em dash is outside the quotes.

> "In this next slide—"
>
> "Does this presentation go on much longer?" a voice shouted from the back of the hall.

An interruption by a third party, so the em dash is inside the quotes.

NOTE ON YOUR STYLE SHEET:

Will you use em dashes or spaced en dashes for interruptions of this nature?

Quotes within quotes

What happens if one character directly quotes another character? Use the other form of quotes, single or double, around the quoted material, in what is called "nested" quotes.

> "He told me, 'I'll be back in one hour,'" she said.
>
> 'He told me, "I'll be back in one hour",' she said.

Note the placing of the comma after *hour* under the two different sets of rules, US rules in the first line, UK in the second. Note also that you don't put quote marks around *reported* quotes.

> "He told me that he would be back in one hour," she said.

Here she is not quoting the other character directly.

Tailing off dialogue

How do you punctuate that occasion when the speaker tails off into silence? You use an ellipsis, where a character starts to express something but finishes with the dialogue incomplete.

> "You hit a child?" she said. "I think that's really ..."
> "I know," he said.

The character here is unable, or unwilling, to say exactly what she feels about the subject, so comes to a stop mid-sentence. Note that this is different from a character's speech being interrupted.

> "You hit a child?" she said. "I think that's really—"
>
> "I know," he said.

In this instance we know, from the em dash, that he interrupts her before she can finish her sentence. He doesn't want to hear her (we presume) condemnation. In the example with an ellipsis, she comes to a halt mid-sentence, and presumably there's a slight pause before he speaks. There's a subtle differentiation of the male character there. One is presumably more contrite than the other. The character who waits to hear what she thinks, and when she doesn't say, says "I know," as if empathising with her unspoken feelings, seems a very much more empathetic and contrite character than the one who interrupts her. He appears, by not letting her finish, to be less apologetic, or even not very contrite at all. This is where the use of proper punctuation can add very subtle nuances, to characterisation in particular, that readers will pick up on and appreciate.

An ellipsis could also be used where this thought was internal monologue, rather than expressed dialogue.

> He hit a child, she thought. That's really … She shook her head.

You can create the special ellipsis character simply by typing three points in a row, but be aware that sometimes this requires tweaking your software package's default settings. There are more detailed notes on this and other related issues in the *Ellipses* section.

Dialogue tags

In an ideal world we wouldn't need dialogue tags. They only exist to make it clear to the reader who is speaking. Because we're so used to them, the normal "he said, she said" kind of tag is almost invisible. A common mistake is to make much more of the dialogue tag than it deserves, to turn it into part of the narrative instead of being this almost unseen piece of information. There are several aspects to problematic dialogue tags. The first consideration is whether they are necessary at all, and if so, how many.

The need for tags at all

If a conversation is between two people, readers are astute enough to realise who is speaking if it's clear from the outset. You don't need a tag after every line of dialogue, just the odd one or two in a long conversation. If there are more than two people involved, then chances are that you will need more dialogue tags to establish who is speaking at any moment. Even here, though, there are other ways of showing the speaker's identity, one of which is to use *action beats*. Instead of a dialogue tag, the writer will include a physical action in the same paragraph as the dialogue. Because of the "new paragraph for each speaker" guideline, we can easily work out the identity of the speaker.

> "I don't like the look of it," said Adam.
>
> Brianna peered over the lip of the slope. "It's only a real black run for the first few hundred metres. It levels out down there, look."
>
> "You're not chicken, are you?" Charlie started clumping around in his boots, flapping his elbows in and out. "Cluck, cluck."
>
> "Cluck off, Charlie."
>
> "You'll be all right. We'll take it slow," said Brianna.

There are only two dialogue tags in these five lines of dialogue between three people, but it's fairly obvious who is saying what. In our reader's mental shorthand, we see a name in the same paragraph as a piece of dialogue and we know who it is talking. The beauty of this method is that you can provide more character and colour, using appropriate action beats to add depth to the conversation, than you can with the dialogue alone. See how flat the conversation becomes if we take the action beats out and substitute simple dialogue tags.

> "I don't like the look of it," said Adam.

> "It's only a real black run for the first few hundred metres. It levels out down there, look," said Brianna.
>
> "You're not chicken, are you?" said Charlie. "Cluck, cluck."
>
> "Cluck off, Charlie," said Adam.
>
> "You'll be all right. We'll take it slow," said Brianna.

Once again, the use of action beats shouldn't be overdone, but it avoids the unwanted "he said, she said" sing-song repetition that begins to resonate even through this short conversation if the rhythm and variety of dialogue isn't mixed up a little. It's sometimes tempting to break up this repetition by adding dialogue tags in the middle of sentences. In an earlier example we used a line illustrating punctuation within quotes.

> "I'm absolutely dying," said Charles, "for a pint."

Where you put the dialogue tag within a sentence can have a significant impact on the impact of a line of dialogue. In the above example, the reader is left hanging for a moment (wondering what Charles is dying of while they process the dialogue tag), until the answer is revealed in the second half of the sentence. If this were written more normally this subtle hesitation wouldn't exist.

> "I'm absolutely dying for a pint," said Charles.

Don't scatter dialogue tags through the middle of lines of dialogue without considering their effect on the natural rhythm and cadence of the speech. Dialogue tags are generally better off at the end or the beginning of lines of speech, where they're almost invisible to the reader. If a conversation has developed a bit of a sing-song "prompt and response" sound to it, it would be better to experiment with action beats, or to omit the dialogue tags completely, than try and artificially mix things up by introducing mid-speech tags.

Unusual tags

A common problem is to create a dialogue tag out of a non-vocal verb. It should be fairly obvious from the context of the conversation what state of mind the speaker is in—if they're angry, upset, overjoyed, afraid. If it isn't obvious, then as a writer you should be asking yourself why it isn't obvious. The actual words spoken are the major clue, but your reader should have some notion of how the speaker is feeling from the plot, what they know about the character at that point, what their interaction with this other party to the conversation has been up to now. Are they an enemy, a friend, a lover, a threat? Readers will pick up on the slightest nuance of conversation, just as they would in real life, so it's quite possible to have a situation where the character is saying one thing, but the reader knows that deep down the character means something entirely different.

Problems arise when the writer doesn't have the confidence in their ability to draw character, or carry a scene, and so they bulk up the dialogue tag with a load of verbal or adverbial emotional weight that the dialogue tag is not designed to carry—not designed to carry, at least, and remain invisible.

How do they do this? Instead of a simple "he said, she said" conversation, we get dialogue overflowing with rather startling verbs.

> "I love you," she smiled.
> "I love you too, but I worry that I love you more than you love me," he fretted.
> "I think I love you more," she calculated.
> "Thank goodness," he ejaculated.

If there was a full stop/period after "goodness" in that last line, and the "he" was capitalised, we'd get an altogether more ... ahem ... adult interpretation of that last line, but perhaps you can see how an unusual verb used as a tag takes on a significance out of all proportion to its weight in the sentence.

The important point is that with most of these verbs, they aren't vocal verbs at all—you can't "smile" words. You may be smiling as you speak, but you still have to speak.

What about verbs that *are* used in vocal situations, like whispered, shouted, cried, breathed (arguably), roared? It's quite possible to use these as dialogue tags, but as with all things, moderation is everything. If you have pages of conversation where everyone is shouting, roaring and crying at each other, you begin to sound like you're writing the soundtrack for a zoo. Most of these more exotic dialogue tag verbs are much more visible to the reader than a simple "said," and most of the nuance of how a character is speaking should be conveyed by what they say and what the reader knows of the character's mood. All those "roaring" and "shouting" verbs are just another example of "telling," rather than "showing." Show us how angry he is with his words and his actions, the advice goes, rather than simply tell us he's shouting.

However, is "he lowered his voice and said" less obtrusive than "he muttered"? Lots of writing advice recommends using descriptive verbs like "slouching" or "strutting," instead of boring old "walking," as much better writing. Doesn't strutting suggest the style and emotion behind the movement far more efficiently than some more elaborate "showing"—"he walked with his shoulders back, head erect." Should "talking" verbs be treated differently? I don't think they should be. Lots of well-meaning people have focused in on dialogue tags because it's an easy stick with which to beat novice authors. As an editor I see some desperate examples ("No," he declined; "Yes," she agreed), but the problem is invariably that you often don't need *any* dialogue tag. That's much easier advice to try and live by.

Overdoing it

Some dialogue suffers from a mixture of all of the problems I've mentioned above and, at first glance, can seem reasonably okay. But as your own editor, you've got to look through the words as actually written and see what needs to be there and what can be taken out. This passage has a number of problems that perhaps aren't that apparent at first glance.

> "I can't believe you hit a child ..." She tailed off into silence.
>
> "I know," he shrugged.
>
> "Oh my God! What happens when he tells his parents?" she cried, fearfully.
>
> "I'll deal with them," he declared, masterfully.

You might not see it at first, but this conversation is overloaded with descriptive deadweight. Let's examine it one line at a time.

> "I can't believe you hit a child ..." She tailed off into silence.

We already know, from the discussion of ellipses in dialogue punctuation above, that they are meant to indicate a "tailing off" of speech. There's no need to spell it out.

> "I know," he shrugged.

"He shrugged" isn't a dialogue tag at all. "Shrugged" is not a vocalisation; it's a movement of the shoulders—you can't shrug speech. This sentence is actually a comma splice (described more fully under "Punctuation – commas," later on), the joining of two separate sentences ("I know" and "he shrugged") by a comma. To correct it, either omit the phrase "he shrugged" completely, or give its correct status as a separate sentence.

> "Oh my God! What happens when he tells his parents?" she cried, fearfully.

You don't need any dialogue tag here. We've established that it's two people having a conversation. If it were him speculating on what would happen when the parents find out, the dialogue would have continued on the same line as "he shrugged," so it must be the woman talking, therefore we don't need a dialogue tag (meant only to clarify who is talking, remember?) at all. We certainly don't need a verb like "cried" when she clearly exclaims the first phrase of her speech, "Oh my God!," and we don't need an adverb like "fearfully" to describe how she cries. There are not many ways to cry something, but "fearfully," when she's clearly afraid of what will happen when the parents find out, is fairly obvious from her words.

> "I'll deal with them," he declared, masterfully.

Here again, we don't need a dialogue tag at all. He is responding to her question, assuring her. Because of the flat finality of his words, we can sense the way he speaks them, so we don't need the "declared," and we can deduce that he's fulfilling the strong, reassuring role without it having to be spelled out for us ("masterfully"). Having applied these principles to this bit of dialogue, what does it look like, edited?

> "I can't believe you hit a child ..."
> "I know." He shrugged.
> "Oh my God! What happens when he tells his parents?"
> "I'll deal with them."

Can you see how almost none of the emotional weight of this passage is lost by getting rid of all the extraneous verbiage? The conversation is clear to follow (you could start with a "she said" if you felt it necessary, but we presumably know, by this time in the book, that it was he who hit the child, not her), and by getting rid of all the other dead weight, it's easier to concentrate on the emotions behind the speakers' words. This brings us in closer to the characters and, just by eliminating words we don't need, we've cut the word count down by nearly a third. Let's be clear: cutting word count is not an end in itself, but when we can achieve that by cutting words which have no real use, clutter up your writing and, far from adding value, actually weigh the prose down, that's a great result.

Adverbs and dialogue

Briefly focusing on adverbs ("fearfully," "masterfully"), it was Stephen King who said, "The road to hell is paved with adverbs" in his memoir *On Writing*. Before that, a writing style guide called *The Elements of Style* by Strunk and White had already blacklisted adverbs (and adjectives) and commanded several generations of writers to solely rely on nouns and verbs, advice reinforced by the exhortations of thousands of English teachers the English-speaking world over. This is still widely quoted as a "rule" and is often used to bludgeon novice writers into thinking that using adverbs is one of the gravest sins. That's not what King said, Strunk and White weren't advising novelists, and your English teachers were trying to teach you to submit clear and concise essays on the Tudor kings or the Gettysburg Address in an exam situation, not give you advice on writing your current vampire-mermaid romance trilogy.

"She cried, fearfully," above, is an example of poor adverb use. It adds nothing to the words the character actually speaks, and just bogs the reader down with another word we have to process in order to absorb the same amount of information. But "I'll happily take the train instead of fly" is an example of perfectly good adverb use. Some authors go overboard trying to avoid the use of adverbs and write a lengthy adverbial phrase instead. "She pressed softly down on the wound to stop the bleeding" becomes "She pressed on the wound with a gentle pressure to stop the bleeding." This does nothing but add to word count. "Softly" perfectly describes her actions; why substitute the more clunky, "with a gentle pressure"?

The reason for mentioning adverbs specifically under dialogue is that often the most egregious use of adverbs is as part of a dialogue tag. Writers who know not to use weird verbs, who usually use "said" and use action beats sparingly, still lose confidence that they are conveying exactly the right mood. They turn to adverbs to add some colour to their dialogue.

> "I can't run any further," she said, breathlessly.
>
> "We have to. We're dead otherwise," he said, flatly.
>
> "I'll slow you down. There's no point in both of us getting eaten," she said, resignedly.
>
> He looked over his shoulder, then pointed. "See? There's a light ahead. We can make it," he said, hopefully.

Each line ends in an adverb. It's a slight exaggeration of the problem for effect, and not many writers would be quite so blind to leave this as is, but I've edited otherwise well-written novels that run close to this.

There are various means by which this writer could get rid of all the adverbs. They could use more exotic verbs instead of "said," or they could add some action beats to make more visual sense of the conversation. They could even add a few words to the dialogue to make it more involving.

> "I can't run any further," she called after him.

> He came to a stop and turned back to her. "We have to. We're dead otherwise."
>
> "I'll slow you down. There's no point in both of us getting eaten."
>
> He looked over his shoulder, then pointed. "See? There's a light ahead. Come on. You can make it."

This is just one potential solution of many, but what have we done? We've dispensed with all the adverbs. We've added a few action beats to give a physical dimension to the conversation (otherwise the danger is that the scene seems very static, whereas in a chase situation we really want to add some fluidity and pace to the dialogue). We've also added "Come on" to his dialogue, to give a feeling that he's encouraging her, that he's genuinely optimistic about their chances. (In the first example, it sounded as if he didn't really believe what he was saying himself.)

Grammar, dialect and foreign words in dialogue

People don't speak in perfect sentences. They repeat themselves, pause, stop and start a sentence over again when they realise it isn't coming out quite right. There are some people in the public eye (invariably highly educated and extremely literate) who do seem to have an effortless command over the language and can speak in perfectly modulated sentences, but they are in the tiny minority. Does that mean that you should replicate every flaw and foible in your characters' messy utterances?

Definitely not. When writing advice says to make dialogue as realistic as possible, it doesn't actually mean that. What it means is that, when spoken out loud, it sounds as if your dialogue is what someone might say if they were one of that tiny minority who can speak flawlessly at the drop of a hat, or if they were reading from a script. Many of us speak a little more like this.

> "I dunno. It's not like ... Not really sure I can be bothered, really, you know? I mean ... maybe. Is Rachel going? It's like, I had a really shit day and ... I know I said I would."

That might be how someone might prevaricate over an invitation for a night out, but it would get extremely tedious, very quickly, to read that kind of fractured and repetitious dialogue for very long. That's not to say some writers haven't done it, and made a great success out of it, but it's hard to do.

It might be better to leave a couple of words in to indicate the tone of the speech, but to eliminate most of the actual repetition.

> "I dunno. Maybe. Is Rachel going? I've just had a really shit day and ... I know I said I would."

This version eliminates all the repetition and two-thirds of the ellipses, but retains all the information that we might need to know (she's feeling ambivalent about going, that if Rachel is going that might sway her, that there's a reason she's not keen on going out, and her acknowledgement that she's letting people down if she doesn't). With the inclusion of "dunno" at the beginning we still retain the sense of a very informal conversation between friends.

That neatly introduces the concept of dialect. Another common question among novice writers is whether to include dialect, and if so, how much. If a character talks with a particular regional accent, how much of that speech pattern should you replicate?

Like many things, less is more. Never forget that you are trying to communicate, when writing dialogue, not confuse readers. If the dialect is so idiosyncratic that it needs translation, then you're effectively writing in a foreign language. This will slow most of your readers down as they try and decipher what you are phonetically spelling out, and will cause many of them to put your book down (or back on the shelf in the bookshop) and never pick it up again. Phonetically spelling a regional accent can also look like caricature, especially if you're not from that region yourself. The people who do hail from that region, the few who understand how inaccurately you might be parodying their speech patterns (unless you know them very well yourself), may well resent you for writing it out like that.

Invariably it's better to perhaps have one or two keywords dotted around in a particular character's speech, to remind us of their origins, than to try and reproduce it word for word. So someone from the East End of London might say "ain't" instead of "is not." Someone from Scotland or Ireland might say "ye" instead of "you" in informal speech. Someone from the southern states in the US might address people as "y'all," but even with these minor tweaks, be careful you don't create more problems than you solve. I've seen heated disagreements online between people *from* the southern states in the US (who therefore should know) as to whether “y’all” can be used to address a single person as well as a group of people.

Have writers ever written out regional dialects in full? Of course they have. Irvine Welsh wrote his Edinburgh-based novels like *Trainspotting* in a mixture of Scots, Scottish English and British English. Some people find the authenticity this lends the prose (and it’s not just the dialogue, even the narrator talks in dialect) magnificent. Others find it unreadable. Will Self wrote *The Book of Dave* in a dystopian future where most of the dialogue of certain characters is written in a phonetic Estuarine English that is quite difficult to decipher until you get used to it. It’s literary fiction so he’s not breaking any rules, but it’s not an easy book to read.

The same is true of foreign languages. Unless you expect all your readers to be bilingual, then writing entire sentences in even a commonly learned foreign language like French or German is going to stop many readers dead in their tracks while they reach for a dictionary, or Google Translate, and that’s if they bother. Most of them won’t, and whether they carry on reading is really a question of how annoying they find it to keep having to skip bits of your book that might, for all they know, be crucially important to the plot. This is the antithesis of an immersive novel. You really have to ask yourself, is it worth it for the “authenticity”? Other fudged solutions, like writing out the English translation immediately afterwards, are also clumsy and artificial and merely serve to remind the reader that they’re reading a book. Those who know the other language are going to be irritated by the translation. Those who don’t know the language may well be offended by the fact that you’re putting them in a situation where they’re reminded that they didn't pay much attention to French in school.

If you want to convey an international flavour, use the odd foreign word or phrase that is easily understood, "monsieur," "nein," "bon dia," to ground the speech in a foreign idiom in the reader's mind. Do you need to put these words in to italics? No, they're real words, just not English words. With those foreign words I'd suggest, as a mark of respect for the nationality of the people whose word it is, that you respect their spelling and punctuation, so include the accent on café, for example.

Please resist the urge (unless you're writing dialogue in a particularly old-fashioned kind of farce) to write in "foreign phonetics," that is, to have French people say "Iz zis ze way to ze station?", or Germans to mutter "Ve haf vays off makink you talk." It was funny in the 1970s, perhaps, but we've moved on a bit from then, haven't we?

With all of these issues, grammar, dialect and foreign words and phrases, think about what you're doing when you write a conversation between two characters. The precise pronunciation of the words is rarely of importance. What *is* important is what the other party to the conversation understands and therefore what the reader gleans from the conversation. If you want to add some colour to the dialogue, then by all means use all of these techniques, but use them sparingly. They are terms of description, essentially, and as we discussed in the section on description in "show, don't tell," you shouldn't overdo it.

Contractions

It used to be the case that a contraction was a style issue, that you were making a point when using a contraction that the passage was supposed to be read informally and casually, almost slang, in a sense. But I think that contracting "not" after have, could and should, for example, is almost invisible, these days. It also doesn't stress the negative.

> She couldn't believe his rudeness.

We get the feeling that although she might have been irritated, she wasn't that perturbed or surprised by his manner—she might even have been slightly amused, or turned on. If the expression isn't contracted, we get a very different sense of the phrase.

> She could not believe his rudeness.

This brings a much more formal register to the sentence and, therefore, our sense of the depth of her outrage. We get the distinct impression that in fact she was deeply offended.

Many basic grammar and spell-checkers highlight the use of contractions as poor writing, and prompt a writer to change them to the full expanded form, so *can't* becomes *cannot*. In formal writing, such as business correspondence, that advice generally holds good—most grammar-checking software is designed with business users in mind. However, for fiction writers, such software cannot anticipate how a character in your book would talk (which is yet another reason why novelists should use such software with extreme caution).

In the following passage, Tommy, a gun-toting gangster, threatens a member of a rival gang.

> I can't see why I shouldn't plug you full
> o' holes.

For this to be expanded out to its correct spelling entirely ignores the cadence and personality of the dialogue.

> I cannot see why I should not plug you
> full of holes.

The simple contractions in the original are unobtrusive and read very smoothly. Why spell them out in full and lose all that characterisation?

Longer and more elaborate contractions can start to get both unwieldy to write and awkward to say:

> She shouldn't have done that.

There the contraction is almost invisible, but you might take it a step further.

> She shouldn't've done that.

Here the contraction, with its twin apostrophes, starts becoming rather prominent.

Contractions using pronouns are also pretty ubiquitous these days, especially with the *to have* and *to be* verbs. "I've," "I'd," "I'm" and "you're" for example, are very common, to the extent that writing it out in full, "I am going out tonight," begins to sound either as if the speaker is not too sure if they are going out, or is defying some kind of authority by stressing the "am"—"I *am* going out and there's nothing you can do to stop me."

In conclusion, dialogue that doesn't use contractions sounds extremely formal and rather stilted, to modern ears. That formality may suit your character or setting, but if so, it's a style choice. Dialogue written with contractions generally aids the flow of reading, sounds far more natural, and, importantly, can illuminate a character's personality in a very organic and unobtrusive way.

In narrative, contractions can be slightly more difficult to justify, but here, genre and voice will play a part. In light-hearted or fast-paced fiction, using common contractions like *can't* or *it's* (be careful with *it's*, obviously!) is extremely unobtrusive. In weightier, more profound writing, it might be that *cannot* and *it is* should more properly be written out in full—it's all about tone and style. In this book, for example, I make frequent use of contractions. I am, of necessity, laying out rules and guidelines and best practices. It would be extremely easy to come across as rather pompous and didactic if I wrote out *it is not advisable* in full, instead of *it isn't advisable*. It's a subtle difference (see what I did there?), but one that makes a big impact on the tone of the writing.

NOTE ON YOUR STYLE SHEET:

You might put a note on contraction use. Contractions allowed only in dialogue, or more generally, in the narrator's voice too? And what level of contractions?

Inner monologue

The presentation of interior or inner monologue, a character's direct thought, is determined by the PoV.

Interior monologue in a close PoV is usually written in italics to distinguish it from narrative or normal dialogue.

> *I wonder where she's hiding?* He swung the katana in the air with a satisfying "swoosh."

The direct thought, "I wonder ..." is written in an italics, with no other punctuation around it. The paragraph then seamlessly moves on to an action beat. In a more distant PoV, it can be written in roman, with an appropriate "he thought" or "she wondered" tag after it.

> Where is she hiding? he wondered, as he swung the katana in the air with a satisfying "swoosh."

Again, there's no other punctuation, and the normally sentence-ending question mark doesn't end the sentence. There's a third option, with free indirect style, if you remember our discussion about this in the PoV section in Part II. Here the thoughts, obviously those of the character rather than the narrator, are written in roman, again, and blended with the narrative seamlessly.

> Where's the little bitch hiding? He swung the katana in the air with a satisfying "swoosh."

Some readers express irritation, or even discomfort, if there is too much italicised text in a book. It's true that inner monologue, like any stylistic touch, shouldn't be overdone. If it is, it tends to draw attention to itself and bring the reader out of the story. The odd word or phrase is generally enough to bring us close in to the character's mindset.

Another consideration is font. There are certain fonts whose italics are very clear and easy to read (I happen to think this font, Georgia, has particularly clear italics) and others which don't read with as much clarity. It's a discussion you should have with the person who is typesetting or designing the interior layout of your book when the time comes. Make them aware that, if your book is italics-heavy, they need to choose design options that make those italic sections as easy to read as possible.

NOTE ON YOUR STYLE SHEET:

How are you going to denote interior monologue? With italics, or using the free indirect style, or with thought tags?

Telepathic dialogue

A frequent question posed by fantasy writers is "How do I show telepathic dialogue between my characters?" Since telepathic communication is thought, it seems sensible to suggest that you deal with it in the same manner as you do with interior monologue, to be consistent. In a close PoV this would be italics and, in practice, this is the format that you'll find in most fiction that features telepathic communication (a good example being the Anne McCaffrey *The Tower and the Hive* series).

If your book is written in a more distant PoV you could write the telepathy out in roman, with "he thought" tags.

The indirect free style approach wouldn't work in a "thought conversation," because, by its nature, the indirect free style narrator takes the PoV of one of the characters. To swap PoVs in a thought conversation going backwards and forwards between different characters would get very confusing very quickly. You'd essentially be head-hopping, which is a poor use of indirect free style, let alone telepathic communication! (In any kind of thought conversation you *are* hopping from one head to another, so you need to make sure that it's only the thoughts that hop, not the PoV! In a close PoV situation, one of your characters is going to be the PoV character. Of the other character, make sure it's the "transmitted" thoughts that are transferred, and not the character's own private thoughts—presuming they have any!)

Bold type is another possibility for showing internal thought, but again, font choice might make a difference in how well that looks on the screen or in print. It's difficult to get away from the impression that if something is written in bold type, it means shouting. (If your character is always shouting, then fair enough!)

In all of these styles there remains the problem of showing who the telepathic conversation is between, who the recipient of the telepathic thought is. If there are two people in a scene having a normal conversation, then it's obvious that the vocal conversation is between the people in the scene. But presumably a telepath might be communicating to anyone else, including people who are not physically present, depending on how the "rules" of your telepathic world work. So how do you indicate the target of the telepathic "message"?

Perhaps in your world telepathic communication is not in literal words, but moods or senses, that anyone in the vicinity with the same gift could pick up. That sidesteps the issue. But if your telepaths "think" in sentences to each other, then you'll have to work out a method of directing those conversations. Ken is at a party, standing in the kitchen with three girls, Milly, Molly and Mandy. He thinks, *If you leave now, and wait for me behind the bike shed, I'll follow you in a minute.* How do you let your reader know which girl he "thought" that at? If you want to avoid clumsy stage directions, like "he thought at Mandy," you'll have to work hard on the context to make it quite obvious who the telepathy is between.

NOTE ON YOUR STYLE SHEET:

If your characters indulge in telepathic communication, how have you decided to denote that? Using italics, or bold type, or some other method?

Maid and butler dialogue

What is "maid and butler" dialogue (sometimes called "feather-duster dialogue"), and why is it a poor writing style?

Where does the term come from?

Without getting too technical, classical scholars will be aware that the origins of the prologue, to which maid and butler dialogue relate, date back to Euripides and the Ancient Greeks. The idea that the scene of a stage play should be set at the very beginning of the play by a narrator talking directly to the audience, or by two minor characters having a conversation, certainly predates Shakespeare.

What happens?

The curtain goes up. A banqueting hall, dirty dishes on the table, empty bottles, glasses, streamers and half-deflated balloons.

Two characters enter, one carrying a mop and bucket, the other a brush and a rubbish sack. They begin to clear up the mess.

Maid: Well, that was certainly a party last night, on this the fifth year of Queen Georgina's reign.

Butler: It was. All the gentry from across Northumberland attended, with carriages at dawn. The duke's only daughter, Jezebel, had a fine eighteenth birthday celebration.

Maid: So sad that she is a thoroughly spoiled and selfish child.

Butler: Yes. The duke has had to indulge her wish to go shopping this morning, as if she hadn't already got enough presents.

Maid: Yet Lady Southport didn't accompany them, staying at home and complaining of a headache.

And so on. These two characters are telling each other things that they both know for the benefit of us, the audience. We eavesdrop on their conversation (if it can really be called that) and we establish the basic premise of the play, who the major players are and what the major plot issues are likely to be. It's a form of exposition, of "telling" rather than "showing."

In a novel, if there is a "maid and butler" dialogue problem, it is rarely going to be this blatant. In a novel opening that I was critiquing, one character says to another, "Well, that's the last time you'll need to do that long commute from Dublin on a Friday evening." Although there's nothing wrong with the sentence, when you think about it, you'd be very unlikely to say that to someone who's just walked in at the door having driven the width of Ireland. The traveller knows where they've come from, and they know what day of the week it is. You'd be more likely to say, "You made it! You must be tired. Will I put the kettle on, or would you like something stronger?"

The reason this author wanted to have his character say those words is because it *was* the last time the driver was going to make that journey and it *was* an important plot point to get across. But it's still unlikely to be the first words of a greeting. It would be like meeting someone getting off the train at the station and saying, "Well, that six-carriage 5:52 stopping service from Victoria to Bromley looked pretty packed!"

How to look for it in your own writing

"Maid and butler" dialogue normally arises when an author is too obvious in their attempts to influence the narrative. They want to get an important plot point or character development issue across in a conversation between characters, but instead of letting the characters speak, *they* are speaking *through* the characters. A reader will detect this unnatural author intervention a mile off and it will sound artificial. When you have something important for a character to say, make sure that they say it in a natural way, not in a declamatory, blunt fashion. It may take longer to say—"showing" generally requires a higher word count than "telling"—but it will sound far more realistic and still get the message across. Let's have a look at an example. Two friends are talking:

> "Are you going to the party?" Sally said.
> "I can't." Christine shook her head.
> "Why not? Is it because when you were last at that house you were sexually assaulted by Jake's best friend Rob?"

This is the scenario that the author wants us to appreciate. Christine doesn't want to go to the party because of a previous incident there involving Jake's best friend. The two girls both know this, but at this point in the book, we (the readers) don't know about Christine's past, so the author has Sally telling Christine what Christine's problem is likely to be. It sounds very artificial, and that's because it's simply not what one friend would say to another in this situation. So how *should* the author get us to know Christine's motivation for not going to the party? The answer is simply by writing more realistic dialogue. How would this conversation pan out possibly? A more genuine conversation might sound like this:

> "Are you going to the party?" Sally said.
> "I can't." Christine shook her head.
> "Why not?"

> "Because," Christine said, looking away.
>
> "Oh shit." Sally smacked her forehead. "Sorry ... I'd forgotten. That thing with Rob ..."
>
> "It wasn't a 'thing', Sally. He near raped me."
>
> "Ah, hon." Sally put her hand on Christine's arm. "Sorry, babe." She brightened. "But Rob might not even be there," she said.
>
> "He's Jake's best friend. Of course he'll be there."

The merits of the writing aside, I think we should be able to agree that the second conversation sounds more realistic. It gets the same information across and also manages to convey some nuances of the characters concerned. (The way I happen to have written it, Sally comes across as a bit dim and unsympathetic, but her character reaction could have been written differently.) It is longer, but that's the downside of "showing" rather than "telling."

"Maid and butler" dialogue is one of the more problematic writing faults because it combines two weaknesses, that of telling rather than showing, and of having conversations that sound artificial and stilted. When looking through your dialogue, keep alert for anything that sounds a little staged.

Punctuation

A comprehensive punctuation guide is beyond the scope of this book, but there are some common problems I see coming up repeatedly in questions in author forums and in manuscripts I'm given to edit. This section aims to address those common problems in a quick and easily navigable fashion.

If you're intrigued by punctuation (don't laugh—some people are!) then be aware that there are often subtle stylistic differences between certain punctuation usages in newspapers, scientific journals and books, which is why a completely comprehensive guide is unrealistic here. Most novels are edited to one of two standards, the *Oxford Style Guide*, also known as *New Hart's Rules* (*NHR*) for UK/European English speakers, and the *Chicago Manual of Style* (*CMoS*), for the rest of the English-speaking world. In the section that follows I'll term these "UK" and "US" rules, for brevity's sake. Even within those rules there are areas of personal choice (and some presses, like the Oxford University Press in the UK, make their own rules), so the important thing is to be consistent within the book (and/or series). Make a choice and stick to it.

Once again, if you're going to use an editor you can sit back, having discussed your approach with them, and let them get on with the detailed work. You can get on with writing the next book instead. However, if you've made at least an attempt to sort out your punctuation, the next book you write will probably have fewer errors, and the MS you hand your editor will need less work, therefore saving you money.

Instead of trying to elaborate on every punctuation rule, I'll go through some areas that frequently cause writers problems. Remember above all else that punctuation is only there to aid clarity of meaning and, sometimes, of expression.

Commas

Commas are one of the most subjective issues in punctuation. Several generations of writers were brought up to believe that you put a comma anywhere you take a pause while reading. While this advice has a certain natural congruity with actual writing rules, it doesn't hold up to too much close inspection. In certain circumstances, where you would naturally pause while speaking, a comma is necessary. In many situations a comma isn't required. Whether you choose to use a comma then becomes a matter of style, rather than of rules. Is there an overall principle? I'd recommend an overriding principle of not using punctuation that's unnecessary. Anything that intrudes on the flow of the writing without due cause should be left out—that seems to be in line with how modern writing is evolving.

However, we do speak English, and we do pause sometimes, mid-sentence, for reason of meaning or inference, and it might suit your purposes for conveying that meaning to put a comma where there's no good grammatical reason for one. There are certain places where a comma's presence or absence will be almost always interpreted as a mistake, of which more in the following sections.

The Oxford comma

US rules require a serial, or "Oxford" comma, that is, in a list of three or more items, a comma precedes the final conjunction.

> "You can have chicken, beef, or fish."

UK rules don't require it.

> "You can have chicken, beef or fish."

There's no ambiguity there, so a comma after *beef* is unnecessary. However, in the following example, it's not necessarily clear what the author means.

> "I'd like to dedicate this book to my parents, Mother Teresa and Nelson Mandela."

If the author really is the love child of these two icons, then fair enough, but I doubt it! A comma after *Teresa* shows that the phrase is a list of three components.

> "I'd like to dedicate this book to my parents, Mother Teresa, and Nelson Mandela."

Opponents of the serial comma, and UK writers who don't use it, would be better off rephrasing the sentence to avoid the ambiguity in the first place.

> "I'd like to dedicate this book to Mother Teresa, Nelson Mandela and my parents."

Supporters say that if you're going to use a punctuation rule, you should use it consistently. Under US rules it will be expected. Some rather strident grammar-purist readers will take it as a personal insult if you don't include it, and will let you know, via their review. Under UK rules you have the choice. Since excluding it where it's unnecessary but including it where you can't avoid ambiguity requires some thought, many writers take the easy option and include it in all cases.

NOTE FOR YOUR STYLE SHEET:

Are you adopting the Oxford comma, or only including it if needed for clarity?

Comma splices

Don't use a comma to join what are two complete sentences together. This is called a comma splice, or run-on sentence.

> I was late for my flight, I still made it on to the plane.

Instead, separate the two sentences with a replacement full stop/period, or the addition of a conjunction, called a co-ordinating conjunction.

> I was late for my flight. I still made it on to the plane.
>
> I was late for my flight, but I still made it on to the plane.

A corollary of that rule is to use commas before coordinating conjunctions. You might have heard of the mnemonic FANBOYS, meaning the words *for*, *and*, *nor*, *but*, *or*, *yet* and *so*. If these separate two main clauses (i.e. phrases that can stand alone as a sentence, as above) then use a comma before the conjunction. However, if the component parts of a sentence are very short, then the comma can be omitted in front of the conjunction. The above example is marginal, in truth.

> I was late but I just made the flight.

In this even more abbreviated example the meaning is quite clear without the comma so, in the interests of leaving it out if you can, leave it out.

If either one of the phrases on either side of the conjunction is not a complete sentence, then you don't have to use a comma.

> I missed my flight but caught the train instead.

Here, "caught the train instead" is not a complete sentence, so no comma is needed before "but."

Historical note: comma splices used to be quite acceptable. If you've read Appendix II already, I mention the beginning of Charles Dickens' *A Tale of Two Cities*. "It was the best of times, it was the worst of times, it was the age of wisdom, it was the age of foolishness ..." It is an extremely long example of a serial comma splice that would be frowned upon in modern literature. It's a good example of why, even though I'm writing about best practices here, I prefaced this section by saying there's very little written in stone about punctuation rules.

Commas between adjectives

Believe it or not, doctoral theses have been written on the subject of adjectives (technically called "premodifiers") placed before nouns and their associated comma placement, but really there are only a couple of things you do need to know. Firstly, there is no comma after the last adjective in a list. Secondly, only use a comma in a list of adjectives where you could substitute a conjunction like *and* or *but*, and/or where the adjectives can be swapped around and the sentence retain its meaning without sounding awkward. For people who like terminology, these are termed coordinate adjectives.

a modern, fuel-efficient car

a modern and fuel-efficient car

a fuel-efficient, modern car

For phrases where a conjunction would feel awkward, or where swapping the adjectives would either make no sense or change the sense, don't use a comma.

the long summer holidays

is not the same as

the summer long holidays

or

the long and summer holidays

so no comma between long and summer.

a fast Italian sports car

is fine, but

a fast sports Italian car

makes no sense, so no comma anywhere. These are called cumulative adjectives. The general rule of thumb then, is, if the sentence still makes sense and has the same meaning if you can insert an "and," or swap the adjectives around, use a comma.

You don't really need to know much more than that, but for those who would like a bit more in-depth knowledge, here are some other interesting details.

There is an order in which adjectives are generally placed before nouns; that is, the most subjective or general adjectives first, and the most objective or specific closest to the noun. This notion, of increasing specificity, largely determines the order in which a series of adjectives are applied.

Subjective or *qualitative* adjectives, such as *large* or *green* or *heavy*, can be divided into four categories, *opinion*, *physical attributes*, *age* and *colour*. These are invariably placed first in an adjectival phrase, in roughly that order.

a small green dragon

Small is *size*, or category two; green is *colour*, category four. If there's a logic that the adjectives are in this order (and in some instances it doesn't appear that there is any logic), a reason could be that a green dragon is a specific colour of dragon, whereas presumably any colour of dragon can be big or small. So *green* modifies the noun *dragon*, and *small* modifies the phrase *green dragon*. It's best not to look too closely at this analysis though, because there's a similar argument that a small dragon is a specific size of dragon, and green is the colour of that particular small dragon, in which case small modifies dragon, and green modifies the phrase small dragon. It remains the case though, that "a green small dragon" looks and sounds awkward. (Note that the young Tolkien got his knuckles rapped for writing a sentence which included the phrase "a green great dragon." Presumably his logic was that if there are lesser dragons, and great dragons, then it's perfectly acceptable to talk about green great dragons. After all, Tolkien knew a thing or two about dragons.)

While the adjectives *small* and *green* are both qualitative adjectives, they are of different types (physical, and colour), so no comma is needed between them—they are qualitative, cumulative adjectives. However, commas are required when applying several qualitative adjectives of the same category.

> a handsome, tall, well-built young man

Handsome, *tall* and *well-built* are all qualitative physical attributes (category two), are therefore coordinating, so require commas between them. *Young* is another qualitative adjective, but of a different category, age, so it doesn't coordinate, and there's no need for a comma between *well-built* and *young*, in the same way that there's no need for one in the phrase *little old lady*.

Objective or *classifying* adjectives can be subdivided into nationality/origin, material and purpose. These are generally placed last, again in roughly that order, in an adjectival phrase.

> an Italian marble dining table

No commas are required between adjectives of different types, that is, between qualitative and classifying adjectives.

> a small Hungarian dragon
>
> a beautiful Italian car

Just before we move on, let's go back to one of our examples above.

an Italian marble dining table

You might have noticed that there is a slight ambiguity in that phrase as it stands and since clarity should always be uppermost in the writer's mind, that could be problematic. Is it an Italian dining table made of marble (which might come from somewhere else), or is it a dining table (designed in France perhaps) made of Italian marble? We can't tell from that phrase. No rule about commas or adjectival order should trump clarity. If it's a dining table made in France, of Italian marble, then no amount of tweaking and shuffling word order is going to resolve the ambiguity in that adjectival phrase. It should be rewritten.

And what about numbers? Numbers go before everything, so there are four small green dragons, not small four green dragons.

Believe it or not, there are even more complexities in the adjectival ordering discussion—we can bring up subsective adjectives, privative adjectives and more—but that's getting in to the realms of doctorate-level linguistics and beyond the scope of this book.

In summary, respect the order of adjectives: [number], opinion, physical attributes, age, colour, nationality/origin, material and purpose—*four beautiful slender old blue Flemish porcelain stem vases*. If you have two adjectives of the same classification, they need a comma or conjunction between them, but if they are of different classifications, as in the example in the preceding sentence, you don't need any commas.

Parenthetical commas

In more complex sentences there will quite often be non-essential information, a phrase that, were it to be omitted completely, would still leave a complete sentence behind. It's common to bracket that phrase with what are called parenthetical commas.

> John's apartment, which was four floors up, had a beautiful view.

If you take out "which was four floors up" you still have a complete sentence.

> John's apartment had a beautiful view.

In the same way, introductory, interrupting or afterthought phrases are often offset with commas.

> Sure, I'd love to come to your gig.
>
> The music at the gig was, frankly, awful.
>
> I wish I'd never gone to the gig, to be honest.

If the phrase is very short, then it's not breaking any rules to omit the comma, and in the last two examples above it could be left out without any real impact on the meaning or cadence of the sentence.

That and which

Following on from parenthetical commas, the treatment of *that* and *which* with commas is similar. Use *which*, with a comma preceding it, if the phrase that follows is non-essential, as in the previous example.

> John's apartment, which was four floors up, had a beautiful view.

If John had two apartments, one in the basement and one four floors up, you would use *that*, with no commas.

> John's apartment that was four floors up had a beautiful view. The apartment that was in the basement only looked out on the bins.

Here it's specific apartments being talked about. The information that comes after *that* is essential to understand the sentence. There's another US/UK difference here. UK writers tend not to adhere to the *that/which* rule to the same degree. You'll see *that* preceded by a comma, and *which* with no commas, in UK fiction. Under US rules, a comma before *that* will be frowned upon.

Vocative commas

When a speaker directly addresses a specific person, that person's name (or title) should be offset by what is called a vocative comma. The comma can come before, after or at both ends of the person's name or title, depending on where the placement of the name is in the sentence.

> "I don't know, John."
>
> "Jack, can you pay me?"
>
> "If I drove over, Jack, can you pay me?"

Removal of the comma leads to very different connotations.

> "I don't know John."

"If I drove over Jack, can you pay me?"

If the comma is omitted, the sentence could be misinterpreted to have a completely different meaning: the speaker doesn't know someone called John. The reason there are commas around a name is that an addressed person's name is always parenthetical; it's an interjection. More on parenthetical phrases in a minute.

Technically, when you begin a letter or email with a "Hello Mary" address (instead of the more traditional and formal "Dear Mary"), there should be a vocative comma between the "Hello" and "Mary," but you rarely see it used in anything but the most correct correspondence.

"Hello, Mary,

Thanks for getting in touch."

The reason there isn't a comma between "Dear" and "Mary" is that dear is an adjective that describes Mary; it's not a form of address.

Commas in dialogue

It's not as if all the rules go out of the window when using commas in dialogue, but a comma may be used to indicate a pause in a piece of speech where you might not technically need a comma. Adding a comma could lend quite a different nuance to the speech.

"I can help," she said. "That is, if you want my help."

The second sentence in this example doesn't need a comma, but the true sense of uncertainty, of not being sure if help is what is wanted, is subtly weakened without it. There's an argument for using an em- or spaced en dash there (see later, under *dashes*), instead of the comma, but stylistically, that looks a bit like punctuation overkill.

> "I can help," she said. "That is—if you want my help."

In dialogue, comma usage can begin to mimic the old adage of marking a breath taken, or a pause. That alone isn't a valid reason. Only include a comma in such instances if the hidden meaning or nuance behind the dialogue you want to convey is missing without it.

Full stops/periods

If commas were a marathon, periods/full stops (I'll call them *points* in this section) are a gentle stroll! There's not much ambiguity about closing punctuation, except sometimes where to put it, and whether to include it in certain situations. One thing common to all uses of points—only one space after them. Traditional typesetting would generally use a wider space after the end of a sentence than between words. To mimic this presentation, with the advent of the typewriter, typists would double-space after every point. This wide spacing was slowly phased out in the printing industry over the course of the twentieth century, but it was still common practice in typing schools until quite recently. With computers and sophisticated word-processing systems it's no longer necessary, and often the first task that a proofreading editor will do on an MS is to eliminate all instances of duplicated spaces. (The same applies to spaces after question marks and exclamation marks.)

Placement in quotes

Under US rules, if a sentence ends with a quotation, be it a straight quote or dialogue, the point is always placed inside the quotes.

> When I asked him, he said "last Tuesday."

Under UK rules the punctuation only belongs inside the quotes if it belongs to the quote. In this example it doesn't.

> When I asked him, he said 'last Tuesday'.

But,

> When I asked him, he said, 'I'll see you next Wednesday.'

Here the point belongs inside the quotes—it's a full sentence. There is no further point after the quotes. Similarly, note that there is no further punctuation if the quote ends with a question mark or exclamation mark.

> When I asked him, he shouted "last Tuesday!"

NOTE FOR YOUR STYLE SHEET:

US or UK rules for terminal punctuation within quotes?

Placement in parentheses

Here US and UK rules don't differ. If the parentheses enclose a full sentence, then the point belongs inside the parentheses.

> (Robert usually crashed.)

If the parentheses include a full sentence that in turn is part of another full sentence, then the point is outside the brackets at the end of the enclosing sentence.

> It was odd seeing him on the podium (Robert usually crashed) instead of the medic's tent.

If the parentheses enclose a fragment, then the point is outside the brackets.

> It was odd (seeing him on the podium).
> He usually crashed.

With other terminal punctuation

If the sentence ends in a question mark or exclamation mark, no further point is needed. If it ends in a construct requiring a point, such as an abbreviation like etc., or an ellipsis, then no further point is required.

Semicolons

Semicolons are a break in a sentence stronger than a comma, but not as strong as a colon or a point. They're usually used to link two sentences that are closely related to each other, and are quite often a possible solution to the comma-splicing or run-on sentence problem mentioned in the *commas* section.

> I was late for my flight; I had to run to the gate.

Both parts of this sentence can stand alone. Although they are directly related, it would be incorrect to link them with just a comma, and a full point might seem to interrupt the flow of the linked ideas.

Semicolons can also be used in a list situation to clarify the elements of a list that might already be punctuated with commas.

> We thought we were secure: all the doors and windows were locked; the windows downstairs were also boarded up, those upstairs just shuttered; the hatch into the cellar we'd barred from the inside; and we lit a fire in the main fireplace, which had the only chimney big enough for them to crawl down.

In informal writing, and therefore quite often in fiction, semicolons can be replaced with em dashes.

> I was late for my flight—I had to run to the gate.

Since there's a slightly more formal feel to a semicolon, I tend to recommend that authors avoid using semicolons when writing dialogue, and use em dashes instead. Then, elsewhere in the narrative, using semicolons instead of em dashes can be just about feel of the flow of the sentence. That isn't a rule, however, and the voice of the writer and the genre will play a part in deciding whether the slightly more formal use of semicolons is more or less appropriate.

Colons

Colons have a fairly limited use. They can introduce a list of elements separated by commas or by semicolons (see the "We thought we were secure ..." example above in *semicolons*).

They can also separate parts of a sentence that are directly related to each other. When using a colon in this manner, although the clause after the colon can be a full sentence, it doesn't have to be.

> The finest examples in the car collection were all Italian: Ferraris, Lamborghinis, even an old Alfa Romeo Spyder.

A neat rule of thumb for colon placement in this type of phrase is to check whether the phrase "for example" or "namely" can be substituted for it.

> The finest examples in the car collection were all Italian, [for example,] Ferraris, Lamborghinis, even an old Alfa Romeo Spyder.

If it can, as above, then a colon is a good fit.

It's also possible to use a colon to isolate a single word or short phrase at the end of a sentence, for dramatic effect.

> There was only one word to describe the approaching horde: zombies.

Whether the first word after the colon is capitalised varies between US and UK versions. If the word is a proper noun, then it is capitalised in both jurisdictions. If it is not a proper noun but introduces a full sentence, then it is capitalised under US English rules. In every other circumstance the word is lower case. UK English retains the option to capitalise in certain specific circumstances (introducing the subtitle in a book's title, for example. This book's subtitle is "Incorporating: A style guide for fiction").

Apostrophes

Apostrophes are the delinquent child of the punctuation world, the five-year-old with a box of matches in the hayloft, causing grief and aggravation out of all proportion to their size and importance. There are two primary uses of apostrophes, and both are roundly abused. It might help to note that both uses derived from the same evolution in writing.

Contractions

The principle use of apostrophes is in contractions. They simply denote a missing letter, or letters. "Had not" is contracted to "hadn't," the apostrophe in place of the missing vowel. "I am" is contracted to "I'm," same story. "Should not" is contracted to "shouldn't" and "should not have" is (sometimes, daringly) contracted to "shouldn't've" (but you'll know what I think of that if you've read the section on "Contractions" in Dialogue). Being English, there are of course exceptions. "Will not" is contracted to "won't," "shall not" is contracted to "shan't."

If, in addition to these standard contractions, your characters are eliding letters in their dialogue, the correct way to write out the speech would be to use apostrophes where they've missed a letter.

> "D'ya want some ham an' eggs?"
>
> "You're 'avin' a laugh, ain't ya?"

The apostrophe is always the closing single quote, never the opening one, even if it goes at the beginning of a contraction like in the middle of the phrase "rock 'n' roll." Some word processors will automatically assume that a space followed by an apostrophe means you are opening quotes, and will insert the opening mark. To get round that in Word, type CTRL and the apostrophe key twice to generate the closing quote in front of a letter.

Possession

The other use of the apostrophe is to indicate the possessive, but it might be interesting to understand where that comes from. We find out that it's actually very much related to the elision of a letter.

In the Middle English of Chaucer's day, there were no apostrophes. The possessive was almost always indicated by adding *-es* to the word or name in question, so Chaucer started the Canterbury Tales thus: "Heere bigynneth the Knyghtes Tale." In time, the *e* was dropped in favour of an apostrophe, so we'd now write "Here begins the Knight's Tale," completely in line with the rules we just established for contractions. (Note we still do add *-es* to a name or word ending in *s* to form the plural. If we're talking about the family of Mr and Mrs

Williams and their five children, it's "the Williamses," so we haven't moved on that far from Chaucer.)

Bearing that in mind, how do we form the possessive in modern usage? After a single noun and after the rare plural that doesn't end in *s*, we use an apostrophe and the letter *s*, but just an apostrophe after a plural noun.

> Nigel's car was used in a bank robbery.
>
> Women's rights should be enshrined in the constitution.
>
> It was all the banks' failure to self-regulate that resulted in the crash.
>
> The party is at the Williamses'.

Timespans can catch people out. Be careful to note whether you're indicating a single period, or several periods.

> In a year's time

But

> In twelve months' time

Although these two phrases describe the same length of time, "a year" is singular, whereas "twelve months" is plural.

If the possessor noun or word ends in a pronounced *s*, general advice would be to add an apostrophe and an *s*, as in "boss's office" (but see "Williamses' " above). Some US style guides differentiate on this, however. If the object of their possession begins with an *s* they say drop the trailing *s*, so "boss's office," but "boss' secretary." They don't seem to all agree though, so it's open to author choice. It's probably easier to be consistent.

However, there are many exceptions and special cases—far too many to go into here. For example, if words and names end in a pronounced *eez* sound, as in many Greek names, or end in a silent *s*, as many French names do, then you can omit the trailing *s* ("Archimedes' theory," "Descartes' writings"). It's normally "Jesus's sandals" but it can be written as "Jesus' sandals." Proper nouns and place names have an accepted spelling that, if in doubt, you'll just need to look up in your adopted dictionary (Lord's Cricket Ground, Johns Hopkins University).

The key thing I do want to mention here is that you never include an apostrophe on a possessive pronoun, theirs, yours, ours and the dreaded its.

It's horribly easy to write "it's" when you mean "its," and if you find you're very prone to doing it, it might be worth a "search" function in whatever word-processing program you use, calling up all instances of the possessive "it's" and working out if they're correct. The test is to expand "it's" out into "it is," for which it's the contraction. If it doesn't make sense, then you've got it wrong.

> The fox eyed it's breakfast from the safety of the hedge.

Expanded out, this sentence clearly doesn't make sense.

> The fox eyed it is breakfast from the safety of the hedge.

It's a possessive pronoun—no apostrophe.

> The fox eyed its breakfast from the safety of the hedge.

What's called the "grocer's" apostrophe is where a market stall-holder will include an apostrophe in a plural, leading to horrors like "Five apple's for a pound." This is never right, and must be the most common mistake in punctuation.

When you go through your MS, keep an eye out for these little devils, apostrophes. When you see one, ask yourself, what letter is it replacing? If it's not replacing a letter, what is it doing there? Is it really representing the possessive, or is it one of those five-year-olds in the barn with the matches?

Dashes and hyphens

Dashes and hyphens are another problematic area where many novice writers are genuinely unaware that there are different uses for each type of dash, and that the hyphen is not ubiquitous. Here I'll go into the most common uses of each type of mark and their associated punctuation, if any.

Hyphens

A hyphen is the shortest of the dashes, and their use is actually quite limited. There are two classifications of hyphen, *hard hyphens*, which make compound words and phrases out of shorter words, like machine-gun, or drip-proof, or *soft hyphens*, that indicate that a word continues on the next line. If you're using a modern word-processing package like Word you shouldn't need to worry about soft hyphens at all; the program will do the layout of the page for you.

When you might need to think about hyphens is when forming a compound word. That word can be a compound *noun*, *verb* or *adjective*, and the overriding consideration for hyphenation is for clarity. If you don't need a hyphen, there's no need to put one in.

Consider the first half of this sentence.

> Twenty year old girls ...

Is it talking about twenty toddlers celebrating their first birthday? No, because the sentence continues

> ... sometimes abuse alcohol.

Proper hyphenation resolves the ambiguity.

> Twenty-year-old girls sometimes abuse alcohol.

Another example.

> I'd like to recover the sofa.

Was the sofa stolen? Did it fall down a well? Hyphenation clarifies the meaning.

> I'd like to re-cover the sofa.

Hyphens are frequently used to create compound words. Whether or not you use a hyphen varies depending usually on what the grammatical components of the compound are.

COMPOUND NOUNS

Compound nouns are generally pretty straightforward. They will be listed in a good dictionary (although check that it's up to date—hyphenation evolves, as I'll mention later). They can be closed up, *toothpaste*, open, *ice cream*, or, rarely, hyphenated, *city-state*. How they are written generally depends on current usage, and if you're not confident, best and quickest just to look it up.

COMPOUND VERBS

Compound verbs are also generally straightforward. They can be closed, *to breastfeed*, hyphenated, *to court-martial*, or, in the case of what are properly known as phrasal verbs, open, *to break in*. Again, these should be listed in a reliable dictionary, as long as it's up to date.

COMPOUND ADJECTIVES

The basic rule is: hyphenate if it comes before the noun to which it relates, open if after. So,

a quick-thinking fireman

but

the fireman was quick thinking

Why is that? It boils down to ambiguity again. With the adjective before the noun the phrase can be interpreted in a number of different ways.

a quick thinking fireman

Is this a fireman who is particularly fast on his feet, who happened to be thinking? What's important is that his *thoughts* were quick. This ambiguity doesn't exist where the adjective is used after the noun.

The main exception to this rule is where one component of the compound is an adverb. This can be a word ending in –ly,

the quickly deflating bouncy castle

or another adverb, like *very*

a very large cake

or *much*

the much admired pianist.

PREFIXES

Use a hyphen to join a prefix to another word, like *post-apocalyptic*. However, here usage is changing. More and more commonly, words that used to be hyphenated are closed up. Consider *co-operate*. Some diehards still hyphenate co-operate, but most writers now close this up to *cooperate* even though the prefix ends with the same vowel the other word starts with. In the days when the rules of hyphenation were more rigid, this would definitely have been frowned upon.

If you find these tiny distinctions too hard to deal with, Word will highlight words or phrases that it thinks should be hyphenated, or should not be, and it usually gets it right.

EVOLUTION

I mentioned at the outset that hyphenation is one of those areas of the language that is constantly evolving. The evolution of cooperate took place over a couple of centuries. Research can show you that at around 1720 no one wrote cooperate, but the closed up version began to gain the ascendancy in the early twentieth century, and is now in the distinct majority.

Modern words evolve even faster. *Website*, all one word, has always been more popular than the hyphenated version, *web-site*, or even the open version, *web site*, but now it's vastly more common than either of the alternatives.

The only way to make sure that your compounds are up to date is to check with your dictionary of choice, or, if you're really keen, to check with a style guide such as *CMoS*. The hyphenation table of the current version of *CMoS* runs to nine pages and includes things beyond the scope of this section, like compass points (*northeast*, but *east-northeast*), proper nouns (*African American* but *Franco-Prussian War*) and dozens of prefixes.

Even the *CMoS* guide, which is updated regularly, quite often redefines current usage, so there are few constants. There are also some strange outliers in real life. The editorial style guide for the *New Yorker* magazine, for example, insists on hyphenating "teen-ager." There is an archaic word meaning something to do with hedging, I believe, called teenage (presumably pronounced *tinnidge* in this usage), so they choose to break up and hyphenate a word universally understood as a gawky adolescent, from this overused synonym for rural boundaries, for the benefit of their extensive agricultural historian readership, who might otherwise get confused.

Rather than worry too much about it, especially in fiction, try to adhere to one particular usage. Don't say *homemade jam* in one chapter, and *home-made pickle* in another. It's very easy to be inconsistent, especially if those terms can occur chapters apart, and while it's not the end of the world, that kind of inconsistency marks out an amateur MS. If you're expecting people to pay money for your book, then you're a professional writer, not an amateur.

NOTE FOR YOUR STYLE SHEET:

It's a problem that will probably concern non-fiction writers more than fiction, but if there are compound words and phrases you use more than once or twice, you might consider specifying whether you are using the hyphenated or non-hyphenated version of a word where there is a choice. If you're writing a book on self-sufficiency or crafts, for example, you might decide which version of "home-made" you're going to use. You can then check whether you've kept this consistent in every occurrence in the manuscript.

En dash (or en-rule in UK English)

The en dash is a slightly longer line than a hyphen, usually about double the length. This is largely a "joining" mark.

Use the en dash when you're indicating a range of numbers, for example, "*the Second World War, 1939–1945*" or a relationship between two otherwise unconnected words, "*the Mayweather–McGregor fight*," or "*the London–Istanbul train*." In this latter sense it's used as a replacement for "and" or "to."

In UK English, some writers use a spaced en dash (a dash with a space on either side of it) for parenthetical clauses.

> The princess – she had been awake half the night – came downstairs in a terrible temper.

En dashes can be used in this way instead of commas (see parenthetical commas, above) but it's better to use them only when the parenthetical nature of the interruption needs to be stressed. Too many en dashes littering a page is not great typography.

In UK English spaced en dashes can be used in instances of interrupted dialogue. Whether the en dashes go inside or outside the quotes depends on whether the dialogue is being interrupted, or whether the writer is merely introducing an action beat in the middle of the dialogue.

> 'In this next photo' – she clicked the remote – 'you can see the lion approaching the tent.'

In this case the dialogue is not being interrupted—the speaker is doing something while speaking, an action beat.

> 'In this next slide –'
>
> 'Does this presentation go on much longer?' a voice shouted from the back of the hall.

In this case someone else is interrupting the speaker. The en dash belongs to the dialogue, so goes inside the quotes. Note that while there is a space between the text and the dash, there is no space between the dash and the quote marks in this example. En dashes can also be used to emphasise the end of a sentence.

> "There was one thing alone that interested Billy – guns."

In this last example the en dash is acting like a colon. Many writers feel awkward using colons and semicolons, and here an en dash feels perhaps less formal.

There's not a dedicated key for the en dash on most computer keyboards, but you can generate one in most word-processing packages by typing one word, a space, a hyphen, another space and then another word. If you watch carefully, the hyphen you typed will suddenly stretch into an en dash, like Pinocchio's nose. Alternatively, hold down the Alt key and type 0150 on the keypad.

Em dash (or em-rule)

The em dash is generally twice as long again as the en dash. The sure-fire way of creating an em dash is to use Alt and 0151 on the numeric keypad. US publishers (and the Oxford University Press in the UK) choose to use closed up em dashes (em dashes without any spaces) where other UK publishers might use spaced en dashes. So the examples given above would read as follows.

> "The princess—she had been awake half the night—came downstairs in a terrible temper."
>
> "In this next photo"—she clicked the remote—"you can see the lion approaching the tent."
>
> "In this next slide—"
>
> "Does this presentation go on much longer?" a voice shouted from the back of the hall.
>
> "There was one thing that interested Billy—guns."

Em dashes can also be used to signify the omission of an entire word, or part of a word.

> "Baby J— was rescued by emergency services and is now living with foster parents."

NOTE FOR YOUR STYLE SHEET:

Are you going to use spaced en dashes, or closed up em dashes where necessary?

Quotes

In fiction, the most common use for quotation marks is dialogue, and because there's often a lot of dialogue in a novel, it takes an inordinate amount of time for an editor to sort it out if it's wrong. If you're going the editor route and you can hand over an MS with the dialogue already sorted, you will save yourself a considerable amount of money in editing fees.

I covered most of the issues to do with quotes in the section "Dialogue punctuation." There remain just a couple of isolated issues.

Scare quotes

Scare quotes, where the quote marks are used euphemistically, or for stress or clarification, are of the same type as the primary quote marks used for dialogue, so double under US rules, or single under UK rules. The only exception to this rule is if the matter being emphasised is within dialogue, in which case the "nested quote mark" rules apply.

> "This is dull," he said. It was one of those "modern" plays, with almost no set and only two actors.
>
> "How dull. It's one of those 'modern' plays," he said.
>
> 'This is dull,' he said. It was one of those 'modern' plays, with almost no set and only two actors.
>
> 'How dull. It's one of those "modern" plays,' he said.

Block quotes

Sometimes it's necessary to have a character quote a long passage, perhaps of a letter, or diary, reading aloud to other characters in a scene. The quoted matter needs its own nested quotes, so it's clear what's being quoted and what is being said. However, if the passage runs on to multiple paragraphs, this treatment can look quite messy, with the duplicated nested quotes starting each paragraph. It might be more appropriate to treat this as a block quote, in which a chunk of text is set apart from the main body text by means of indentation or italics or a different font. There are various different styles, some using quotes and some not, but the indentation or differentiation by other means from the body text means that the nested quotes aren't necessary.

In this book my examples are styled in a kind of block quote format. Some are multiple paragraphs, and they are indented both left and right from the body text so that it's quite clear what constitutes the example. I don't feel the need to further put them in italics or a different font.

NOTE FOR YOUR STYLE SHEET:

If your book includes a lot of block quotes and you have a particular preference as to how they should appear, you might want to specify the formatting.

Ellipses

The most common usage of an ellipsis in fiction is to mark a tailing off of speech or thought, where a character starts to express something but finishes with the thought or dialogue incomplete, which I've already covered under "Tailing off dialogue" in the dialogue section.

In certain narrative styles an ellipsis might be used to generate suspense.

> The cellar door creaked open ...

This type of narrative is quite common in children's books, but it's a bit "leading" and coy for adult literature. The viewpoint is not grounded in a character point of view, but more that of an omniscient narrator telling us what is happening, and also, how to feel about it.

The other main reason to use an ellipsis is in non-fiction where the author might want to quote part of a passage to elaborate on a point, but not the whole sentence. Here an ellipsis indicates missing text.

> "We shall fight them on the beaches ...
> we shall never surrender ..."

Ellipses, capitalisation and other punctuation

There's no need for a point after an ellipsis if the sentence ends with one. However, if the sentence would normally end with a question mark or exclamation mark, they are added after the ellipsis.

> "Did you really think ...?"
>
> "They're in the room, they're ...!"

If the sentence carries on, so that the ellipsis records a pause in the thought or dialogue rather than a complete break, the first letter of the phrase after the ellipsis should not be capitalised. It's a continuation of the same thought/speech, even though if you removed the ellipsis it would look awkward.

> "You hit a child?" she said. "I think that's really ... how could you?"

If the ellipsis represents a termination of the thought or dialogue, then what follows is a new sentence and should be capitalised. In the example above

> He hit a child, she thought. That's really ... She shook her head.

Her shaking her head is not part of the thought—it's a new action, so represents a new sentence (otherwise you might think that she is *thinking* "She shook her head").

If the ellipsis is part of a single thought or dialogue, but splits two complete sentences, then the part after the ellipsis shouldn't be capitalised, but I'd consider whether an ellipsis is appropriate. If ellipses are used every time a character draws breath they can quickly become obtrusive. It might be that inserting an action beat like "He paused" is a better method of indicating the break.

> "I'm not sure ... do you think so?"
>
> "I'm not sure." He paused. "Do you think so?"

Ellipses and styling

The presentation of ellipses gives even editors conniptions—there are a number of ways of styling the actual punctuation mark, all of which are okay, as long as you're consistent. If your MS ends up with a publisher who uses a different method of presenting ellipses, then all methods are eminently substitutable by someone who knows what they're doing with the "Find and Replace" feature in Word. So choose a styling that appeals to you and is easy to implement, and stick with it.

Most word-processing software can be set to default so that typing three points in a row creates what is called the ellipsis *glyph*, "…", a single character that has its own spacing. Some style guides (notably *CMoS*) recommend typing out three points with spaces in between, so ". . .". Others recommend three separate points but with slightly narrower spaces between them, so ". . ." (created by typing a point followed by Ctrl Shift Space and repeating). There are other complications with what are called non-breaking spaces, so that a line doesn't break in the middle of an ellipsis on an e-reader with flowable text, which leads me to suggest that the simplest method is to create the glyph by typing three points in a row.

Some styles then insist on the ellipsis being closed up to surrounding text, and yet others insist on a space preceding the ellipsis, and following it if followed by text, but not if followed by other punctuation (likely to be a question or exclamation mark, as we saw above). Again, a space followed by three points followed by another space (if appropriate), is easy to type and identifiable to any book designer it they feel the need to change it. Some examples of that style in different situations follow.

> "Me neither ... but perhaps ..."
>
> "You said ...?"

NOTE FOR YOUR STYLE SHEET:

Which typography are you going to use for ellipses, the glyph, or three spaced points, or some other variant? It's important to be consistent because if you decide to change your style (because you discover compatibility issues with some e-readers, for example) if they're all the same format it's a ten-second job. If they're not, it becomes much more complicated to sort out.

Other punctuation matters

Inner thoughts

The presentation of inner monologue was discussed in the dialogue section earlier. To summarise, there are three common methods for denoting inner thoughts, or interior monologue, as it's more correctly termed.

The first and perhaps most common is to use italics for the expressed thought. Some people don't like italics; some people have a problem reading them. Large blocks of italic text can be problematic, particularly in certain fonts, so if there are lengthy blocks of thought in your book, this might not be a suitable method.

> She looked at Warren. *I'd forgotten he was so tall.*

This is a very intimate rendition of thoughts, which is why it's so popular. There is no narrative distance between the reader and the character at all; we simply read as the character thinks.

The second method is to write them out in normal roman script as you would dialogue (without the quotes) and use various thought tags to indicate that this line is what she is actually thinking.

> She looked at Warren. I'd forgotten he was so tall, she thought.

The "she thought" tag is not quite as invisible as the "she said" dialogue tag, and this method definitely introduces a narrative distance between the reader and the character. But it is unambiguous, and avoids the use of italics completely.

You could use a hybrid of both methods, and use italics with thought tags.

> She looked at Warren. *I'd forgotten he was so tall*, she thought.

However, this seems to combine the problems of both methods, introducing some narrative distance *and* using italics, so is not to be recommended.

If you are writing in a very close third person perspective, it might be possible not to draw any typographical distinction between internal thought and narrative.

> Really? Curry again? She sat down. "Yum," she said.

This is the free indirect speech style I mentioned when talking about PoV. It's quite possible to do this with a very close third person perspective, but it would be very easy to lose the reader if it's not done well.

In a first person perspective (or a third person PoV limited to one character) the story is viewed from a single character, so it's easier for the writer to introduce internal thought invisibly.

> Reznik walked straight into the plate glass window. That's got to hurt. I laughed like a drain.

We know it's internal thought, and we know who's doing the thinking because we only have one PoV. Even then, there's an argument for it to be made clearer with one or either of our two methods above.

> Reznik walked straight into the plate glass window. *That's got to hurt.* I laughed like a drain.

> Reznik walked straight into the plate glass window. That's got to hurt, I thought. I laughed like a drain.

Texting

Very much a problem of our age, I'm not sure that the publishing world has arrived at an "agreed" method of representing social media texts in fiction, so it's up to the author (and publisher, if they have one) to come up with a workable solution.

There are some considerations to take into account. Anything can be done in print copy. The obvious solution would be to have the texts in a different font, perhaps a sans serif font like Calibri or Arial. When transposing to ebook, however, most e-readers allow the user to specify their own font, and it might be that, unless the e-reader is capable of maintaining the differentiation, that formatting is lost. Other more ubiquitous solutions might be to have the texts indented, or in a bold or italic type.

A clever solution in one ebook published in 2016 was to have the texts from the main character indented left, and the correspondent's text flush right, so the ebook page looked like this.

> I dunno. You sure?
>
> Absolutely. What could go wrong?

This has the added bonus of visually approximating some popular social media apps. There are other slightly more subtle solutions. Another book published in 2016 had texts in-line, in italics.

> *You awake?* the text said.
>
> *No*, I texted back.

This is good, but might run in to problems if the italics solution is already being used to denote interior monologue, for example. How do you differentiate between thought and text?

> *Yeah, I'm going to the prom with him*, I texted back. *I'd love to see your face.*

Does she text *I'd love to see your face*? Probably not; it's more likely to be what she's thinking privately as she presses the send button, but there's ambiguity there.

Another solution is to run text conversations in block quote style, perhaps with texting-style attributions.

> **You awake?** Caller ID withheld.
>
> **Depends who's asking.**
>
> **Grinning emojis.** *It must be him.*

Be inventive, but also, don't overdo it. Anything that breaks the reader out of the story to admire your presentation is not a good thing, however clever it is.

Emojis

Talking of emojis, fiction has generally not moved to accepting emojis, despite their ubiquity in social media, and I'm not sure they will any time soon. They are images, rather than letters, and there is the simple practical issue that, while they could be reproduced at some expense in print books, they would likely cause significant formatting problems between different platforms of e-reader for ebooks. As a shorthand for expressing an emotion they're very useful where space and time is limited, in texts and social media posts, but authors really shouldn't be using them.

Another thing to consider is that fashions and trends change, sometimes very quickly. Consider phone ring tones. Phone ring tones were a big industry around the turn of the twenty-first century and many phone users spent a long time worrying about, and often spending money on, audio clips designed to make their phone's ring "unique" and "interesting." But the market has matured, and nowadays when a mobile phone rings in a crowded place, it's almost always a classical ring tone that sounds like an old land-line handset (and ironically no one knows who's mobile is ringing and we all reach for our phone).

Who knows whether the trend for ever more elaborate and specific emojis and GIFs might not exhaust itself in a few years' time? In which case, unless it's important that your book take place in precisely this moment in history, extensive use of them in your story will date it very quickly.

The interrobang/all-caps

The interrobang, ?!, sometimes seems really appropriate, especially in dialogue when a character is asking a question aggressively, or makes a statement in a questioning way. Similarly writers can be tempted to use ALL-CAPPED words to express particularly loud or stressed words, especially in dialogue. Their use is generally frowned upon, however, even in modern literature. Any mark or indication that tells us more about the words on the page than a simple punctuation mark is, ultimately, drawing attention to itself. The reader is made instantly aware that they are reading a book, not experiencing the story.

> *The common punctuation marks are almost invisible. They are only there for clarity, or comprehension, not to tell us more about the book than the words in it.*

With the development of the new world order of self-publishing, these may catch on, in time, but I think serious writers will continue to adhere to the principle of punctuation being as invisible as possible. The interrobang draws attention to itself and says "look at me—I need interpretation too." An all-caps word stands out on the page, even if it is in "small caps," capital letters roughly two-thirds the height of a normal capital letter (however, note "words on signs" later on). To writers who want their words alone to tell the story, punctuation that interjects with that "look at me" message is an anathema.

If you think about it, writers communicate ideas and emotions through words. Musicians communicate ideas and emotions through notes. Writers using all-capped words to indicate particularly shouty bits of dialogue are the same as the pianist leaning back from the keyboard in the middle of Rachmaninoff's Prelude in C-sharp Minor and yelling "Fortissimo." It should be patently obvious at this point in the performance that he's thumping the piano with everything he's got (it *is* a percussion instrument, after all). If the writer is doing their job, we shouldn't need the all-caps. We readers should be (mentally) screaming the words aloud, along with the character.

Sentence construction

Part of the copyediting process is looking at sentence structure. It's perfectly possible for a sentence to be properly punctuated but still have some grave problems. It's hard to see in your own writing, where you know exactly what you meant to say but have actually written something slightly different.

Dangling modifiers

The most insidious of all of these problems is the dangling modifier. The problem is best illustrated with an example. Here's one taken from one of my own pieces that I wrote for the *Irish Times* about editing companies, that I didn't notice at the time, and neither did anyone at the *Irish Times* (where you can see the original in their archives, much to my enduring shame!)

> The feedback she received told her nothing useful, and then tried to sell her further editing services.

It's really quite obvious, pulled out and examined in isolation. The feedback she received wasn't any good, but it wasn't the *feedback that she received* that tried to sell her further editing services. It was the company that gave her the feedback. I revised the version on my blog, subsequently.

> The feedback she received told her nothing useful, and the company then tried to sell her further editing services.

Now you might say that *contained in* the feedback she received was the bait that she needed further editing services, and you'd be right, but you'd also just be being nice. If I was in the dock and trying to defend the sentence on those grounds I'd probably have to substitute an "also" for the "then."

> The feedback she received told her nothing useful and also tried to sell her further editing services.

(I suppose I could ask the Culture Editor at the *Irish Times* to get it fixed for me but hey, it's a good example of why even editors need editors, so I'll leave it stand!)

Here's another example of a dangling modifier.

> Driving his dad's Chevy to Vegas, storm clouds brewed over the desert.

Atmospheric, ominous ... and wrong. The storm clouds were driving his dad's Chevy? No, *he* was, but this sentence implies otherwise. How do we correct something like this? There are a number of options. We can change the order of the phrases that make up the sentence.

> Storm clouds brewed over the desert as he drove his dad's Chevy to Vegas.

That's a bit flat, and now we can feel what the author intended with the original phrasing.

> Driving his dad's Chevy to Vegas, he saw storm clouds brewing over the desert.

This is closer to the sense of the original. But you'll remember from our conversation on filtering that "he saw" is a filter and to be avoided if possible (it distances us from the character's experience).

> The Chevy rumbled east, into the desert. The setting sun threw massive black storm clouds ahead into sharp relief.
>
> "Thanks for the 'loaner', Dad," he muttered as he squinted through the windshield. Then he grinned. "Looks like we're going to have a wild night in Vegas."

Once again, we've fleshed this out. There are forty-six words in this final version compared to the original eleven, but this last passage isn't a strict replacement of the original anyway. It adds a lot of colour. We get the feeling by his sardonic use of the word "loaner" that his dad may not have been entirely complicit in his use of the car. We get his feeling of anticipation about the wild night ahead, and we can then contrast that with the black storm-clouds that are boiling on the horizon. In this version he's talking out loud, but it could equally well have been written in interior monologue. The original text now reads as rather flat and uninteresting.

Sentence stumbles

Sentence stumbles occur when you're reading along and you come to a sentence which makes you stop, frown for moment, and go back and read it again. They can happen for any number of reasons.

Outright error

The easiest and most obvious sentence stumbles to identify are caused by outright error—if you've missed a word, or duplicated a word, or the punctuation is incorrect, or there's some other simple technical objective error. If you followed the advice at the very outset to read your manuscript in a different format than you wrote it, perhaps with a different font, or a different size or page orientation, you are giving your brain a lot of help spotting errors of this nature. There is no other option than to work through, slowly and methodically, to try and catch as many of those errors as you can. But there are other more subtle problems that may not be errors that will still cause a reader to stumble over a sentence.

Unintentional wordplay

Unintentional wordplay can be disconcerting. The words you have used might not actually be wrong, but used in close proximity within a sentence or paragraph, they combine to create unintended effects. They include unintentional rhyme, unintended alliteration, repetition of phrases or unusual words (particularly in close proximity). All these things are obtrusive, to the reader. They stand out from the smooth flow of words, and as soon as the reader becomes aware of them, the illusion slips and they remember they're reading a book.

> The principal paused. He looked over the top of his podium. "I have to say ..." He paused. "It is with considerable opprobrium ..."

I think you'll agree that sounds like something out of a Gilbert and Sullivan operetta. There's repetition ("paused"), alliteration, ("the principle paused") and unintentional rhyme all within the two sentences.

A word might not mean what you think it means, or it might have nuances that you haven't considered. This is particularly true if your book is likely to be read by someone from a different culture, and becomes very important in a non-fiction work (see the section "Sensitivity issues," later on). Of course the problem here is that, unless you have some kind of "lightbulb moment," you are likely to continue thinking it means something else, and continue to be unaware of unintentional nuance. This is another situation where a second set of eyes is so valuable.

Capitalisation

The rules on capitalisation in fiction are not as rigid as in non-fiction. The general rule, of course, is to only capitalise proper nouns, i.e. names. In some genres, such as fantasy or science fiction, capitalisation rules are bent to accommodate a more weighty meaning. Think about *the Force* in Star Wars. The word "force" isn't a proper noun, but in the Star Wars oeuvre it becomes one. Fellowship isn't a proper noun, but in *Lord of the Rings* "the Fellowship" acquires a particular significance. Note that in both of these examples the definite article "the" is not capitalised.

What are common questions about capitalisation?

Names

Most writers understand that proper nouns are capitalised: Fred, Ginger, Mr Holmes. Confusion arises when another word other than a proper noun is used as a name. Mum and Dad are common problems. If it's preceded by a possessive, *my mum*, *his dad*, then the noun is not being used as a name and therefore should have no capital. However, if it is being used as a name, *"Hi, Mum,"* then it should be capitalised. There's a generational difference when applied to familial titles though—something to do with "respecting your elders," I suppose. The above rule applies if you're referring to people of an older generation. When referring to people of the same generation, it's generally not capitalised even if you could argue that the word is being used as a name, so "Hey, sis," or "Howya, bro?" Other examples: *his aunt*, but *his Aunt Beatrice*, because that's her name, *my brother*.

When does a nickname or an endearment come to be regarded as a proper noun? It's a difficult question to categorically answer. A good rule of thumb is that if a character refers to a third person in conversation about the nicknamed character, *using their nickname*, then it's being used as a name, and should be capitalised. In the *A Game of Thrones* series, for example, George Martin uses this technique frequently; Ser Varys is referred to as the Spider, Gregor Clegane as the Hound, both to their face in terms of address, and in conversations between various other characters.

> *Common nouns can be elevated to proper nouns if they are used as the name of a third party in conversation between other people.*

That would tend to eliminate those instances of endearments that, although they may be used frequently by one character to another, are just endearments. The sales rep might call his girlfriend honey bunny in the bedroom, but he doesn't tell his boss that Honey Bunny has booked a romantic weekend away so he needs to leave early on Friday.

Think of it that there are three tests:

- consistency: is that character always or usually referred to by that title
- specificity: is it only that person who is referred to by that title, and
- ubiquity: does everyone (related to that person in the same fashion, if a family term)

> refer to that person by that title, whether that person is present or not?

It must fulfil all three to be classed as a proper noun. Working through a few examples, "bro" is a substitute for an equally non-specific appellation such as "dude" or "mate" or "man" ("I love you, man"). While a particular character may consistently address another as "bro" in place of their name (test 1), it's likely that character calls other people "bro" too, so it fails the specificity test (test 2). "Sis" would be similar. Even though a character might call another person "sis" habitually (test 1), and even specifically (test 2) if they had no other sisters, other people (schoolmates, teachers etc.) are not going to refer to her as "sis" because it's a relational term, so it fails the ubiquity test (test 3). You could argue that "Mum" would fail the ubiquity test, because not everyone (traffic wardens, shop assistants) is going to call her Mum, but everyone *who is her child* is going to call her Mum.

Nouns of rank

With nouns of rank such as general or king, the rule is to only capitalise when using that title as a name. You would write "The king is in his counting house," but "King John is in his counting house." In phrases such as "All hail the king!" it can be difficult to assess whether you are using the noun as a common noun or as a name. A useful trick is to instead substitute a name in the sentence or phrase, and see if it makes sense. If it does, you are using the noun as a name. If it doesn't, it's just a common noun and you don't need to capitalise it. For example, "All hail the Nigel!" doesn't make a lot of sense, so it's clear that you're not using the noun as a proper noun in that phrase, even though you are referring to a specific king.

If addressing someone as "sir," then again, it's only if that takes the place of a name or prefixes their proper name. So it's, "Take some coffee to Sir Paul McCartney on table five," but, when you get there, it's "Would sir like some milk with that?" (You wouldn't say "Would Paul like some milk with that?" unless the poor old Beatle has lost the power of speech.)

Much of the confusion to do with capitalisation derives from the past, when terms that the author felt required some deference, such as aristocratic or royal titles, were capitalised routinely. (It's the same principle, after all, as calling the Christian god, God). That has carried over into some fantasy writing, where a character might be referred to as "the Priestess" (as in "The Priestess waved her hands over the altar and gouts of flame shot up"). It's not strictly correct, but it's not as frowned upon in the fantasy genre as it would be in other forms of fiction. In general, try to avoid excess capitalisation, even if you are writing fantasy. It can look extremely messy down a page if every other noun has a capital in front of it. If you have a character called "the High Priestess of Lantarth," try and resist the urge to write her as "the Priestess," or even "the High Priestess" in every occurrence. She's really not going to smite you down if you refer to her as just "the high priestess." If another character is addressing her—"Yes, High Priestess"—then certainly. If she's doing something a bit more prosaic—"The high priestess let loose a stentorious belch that startled the temple cats"—then no need.

NOTE FOR YOUR STYLE SHEET:

If you have particular names you want to be capitalised that might otherwise be considered common nouns, you might list them in your style sheet as a reminder to be consistent.

Capitals in chapter headings

The easiest way of avoiding this entire issue is to have chapter numbers, rather than chapter titles. Most bestselling authors do that, but many authors (usually harking back to the books they read as a child) love giving their chapters meaningful titles. That's fine. As I've always maintained, it's your book. But if you want to use chapter titles, you need to understand how to write them, and understand that the capitalisation of words within chapter titles is not random.

It's usual to use what's called *sentence case* capitalisation. The first word is capitalised, but all subsequent words other than proper nouns are lower case. This book, being non-fiction, is structured so that it's easily navigated. I have several different levels of headings for ease of reference. This chapter heading, for example, could have been written as all-caps, CAPITALISATION, to differentiate from the section heading written in sentence capitalisation.

It's unlikely you'll need that level of distinction in fiction, since you will normally only have chapter headings, but it may be that you have Parts to your book (Part One, Part Two). If that's the case, think about how you want to present those titles, having each word either capitalised (Part One), or all-caps (PART ONE).

Title case or *headline case* capitalisation is the other major alternative. The traditional style for the titles of books (and also films, plays and songs), this style dictates that all major words are capitalised, while minor words like conjunctions and prepositions are not. There are some finer details, but the generally accepted rules are as follows:

- Capitalise the first and last words of a title
- Capitalise:
    - nouns
    - verbs
    - adjectives
    - adverbs
    - pronouns (including possessive pronouns, e.g. *my*, *his*, *your*)
    - subordinating conjunctions (e.g. *because*, *since*)
- Lowercase:
    - articles
    - coordinating conjunctions (remember FANBOYS in the discussion about the punctuation of commas?)
    - prepositions
    - *to* as part of an infinitive

This style gives rise to examples like:

> The Curious Incident of the Dog in the Night-Time
>
> The Call of the Wild

On the Waterfront

The Best Years of Our Lives

A glance along the bookshelves in any bookshop would demonstrate the universality of this approach.

A third and less common system is to capitalise each word. This is a somewhat archaic presentation, and has been used for chapter headings in some historical novels (Hilary Mantel's Wolf Hall, for example). However, if you feel strongly that you require a particular format, go with it, but be aware that there are different approaches and stick to one consistently across all headings of a similar type. Annie Proulx, in her novel *Barkskins*, chose to have all lower case chapter headings, with no capitals at all.

NOTE FOR YOUR STYLE SHEET:

Specify the capitalisation you wish to use, for each level of heading and subheading in your book.

Numerals

Whatever you decide on the presentation of numbers in your book, be consistent. In fiction, numbers below a certain limit (commonly 100), and larger round numbers (e.g. a million) are usually written out rather than using numerals. In non-fiction, particularly where there may be a lot of numbers in a scientific or business subject, you might decide to use numerals more extensively. Some scientific contexts only spell out single-digit numbers.

Apply consistency throughout, but be prepared to adapt when problems crop up, such as a list of items some smaller and some higher than your "limit" number. In that case, be consistent within that sentence. In a book using numerals for numbers above 100 for example, you might see a sentence like "There were thirty cavalry, twenty archers and 125 foot-soldiers in the duke's escort." It would make more visual sense, just within this sentence, to make the "thirty" and the "twenty" numerals also. Coming from the opposite direction, if you have two discrete numbers side by side it might once again be better to subvert the rules and write one as a number and one spelled out for visual clarity. "There were 20 two-man teams in the competition."

If a sentence starts with a number, then convention is to spell it out regardless of the limit rule. "One thousand seven hundred and twenty-seven runners started the race ..." You could always try and rephrase to avoid the problem. "There were 1727 runners on the starting line-up ..."

Hyphenate compound numbers over twenty, "forty-four."

Where numbers include an abbreviation of a unit of measurement, they are generally retained as numerals, whatever their magnitude, so "a 7 km walk," but in fiction it would be more normal to spell out kilometre also, so "a seven kilometre walk."

For numerals in dialogue, the rule generally is to spell out numbers, but what's important is to write what the character would actually say, and to make clarity the most important consideration. If someone has been exercising, they're likely to say that they "went for a 5k run." It's probably clearer to write "5k" than it is to write "five k," and unlikely that they would spell out "I went for a five kilometre run." Similarly, if someone is dialling the emergency services, it's probably clearer to say

"Quick! Dial 999!" (it would be 911 in the US) than it is to spell out "Dial nine nine nine!"

NOTE FOR YOUR STYLE SHEET:

Determine your presentation of numbers, and any exceptions to that style.

Decades

If you remember the idea about an apostrophe being primarily used to denote a missing letter or letters, then other apparently unrelated things become clear. For example, the writing of decades can sometimes cause confusion. Is it *the 1950s*, or *the 1950's*? There's no need for an apostrophe after the zero, since nothing has been omitted. If you're implying that a subsequent object belonged to the 1950s, i.e. that it's a possessive construction, then the correct place for the apostrophe is after the "s," since it's a possessive of the entire decade, rather than the year 1950.

> The Chrysler Plymouth Fury was an iconic 1950s car.
>
> The late 1950s' Chrysler model, the Plymouth Fury, was iconic.

Centuries

In fiction it's usual to spell out centuries—*the nineteenth century*—neatly sidestepping the issues with numerals and whether the "th" suffix should be normal script or superscript (the tiny raised letters after the numerals). If you wanted to use numerals to denote centuries (in non-fiction, for example), you would generally use superscript letters in print books but some e-readers have difficulties interpreting them, and they can cause strange line-spacing issues.

If you remember our examination of hyphenation you might remember that the compound noun "in the *nineteenth century*" is not hyphenated but the compound adjective is, i.e. "a *nineteenth-century* church."

Time

In fiction you generally spell out times. "It was three o'clock when his alarm went off," or "It was three a.m. when his alarm went off." Only use o'clock with a round hour. If you want to mention a specific time it's easier on the eye to use numerals, just as you did with complex numbers. "It was 3.37 a.m. when the generator ran out of fuel." Of course, you don't have to mention a.m. and p.m. at all—it should be clear in context—but it can add a precise military or scientific tone to the writing if that's suitable.

When using the digital clock format, either a point or a colon can be used as a separator in UK English, but a colon is normal in US English. Whether to include the points in p.m. or leave as pm is also a style choice.

For more complex times that are spelled out, be careful with your hyphenation. It's *three thirty-five*, not *three-thirty-five*.

NOTE FOR YOUR STYLE SHEET:

You could specify what format you are going to use for times, and the various ancillary decisions like colon or point separator.

Fact-checking

One of the most straightforward tasks in copyediting is fact-checking, and if you don't do it, the probability of readers with specialised or local knowledge picking you up on mistakes is enormous. If your character emerges from Green Park Tube station and starts walking down Oxford Street, it's time you brushed up on your London A-Z. If you're sailing west, straight into the teeth of a howling gale around the Cape of Good Hope in a square-rigged frigate in 1847, you might like to read up a bit on sailing square-riggers. If the climax of your 1928-set thriller is a chase across New York ending in a shoot-out on top of the Empire State Building, just check Wikipedia. Some readers won't know you're wrong, but many will, and they'll point out your errors with glee in their review.

If you have used real facts and figures and locations, particularly in a non-fiction book, now's the time to double-check them. Don't stint on checking things you're "sure about." You might be sure, but you might be wrong. Much as we hate to admit it, our memories are fallible, and it's a much better outcome for you that you find your own mistakes and quietly correct them than it is for someone to call you out on them in public after the book is published. Check everything.

One aside on "writing what you know" that won't be of much use to someone who is now at the self-editing stage of working on their book, but that I need to get off my chest and I doubt whether I'll ever get another or better opportunity: Common writing advice is to tell authors to write what they know, and that writing of their own neighbourhoods, their own people, talking in a familiar dialect using familiar vocabulary, is all going to sound completely and naturally authentic. As soon as you have ambitions beyond that, research comes into play. So much can be found out on the internet these days. We can move down streets we've never been to, looking in shop windows that we've never visited, but these are largely static images. I would say little beats going to the actual location you want to write about. Vision is only one of our five senses. What does the neighbourhood smell like? Is it a dry atmosphere or a humid one? Is there a lot of traffic, and if so, at what time of day, and going where and how fast? How do the locals talk? How fast do they talk, and how close to you do they stand when they talk (personal space varies greatly from nation to nation, and from city to rural neighbourhoods within a country). You're looking for authenticity, and it's often only a few tiny details needed that will give you that authenticity. Those details may not be apparent from a web browser.

You might think your neighbourhood and the people in it are not that interesting or important or worth writing about. This drives you to base your romance in an exotic beach location on a tropical island you've never been to, the detail of whose scenes you research by leafing through travel agent brochures looking at pictures of hotel rooms. Just think instead of your hometown. What is dull and prosaic to you could actually be fascinating to someone who happens to live on the other side of the world, and might be engagingly familiar and comforting to someone who lives just round the corner but to whom you've never spoken. There is a market for all stories set anywhere, and you *are* the expert at where you live. The writers who do look at their surroundings with an open eye, and see the heart and humanity in the people around them (you have intense feelings and ambitions and dreams, don't you? I'm sure your neighbours do, too. What are they?) often tell the most vivid and engaging stories. So don't be so keen to write about somewhere else just because you think nothing ever happened in your neighbourhood. That's the end of my little monologue!

Sensitivity issues

Sensitivity issues affect both content and language. Words have immense power, and we should use them aware of the impact they are likely to have on readers. I don't personally believe that we can rationally expect an author to anticipate *every* possible problem that *every* potential reader might have with a particular plot point, word, or expression, but we should apply *appropriate* sensitivity to what we write, and it may be that the bar for that "appropriate level" is set a little higher than you might think.

There is a slightly different focus between fiction and non-fiction.

In your fictional world, your readers have to accept your characters as you've written them. They may or may not like what your characters do and say, but if they don't like them, they can always just put the book down and walk away; it's your world. If your fiction appears to endorse a particular sexist or racist worldview, and it's written in a PoV which implies that sexist or racist worldview is shared by its author, then you're heading off to the wrong part of town looking for trouble with a big "Hey, wreck my career before it's got going" sign stapled to your forehead.

Does that mean you can't write racist or sexist characters? Of course not. Does that mean any racism or sexism expressed by characters in your fiction should never go unpunished? Of course not. But you need to be aware that if readers come to believe (via the techniques you use to express those characters' views, the PoV in which they are expressed, and the lack of *any* fictional consequences to those characters for making them) that you are holding up a mirror to your own attitudes, then readers will have an open season on you the author, not your characters. On your own head, as they say, be it.

In terms of storyline, the use of rape and violent sexual assault as a plot point is troublingly common. It's troublingly common in real life, too, so you might claim with some justification that it has a rightful place in your thriller. But ensure that it does. Avoid using rape for some spurious "shock" value. Some of your readers will have been raped. There, I've said it. How do you think they will feel when reading your rape scene?

Being sensitive to who your readers might be, and what their experiences might have been before they pick up your book, is a good reason for including a "trigger" statement somewhere prominent in the front matter of your finished book. It's the equivalent of the TV continuity person saying, "The next program contains scenes of a violent sexual nature." People with sensitivities to such issues are then forewarned. They can continue watching at their own risk, or switch channels.

If you've got a violent sexual assault scene in your book, for good reason, then it's only polite to let someone know in advance so that they can make a decision on whether to buy the book. I'm sure no author would intend to cause another book-lover personal distress intentionally. Trigger statements and being sensitive to those experiences your potential readers might be bringing with them to your story is going a long way to making sure that you don't do it unintentionally, either. (That also goes for editors, by the way. If your material is potentially upsetting to some people, you should let an editor know before they start work on your book. We editors are humans too, you know!)

In non-fiction pretty much the same caveats apply, but far more rigorously. In non-fiction, it *is* your opinions that are on view. It might be that you have some old-fashioned ideas about race and sexuality and gender identity. If your book is going to go public it isn't going to be published in the past, or only circulated among friends who just laugh off your rather "non-PC" assertions; it's going to be published in the very modern real world, standing up to modern scrutiny from people who have no idea of who you are and who will have no compunction about telling you where you're wrong and how deeply they are offended. If you know you have opinions and state in the book assertions that others are likely to view as offensive and are going ahead anyway, then have at it. As long as you haven't broken any laws, you'll just endure a mountain of abuse online and in social media. It's a dangerous way to court publicity for your book, but some people do it. This whole section is directed to people who may have completely innocently fallen foul of real sensitivities they didn't know existed, rather than those out to directly confront and court controversy.

There is a trend emerging to hire sensitivity readers to review a book for issues that involve racial, social or sexual minorities. These readers, of that minority themselves, will tell an author whether they feel a book covers the realities of their racial, social or sexual experience in an accurate and non-exploitative manner. It would seem to make sense to me that if you're writing about a minority of whom you're not a member, you would naturally want your writing to be seen as both non-exploitative and accurate, so it seems a win-win for both author and target group.

Other puzzling conundrums

An or a hotel?

An hotel, or a hotel? This rule is often misquoted as requiring use of the "an" version of the indefinite pronoun if the next word starts with a vowel—an igloo. It's actually if the word begins with a vowel *sound*—an honesty box, an hour—and there are plenty of words that begin with a vowel but take the "a" form—university, uniform—because they start with a consonant sound.

The "h" is silent in many words beginning with "h," and therefore some people assume that all words beginning with "h" take "an." Not if the word begins with a pronounced "h"—a hymn, a halibut. One occasional exception is where the accent of the word falls on the second syllable, as in *historic*, or *hotel*. In this case, some people don't pronounce the leading "h" so they are, in fact, being consistent with the "vowel sound" rule if they write "an hotel." If these words crop up in your narrative, use whichever pronoun suits your personal pronunciation—this is one of the myriad ways in which writers can express their "voice" and it's a bold editor who tinkers with it. If these words crop up in dialogue, then use the appropriate pronoun for the character's voice—how would they say the words?

Still struggling with its/it's?

There is no apostrophe in "its." There. That's all you need to know. But sometimes there is, of course. Why? Because someone has written "it is," and contracted it to "it's." The apostrophe is used to denote the missing letter "i." If ever you want to test whether "it's" is correct, insert that extra "i" and see if the sentence still makes sense.

> "The bear dropped it's fish" Correct?
>
> "The bear dropped it is fish." No. Clearly wrong.
>
> It's "The bear dropped its fish."

99% of errors are inserting the apostrophe when none is needed, so if you approach it from the position that there is no apostrophe, you will eliminate more errors than you create.

Words on signs

How do you write signage, what a character reads on a sign? There are a number of different possibilities. You could write them in italics.

> *Trespassers will be shot*, the sign said.

If you're already using italics for internal thought, or for stressing words or both, then another dose of italics might be too much.

You could use quotes.

> "Trespassers will be shot," the sign said.

A problem here could be that if there's not a "the sign said" tag, it might appear that someone is talking.

One neat suggestion that sidesteps both of these issues is to have signage in small caps. This mirrors the typography on many short signs anyway, so adds an air of authenticity.

> TRESPASSERS WILL BE SHOT, the sign said.

Small caps are accessed in the Font dialogue box as an optional typographic style.

Zombie rules

Beware of zombie rules. These are rules that might be invoked by retired English teachers after you badgered them incessantly into reading your manuscript. One of the early headings in this book is a great example of two zombie rules that I've ignored, because there really was no better way to say what I wanted to say that fitted with the conversational tone of this particular book. I'm not saying you can flout all rules of grammar with impunity (there wouldn't be much point to books like this if I did), but knowing when you can ignore the most restrictive rules is a skill that comes with experience.

One of my early section headings, right back in the introduction, was "Who is this book for?" There are two problems here that will have grammar purists gnashing their teeth.

The sentence ends in a proposition. Winston Churchill, the British war-time prime minister, is famously supposed to have castigated an editor who mangled a line in one of his speeches to avoid it ending in a preposition. In the margins Churchill scribbled the retort "This is the sort of English up with which I will not put." I believe it's okay to end a sentence in a preposition in less formal writing. It's how people talk.

The sentence also begins with "who" where, strictly speaking, "whom" is correct. If we answer the question, we would say "the book is for them," or "the book is for him". We would not say that the book is for "he" or "they." Without getting into a discussion about the nominative functions of pronouns, "who" is okay.

Foreign words

I covered foreign words a little in dialogue, when I described characters speaking in a language other than English. It might be, however, that you would like to use non-English words when referring to particular items in narrative or descriptive passages in your book. Should these foreign words and phrases be set in italics, or left in normal roman text?

In non-fiction with foreign words with which the reader may not be familiar, you might choose italics, to ensure that readers understand that this is a non-English word and not a typo. Alternatively you could use normal roman script, but use a footnote to give a translation or more detail.

In fiction, footnotes are problematic, since they throw the reader out of the story while they absorb the information you, the author, are giving them about the world the story is taking place in. While italicising foreign words used to be the norm, there is a modern push not to italicise. There are two main reasons for this.

The simplest and most relevant to a fiction author is that it isn't how people talk. We don't stop mid-sentence and put mental air-quotes around a foreign word, or use a different stress. If a character speaks using non-English words, they don't put on a "funny accent" and say them—they say them in their normal voice. (If your character is quite insular and *does* use foreign words haltingly or stiltedly, because they are unfamiliar with their use and even perhaps meaning, then you have an argument for italicising, or even putting inside quotes-within-quotes).

The second major issue with italicising non-English words is that it's a form of "othering," rendering those foreign words of secondary or lesser importance, of needing to be explained. Many of your readers will be multi- or bi-lingual and will wonder why you've italicised a word that is common knowledge to them.

In most circumstances it should be possible to understand what is meant by a foreign word from context, even if it isn't completely and specifically understood. If you really think that a word may not be understood at all, even from context, or that failure to understand its specific meaning might be problematic, then it might be a good idea to include a glossary of all such terms you use at the end of the book.

One final point: italicising words generally indicates to the reader that they are stressed words (or inner thought, if you're using that methodology). If you have too many different reasons for italicising, there's a risk that it could lead to confusion.

Chapter length

In non-fiction your chapters should be as long as they need to be to deal with a specific issue. The subject matter of your book should itself give a fairly clear indication of how you need to break the book in to chapters.

In fiction the rules are very fluid. I've seen chapters that run on for thousands of words; I've also seen chapters of a single short paragraph. Generally, a significant change in time, place, or scene can be a good place to begin a new chapter. In certain circumstances a change of PoV can also be a good place to call a break.

It should all be about reader experience. Very long chapters can make a book feel slow, which is fine for some genres but not great for others. On the other hand, a very short chapter might rather stand out and say "Look at me, aren't I short!" That could be interpreted as author-grandstanding, rather than a genuine attempt to convey meaningful reader impact.

Have a look at your book. If you've a lot of short chapters it could cause a rather disjointed reader experience, and has the practical effect of increasing page count (and therefore cost) of the book artificially. You might look at where you've broken them up. If the location or time in the narrative doesn't move significantly with the start of a new chapter, or a new chapter only moves the PoV within a single scene, you might think about a sectional divide instead. These often take the form of three spaced asterisks, or an asterisk glyph called an asterism, but they can be any small ornamental symbol you like if they don't cause problems with your book production.

If you've a sequence of very long chapters, do they relate events in single scenes? If they do, are those scenes pulling their weight? If there's a lot happening, then it's reasonable for a chapter to be long and it would be odd to artificially break it up. However, very long chapters can indicate an over-writing problem, scenes bogged down with a lot of exposition or description. Make sure their length is justified.

Conclusion

Well done! You've worked through this entire book and now should have a really tight and well-written manuscript. You have a few options now.

If you're really confident, you can send your manuscript on to some selected agents or publishers. Choose wisely. You're wasting your time submitting to publishers who don't accept un-agented submissions, and wasting your time submitting to agents who don't cover your genre. They really do mean what they say; they're not going to make an exception for you, so don't waste their time.

Alternatively, if you're eager to get your book out there, you can upload it to the various ebook platforms (Amazon/Kindle being the most significant) via their file formatter programs and get cracking. You can do this yourself, or if you find technology a challenge, get someone else to do it for you for a small fee.

As I mentioned at the very outset, the astute author doesn't do this, but goes to a professional editor for their say on the MS that's seen so much work. I provide a hyperlink to my own website at the foot of this section in the ebook version.

Appendix III: Hiring an editor, goes into this process in some detail. Don't forget to mention, and include when you send them your draft, your style sheet. The simple fact that you have a style sheet will impress an editor greatly, make their job easier, quicker and therefore cheaper for you.

But there's no getting away from the fact that an editor is probably going to have lots to say about what you could change to make the book better, and is probably going to point out myriad errors that you, despite all your efforts, haven't even noticed. The process of writing a book has always been a collaborative effort, and it's very unlikely that your book is the very best it can be, just from your own oversight.

However, draw some comfort from the process that you've gone through in self-editing your MS. There are three significant benefits that will arise from all the hard work that you've put in.

Firstly, you're now a much better writer. Many of the lessons you've learned in the course of working through this book will have "stuck," and you won't make those mistakes again.

Secondly, when you do come to self-edit your next book, the process will be much more familiar to you, a lot less daunting, and much quicker, because you are both a better writer and you know what to look for.

Lastly, if you've applied everything that this book has suggested, your draft manuscript (and appended style sheet) is going to be a joy to work on for a professional editor and you will immediately be a treasured client, as well as paying far less for your editing help than an author who has flung a draft together, run it through a spell-checker and called it finished. The little time the editor does need to work on your book is going to be time they can spend really thinking about how your MS could be improved upon, therefore giving you really valuable advice, and not laboriously fixing punctuation mistakes.

If you've found this book useful, I'm delighted. I'd be hugely grateful if you could leave a review wherever you think it might help other authors to decide if they could use it too. And have your say. Was there a question you had that wasn't answered here? Was there something that you felt could be covered in more depth, or explained in a better way? All feedback gratefully accepted by email to the address you'll find on my website, below.

Best of luck with your writing journey!

Richard Bradburn,

Managing Editor,

www.editorial.ie

Making your words work, beautifully

Appendix I: Writing a synopsis

What is a synopsis?

A synopsis is an outline of your entire novel, from beginning to end, summarising the narrative arc of the book and one or two of the major characters in it. It does include the end (any twists or climactic revelations), but doesn't include details of every subplot and minor character—it doesn't need to be comprehensive. The aim is to give the reader a thorough understanding of the outline of your book, without going into too much detail. There are a couple of key elements you're trying to highlight: your book's original and entertaining or informative premise and/or compelling main character, and to demonstrate that the plot has a solid structure that doesn't rely on insane coincidence or acts of God for its resolution ("and he woke up and it was all a dream").

When should I write it?

Writing a synopsis is a great exercise to undertake after you've finished the first draft of your book. Because it encourages you to look more analytically at your book's structure, it can suggest to you at an early stage of the self-editing process that there might be flaws in your plot or character arcs.

How long should it be?

Depends on who's asking for it. Most synopses are one single-spaced page (about 500 words). It's a really tough mental challenge to achieve this, condensing your 100,000-word novel into a few paragraphs, but it's worth doing. A crucial part of the process of objectification of your book (the ability to look at it like a reader or an editor, rather than the author) is to be able to identify the major themes and focus solely on them. If you're writing a synopsis that rambles on for page after page, you're not achieving this focus.

(If you're at a later stage of the writing process and are actually querying an agent or publisher, check whether they have any specific length or format requirements in their submission guidelines. Do not submit a two-page double-spaced synopsis in Lucida Calligraphy font to an agent asking for a single page in single-spaced Times New Roman. Yes, you're trying to sell your book, but also to sell yourself as a competent author who can follow simple instructions and is going to be a pleasure to work with.)

If you can manage it, write a single-page synopsis. You can always expand it if given the leeway.

Where do I begin?

It's a good idea to start with a strong paragraph that outlines the entire story in essence. For plot-driven books, that's a thumbnail of the whole plot. For character-driven novels, it should be a summary of the main character arc. Most people know the story of Star Wars. "A cruel and evil Empire dominates the universe.

Luke Skywalker, a farmhand on a remote planet, joins the Rebellion to overthrow the Empire and restore freedom to the galaxy."

What should I include?

- You need to include the main character(s)
- What their opening situation/problem is
- What inciting incident happens to start the ball rolling
- What they need to achieve as a result of this event
- What forces or characters are opposing their aims and ambitions
- How the crisis is resolved
- How the characters have changed by the end of the book

What should I not include?

- Much description, at all
- Any dialogue, unless the understanding of a key plot point depends on it
- Subplots that don't really determine the progress of the main plot
- Minor characters' names and backstory
- Flashbacks
- Subheadings—this isn't a management summary or a PowerPoint presentation
- Unanswered or rhetorical questions

This last point is a common problem. A synopsis is a private document, for your eyes (or those of an agent or publisher) only. You aren't trying to create a blurb to entice a reader to buy your book—that's a different document (a reader will never see your synopsis). You're simply trying to summarise the major themes of your novel for yourself, as part of the process of self-editing. Eventually you might find yourself in the situation that your synopsis is trying to explain to an agent why they might be able to sell your book. They won't know if they can sell it if they don't know what it's about. Avoid writing a sentence like, "Does Jake manage to find the right girl and settle down in the Big City, or does he end his days sad and embittered, ruminating on what might have been?" It might be an interesting strapline to put in marketing material for your book, but it isn't going to tell an agent whether you've written a romance or a character study, and isn't going to tell a publisher how they would easily be able to market your book to readers.

Any stylistic tips?

The temptation might be to create not much more than a list of plot points. "This happened, which really ruined Hero's day. Because of this, Hero had to try and do this, but Bad Guy wasn't having any of that. After a fight with Bad Guy, Hero eventually won out and managed to do what he needed to do." For the purpose of summarising your book for your own ends as part of kicking off your self-editing process, this (just) might be good enough. If you want the option of using your synopsis with agents and publishers in the future, it's not good enough. Although a synopsis is just a summary, it still needs to show that you've some talent as a writer. Unless the characters are bland and emotionless (in which case you have bigger problems), you need to convey some of the emotion that drives their thoughts and actions to do the things that they do, and some of the tension that drives the plot forwards. Some stylistic tips:

- It's an idea borrowed from screenplays to include the name of main characters in caps on the first instance, identifying that character as significant to the story.
- Don't try and *explain* the underlying theme of the story ("This is a book about the big issues facing us all, love and death and why kittens are adorable"). It should be quite evident, from your summation, what the central theme of the book is, and if it's not apparent, there's a problem with either your synopsis, or worse, your book.
- In a synopsis, you can throw all that "show, don't tell" advice out of the window (if you're unfamiliar with this term then don't worry; we will look at "show, don't tell" at length in the next section). Showing is wordy. Telling is economical. If your main character has a problem with authority, you don't need to describe a lengthy scene where they "disrespect" the headmaster—just say they have a problem with authority.
- Synopses don't need to be written in the past tense, even if your book is. A synopsis written in present tense can be more vivid and compelling in many ways. At any event, use active language, not passive, and keep sentences punchy and informative, not long and rambling.

I've read all that and I'm still stuck

Perhaps an example might help. Most people know the story of Star Wars, and it breaks down very neatly into a classic Hero's Journey plot:

> A cruel and evil Empire dominates the universe. LUKE SKYWALKER, a

> farmhand on a remote planet, joins the Rebellion to overthrow the Empire.

This is the summation, the entire story outline in the first two sentences. Everything that follows is an elaboration on that statement.

> Luke, a bored fly-boy on a remote planet on the outer rim of the galaxy, dreams of being a space pilot and exploring the universe. He discovers a secret message inside a salvaged droid from PRINCESS LEIA, one of the leaders of the mysterious Resistance. The droid's message needs to be delivered to OBI-WAN KENOBI, a loner Luke knows lives alone out in the desert.
>
> Luke is told to get rid of the message by his step-uncle, but in the night, the droid makes its own way out to Obi-Wan. Luke goes to recover it, but Obi-Wan tells Luke of the significance of the message, plans of a new planet-destroying super-weapon, the Death Star, and also of Luke's real parentage and his connection with the Jedi knights who are leading the Resistance against the Empire. It's too much for Luke, and he heads home, only to discover that his step-parents have been killed and their farm destroyed by Empire soldiers looking for the droid. Vowing revenge, he returns to Obi-Wan. They hire an amoral space pilot, HAN

SOLO, who agrees to take them and the droid to Alderaan to get the plans to the leaders of the Resistance. Emerging from hyperspace amidst a field of stellar rubble, Solo's ship is captured by the Death Star (piloted by DARTH VADER, a Jedi knight who has turned to "the dark side"), which has just destroyed the Rebel home planet.

Trapped on the Death Star but evading detection, Luke finds Princess Leia imprisoned in a cell and frees her. Drawing the attention of Darth Vader, Obi-Wan sacrifices himself so that Solo, Luke, the droid and the princess can escape and find the last Rebel base and what's left of the Resistance.

Although they deliver the plans, and Resistance scientists uncover the fatal flaw in the Death Star's construction, Solo's ship has been tracked, and the Death Star emerges from hyperspace, ready to destroy the planet and annihilate the rest of the Resistance. The Rebels launch a brave attack with tiny fighters that seems doomed to failure but, just as all seems lost, Luke, whose days as a bored fly-boy back on Tatooine are put to good use, delivers the missile to a tiny exhaust port leading straight into the Death Star's central reactor. It explodes, and the Resistance can live to fight another day, rewarding Luke, Solo and his crew with

> medals for bravery in a triumphant victory celebration.

That's only 423 words in total, so could be expanded upon, but you can see that the nuances of Han Solo's character are not explored, lesser characters like C-3PO or Chewbacca are not even mentioned, none of the backstory about the Force, or minor dramas like the escape from the refuse chute on the Death Star, are included. But the gist of the story, space opera on a grand scale, is pretty much all there. If this was put in front of a sci-fi agent back in 1976, you'd like to think they might at least have been interested enough to read the MS!

In terms of its relevance to self-editing, your synopsis will be a valuable tool to refer to throughout the rest of the self-editing process. It might even be that, having tried to come up with a synopsis, you've realised that perhaps there is a major flaw with one of your characters, or your plot or your major theme, and that you need to go back and do a little rewriting before progressing with the self-editing stage. This isn't a negative. This is a huge positive, although it might not feel like it. You've uncovered a big problem at the outset, that you can now go and fix before any of the detailed work begins.

Appendix II: PoV in depth

For those authors who have never really looked at point of view in isolation, would like to understand more in depth about what makes PoV so important and what the differences between the various PoVs are and the terminology used, this appendix should cover the basics.

What is point of view?

Why is PoV so critical? PoV is the filter through which the story is told. Your book may be a story very much of one person, their trials and tribulations and achieving their goals and ambitions, or it can be a much more global narrative—what happens to an entire world, or at least a large group of characters. Those ideas are not mutually exclusive. Sometimes stories of global scale and significance are told through the prism of one character's PoV. This might be because the real story that the author wants to focus on is that character's development against the background of global upheaval (as in many war stories), or because, by having a very narrow focus, the author can make the global story much more real and personal.

Human nature being what it is, in real life, stories of great tragedy or disaster (or heroism or triumph) are much more poignant and powerful if we feel we know someone personally involved. An event like the 9/11 terrorist attacks on the Twin Towers might be a brutal and horrific incident, but when our minds confront the tragedy of the loss of thousands of people's lives it's hard to do so in anything other than the abstract. The pain of hearing that story retold comes into much sharper focus if narrated from the perspective of one victim, and the impact on their families and friends of seeing their personal tragedy unfold in real time on their TV screens.

This forms the predominant perspective of much modern fiction, and it's an important point.

> *Modern fiction tends to narrow a story's focus down to individuals and their personal struggles. We can empathise much more readily and deeply with an individual than we can with a group.*

It stands to reason, then, that PoVs that facilitate a very close perspective, for the reader to identify intimately with the character, are now very popular. It wasn't always thus. Most eighteenth- and early nineteenth-century novels were written from a distant perspective, with the narrator of the story very much in evidence as a separate entity to the characters in the book.

Pick up any Dickens volume for example. *A Tale of Two Cities* begins "It was the best of times, it was the worst of times." This is the *opening line* of the book—we haven't met any characters yet—so must be pure disembodied narrator-speak, telling us the setting of the events that are to unfold. Frequently the narrator of a Jane Austen or Dickens novel is very *visible*, has firm opinions of their own on the behaviour of characters, and may comment on events, even guiding the reader as to the correct interpretation of what has happened. *Breaking the fourth wall*, or addressing the reader directly ("... and now, gentle reader, we leave Miss Bennett to her sewing and visit Netherfield, where poor

Jane ...") was very much the trend in the earliest days of the novel. Such a PoV would seem very old-fashioned now, and probably rather didactic and intrusive.

This isn't the place to spend a lot of time speculating on why this shift has evolved, but perhaps early novelists were more conscious of their origins in story-telling around the campfire or the hearth, in which the narrator was a real person sitting on the opposite side of the flickering flames. The modern trend is for the narrator to be as invisible as possible, and novels that don't follow that trend have a slightly more aloof and distant tone. This might suit some genres (perhaps literary or historical fiction), but definitely doesn't suit others.

Having made the decision to write in a particular PoV, it's generally not advisable to change it. Since PoV is so closely linked to writing style, to change PoVs midway through a book would be running a large risk of alienating a reader who has grown used to a particular narrative voice. PoV is also closely linked to the type of story you are telling, and it would be unusual for this to change midway through the book. If the book starts off as a confessional, intimately personal memoir, but by the end has turned into a large-scale epic fantasy, your reader is likely to be confused.

The different points of view

Let's start with a brief look at the different types of PoV and their characteristics. There are four main classifications of PoV, and one of those is so rarely used for book-length MSs that it can be dismissed as an outlier.

FIRST PERSON POV

First person PoV is the reader as protagonist. The writer tells the story from one character's perspective, from inside their head looking out. The reader sees what they see, feels what they feel, hears what they listen to, is encouraged to think what they think. The story unfolds as that character experiences it directly, and everything outside that character's experience is unknown. The "I" pronoun dominates the text—"I thought this, and then I did that"—since the narrator is the character, speaking directly to the reader. Because of this intimacy—the book reads like having a face-to-face conversation—first person PoV is extremely useful for getting the reader really close in to a character's head and generating a great deal of empathy.

(This PoV is shared in the video-gaming industry, where in most video-games with a narrative, the player *is* the main protagonist. The player controls the actions of the protagonist in the story, frequently sees the playing game-scape through the eyes of the protagonist character or very close to them, and is thrown out of the world and the playing experience—the story ends for the player—if and when the protagonist dies. It's not possible to be any more immersive than that!)

Just because a book is written in first person doesn't have to mean that it is written all from the *same* first person perspective. Although that would be usual, it is possible, if done carefully, to write individual chapters and, in rare cases, sometimes individual sections within a chapter, in different first person PoVs. The danger, of course, is that the shift in PoV from one character to another isn't competently managed and leaves the reader floundering, not knowing quite whom they are supposed to "be" at any one moment. Graham Swift's 1996 Booker Prize–winning novel *Last Orders* was written in what we might term "multiple first person PoV" To avoid any confusion, he isolated each PoV in its own chapter, and named each chapter with the protagonist whose PoV he was writing in.

Although it might seem restrictive, it's possible to stretch the boundaries of first person PoV and be very creative. The concept of an "unreliable narrator" is most commonly found in first person PoV stories. The reader only knows what the PoV character knows. What if the PoV character doesn't know the truth? What if the character jumps to conclusions (perhaps in solving a crime) that turn out to be untrue? The reader has been carried along with the character's thoughts on the whole plot. Suddenly, at the denouement, it is revealed that the character was wrong all along.

Even more deviously, what if the PoV character knows something that they choose not to tell the reader? While there's an unwritten but absolute law that the *author* cannot lie to the reader, it's quite possible for characters to lie and cheat and dissemble, or to simply omit certain facts. Agatha Christie famously does this in *The Murder of Roger Ackroyd* where the narrator, Dr Sheppard, details, seemingly objectively, Poirot's progress in solving a murder case in which ultimately it is proven that Dr Sheppard himself is the murderer.

One slight twist to first person PoV is when the narrator is not the main protagonist of the story. This allows the author some leeway about scenes not involving the protagonist, and some objectivity about the protagonist's actions and motives that wouldn't otherwise be possible. Conan Doyle's Sherlock Holmes books are all written not from the PoV of the eponymous hero, but from that of his sidekick, Dr Watson. Part of the charm of the Holmes stories is the great detective explaining how he comes to the conclusions he arrives at. This kind of surprise revelation wouldn't be possible if we were at all times in Holmes' own head. F. Scott Fitzgerald's *The Great Gatsby* is similarly written, not from the PoV of Gatsby himself, but from that of Nick Carraway, who can then observe and subjectively comment on the goings-on that summer in West Egg. This allows us to place the Gatsby character in context, and allows Fitzgerald to express more objectively his own beliefs about the high-society morals and attitudes of the time, which he wouldn't have been able to do in character as Gatsby himself.

WHEN TO USE FIRST PERSON POV

Use first person PoV if your main character's development is crucial to the plot, the story being essentially a character study, and an intimacy with the character being necessary to lend vital depth and complexity. This is especially true if the character has a particularly interesting or unique perspective. The profound but narrow focus of first person PoV is often used in YA or coming-of-age stories, commercial lit fic where the emphasis is on individual personal growth, and some horror, where tension and surprise can be used to good effect.

Iain Banks' debut novel *The Wasp Factory* is a great example of an extremely distinctive voice narrating a particularly unusual perspective on life. Sylvia Plath's *The Bell Jar* contains passages where the narrating character describes with unassailable logic performing actions that are, to the external observer, obvious evidence of psychosis. By being inside an unbalanced mind it's possible for an author to convince the reader that actions, which might seem psychotic if narrated in a third person PoV, are actually entirely reasonable.

First person PoV has an *immediacy*. We experience everything in real time along with the character. We have no perception, apart from the character's own senses, of what's going to happen next. The reader, like the character, doesn't know what's round the corner. Because of this, it can be a great PoV for creating tension.

As reader, we learn about our world, our surroundings and the other people in it, at the same pace the character does, and we share their confusion and sense of foreignness about things we don't understand or that are strange to us. We can only interpret what other characters say to us at face value or, if we are adept at doing so, try to gain clues from their gestures and body language as to what their real feelings are. For all these reasons, first person can be extremely useful in situations where you want to surprise the reader, where you plan a twist in the story that (while it must be plausible and coherent) need not have been flagged. Many stories that relate an alternate truth, or a misperception of reality by dint of insanity or psychosis, are often written in first person PoV (again *The Bell Jar*, by Sylvia Plath, or *Fight Club*, by Chuck Palahniuk, are good examples).

WHEN NOT TO USE FIRST PERSON POV

First person PoV is limited to the experiences of a single character, so it's hard to include a scene in which the character is not present. This makes it unsuitable for large-scale epics where there may be numerous plot developments occurring simultaneously, or where there's a large cast of characters who can't reasonably be expressing everything to the central character in order to move the plot along. Continually writing phrases like "I heard Jim say to Jack ..." would feel very contrived.

It's also problematic when describing a very different world or setting. If you need to explain how a religious order works in a world you've constructed for a fantasy, for example, you have three options. Either the character is part of that religious order and can explain the rites and rituals first-hand, or the character witnesses those rites or rituals as an observer, or the character is told about those rituals by a third party.

If the character is a member of the order, then you're merely narrating a first person PoV, and all well and good. But what about if, in the same book, you need to explain how a particular caste of warriors fight—their training methods, special weapons, unique skills? Is the character also going to be a member of that warrior caste? The character can't feasibly be a part of everything in the world, in which case you'll need to go down the route of options two or three.

If the character merely witnesses those rituals there are two aspects to consider. Firstly they are a subjective observer; they may not appreciate or understand the significance of each rite. Secondly it will be difficult to avoid a rather dull sequential listing of the order of events. "I watched as the priest lit a black candle on the altar. Then I saw him take a knife from a pocket in his robe and nick his own thumb, squeezing a drop of blood into the open beak of the chicken ..." It's all very interesting, but it reads dully, like reportage.

With the third option, the character is told the relevant rituals by someone else, then it becomes an even more remote exercise, and turns into mere exposition. Generally, at least one PoV character needs to be present at a scene that you're going to describe in any detail. Otherwise, why describe the scene in detail at all? Your first person PoV cannot be everywhere at once. If your plot demands lots of different events going on in different locations, it is going to be technically very difficult to write all those scenes from a close PoV and avoid a heap of exposition.

Finally, it might not be an obvious problem, but in a thriller or mystery where the narrator's life is in danger, telling the story in a first person PoV removes any doubt about the fact that the narrator survives. They clearly do, or they wouldn't be here telling you the story. You might contrive an ending where it turns out that their ghost is the narrator, and they grimly recount the awful details of their own assassination/murder/car accident, but that would be a technical challenge to pull off, and only fit with a very narrow range of genres.

Suzanne Collins chose to write the Hunger Games in a first person PoV, so really we know all along that Katniss is going to survive. In some ways that does weaken the suspense, but Collins presumably thought that the immediacy of first person narrative, with the reader's immersion in Katniss's particular and vivid voice, was a good enough trade-off. Instead of worrying about whether Katniss will survive, because we are so wrapped up in Katniss's feelings, we care about her love interest, Peeta, and her other friends in the games, and therefore we share Katniss's feelings about their deaths with the same intensity as she does.

SUMMARY

When to use first person PoV

The story is essentially a character study focused on one person.

Deep empathy and immersion in the character's feelings and emotions is necessary to really understand the story.

When the perspective you want to show may be very unusual, or distorted, dealing in an alternate reality.

First person PoV is particularly prevalent in the YA, romance and commercial lit fic genres.

When not to use first person PoV

In large-scale epics where there are many scenes where the first person character is not present, or can only be present via rather contrived means.

Where the setting (particularly in sci-fi or fantasy) is very unusual and requires more explanation than normal.

Where the narrator's life being in jeopardy is a significant part of the suspense. If they died, how are they telling you the story?

Strengths

Depth of immersion in the character.

Good for creating tension, or plot twists.

Weaknesses

Potentially claustrophobic.

Narrows focus of the story to one perspective, ruling out larger-scale epics and concurrent narratives.

Third person

Third person PoV is extremely common in modern novels, and actually describes a range of PoVs that are all closely related. Third person PoV ranges from being right inside the character's head, often described as "third person limited," to being best imagined as a camera filming events from a position somewhere above and behind the main protagonist, or "third person remote." Here we see events from the character's perspective, but, because we are outside the character's head, we are not necessarily party to the inner thoughts of the character unless they are voiced out loud in dialogue, or we are told their thoughts in inner monologue. We are no longer the character ourselves, but an observer of that character.

There is a seamless continuum from this very intimate *third person limited* PoV character, to what can be a very distant *third person remote* and this continuum is measured in what is generally known as *narrative distance*—the closer and more intimate the PoV, the smaller the narrative distance. To illustrate what is quite a difficult concept, in these following lines, the same scene is rewritten with an ever-smaller narrative distance, that is, with a closer and more intimate PoV.

> A middle-aged woman stood on the end of the platform, in the rain, and watched the train round the bend and disappear into the distance.

This first version is remote and objective. A scene is described, accurately, but it raises little emotion in the reader. The woman is anonymous. We don't know why she is watching the train, but we know it must have some psychological impact because she is standing in the rain, uncomfortable physically, to watch it.

> Jaclyn, standing at the very end of the platform where there was no shelter from the rain, watched the train round the bend and disappear into the distance.

In this second version the woman is no longer anonymous. She is named, and the rain is described not as an absolute, but in reference to the character (there is "no shelter" from the rain).

> She watched from the end of the platform as the train that carried her hopes and dreams rounded the bend and disappeared into the distance. Rain mixed with her tears, and fell splashing on the concrete.

Now we are solidly in her PoV. She is no longer named, because we *are* the character. Her emotions are shown (rain mixing with her tears), and the reason she is watching the train disappear into the distance is mentioned, although not elaborated upon (her hopes and dreams).

> Sobbing, she stood as close as she dared to the tracks, while the rain poured and the train clanked and groaned out of sight round the bend, carrying beautiful, tragic Harry away from her.

In the fourth version we are very much in her close PoV. She is sobbing. We begin to lose some of the more objective detail (about her standing at the "end of the platform") and substitute it with personally relevant detail ("as close as she dared to the tracks"), which tells us much more of the emotional significance that the scene holds for her. The rain and the disappearance of the train are mentioned, and now emotive verbs are used to describe the train's movement ("clanked and groaned"), but greater stress is placed on what the disappearing train means, "carrying beautiful, tragic Harry away from her."

> She blinked from the rain, or her tears. *If only I'd said ... if only we'd had more time. Oh, Harry.* The train clanked and groaned inexorably out of sight, leaving her bereft and broken at the end of the platform.

Now we are very focused on her experience of the scene, in a close third person PoV. Everything is described, if you look closely, in relation to the character. We don't hear about the rain objectively, only that it makes her blink, and we're not even sure, as she isn't, whether it's the rain or her tears. For the first time we hear her internal thoughts about what is happening, and those thoughts are, of course, entirely subjective and relevant to her emotions. The train clanks and groans "inexorably" rather than just leaving, an emotional tonality that has been missing from the previous versions.

An accomplished author knows more or less instinctively how to manipulate this narrative distance. Too much extremely close third person PoV can be as claustrophobic as a first person narrative. Everything in the book being interpreted from a single perspective means that the reader is not allowed any break from the PoV—it can be a little relentless. On the other hand, not enough close personal detail means that the reader is not being encouraged to live the story, and may fail to bond with the main character.

Similarly to an inventive cameraman in a film, effective use can be made of the emotive power of narrative distance by focusing in and out of a character's PoV. In intimate or very emotional scenes, the reader's immersion in the character is best served by a close PoV, but to avoid a sense of claustrophobia or exhaustion, it's good to lighten that close PoV regularly with a little more narrative distance, to give the reader a breather. As an example, let's add another paragraph to the last passage.

> She blinked from the rain, or her tears. *If only I'd said ... if only we'd had more time. Oh, Harry.* The train clanked and groaned inexorably out of sight, leaving her bereft and broken at the end of the platform.
>
> ***
>
> The autumn passed slowly. There was no word from Harry and, although he'd given her the address of the Mission, her letters went unanswered.

The narrative distance has increased hugely. In the first paragraph everything in the scene is related to the character. In the second paragraph (after a section break, to denote a significant shift in time or place) the perspective is quite distant. The passing of the seasons is noted, but we don't hear what the character was doing for that period and although we gather that she was writing to Harry, the actual letters she wrote are unspecified. This kind of passage acts as a hiatus, a moment for the reader to get their metaphorical breath back before diving into another close perspective scene.

In the same way that first person PoV can be used to relate the experiences of more than one character, a book written in third person need not limit itself to a single character. Different characters can relate individual chapters or scenes to give a varied and sometimes conflicting viewpoint on a story. This can be used to great effect in crime (where perhaps we alternate between the PoVs of the criminal and the detective), romance (where we alternate between the PoVs of the main characters showing the different views on how the romance is progressing) and large-scale fantasy epics, where there's a large cast of significant characters, all with their stories clamouring to be told.

Third person limited PoV (sometimes called *third person close*) is very similar to first person in many ways. We observe the world and events subjectively through the eyes of a single character. Nothing that happens outside the experience or view of that character is described to us and, having been filtered through the lens of the character's subjective perception, we can't be entirely sure that we know the exact truth about the situation the character describes. They may have made mistakes of perception or interpretation. They may have been lied to by other characters. They may have jumped to conclusions that ultimately are proven false. We are not privy to any knowledge that the character does not know.

Although our reader's overall perception of and immersion in the story is almost identical to that of first person PoV, there is a slight increase in distance from the character. The portrayal of emotion in another, however closely we are following that character, can never be quite as intense as if it were happening to *us*. In a very traumatic story where the author doesn't want the emotional element to overpower the book, telling the story from a third person PoV instead of a first person PoV can subtly dial down the intensity. When John Boyne wrote *The Boy in the Striped Pyjamas*, he chose not to write it in first person, even though that might have been the more normal choice for a YA book, perhaps because the already harrowing story would have been too much for his intended audience in a first person PoV.

Third person remote PoV is a more objective narration of the story. We are not so closely involved in the character's thoughts and feelings. To elaborate on the camera analogy, the camera has pulled back from the intimate "parrot sitting on the pirate's shoulder" kind of relationship with the protagonist that we were in a close third PoV, and is now an overhead shot, tracking the character from above as they move through a busy marketplace.

In a remote third PoV, less time is spent dwelling on the character's thoughts and emotions, and more on action and dialogue.

WHEN TO USE THIRD PERSON LIMITED POV

Third person limited PoV is ideal to use in a situation where the story is closely focused on the progress and development of one character, or perhaps several, but has significant plot-driven elements.

It lends itself very well to fantasy, where the story relates a single individual's *hero's quest*, but where occasional interludes in other characters' PoVs may be necessary to further the plot in absence of the main PoV character. However, too many changes of PoV to other characters are ultimately going to detract from the immersive experience of the hero's PoV. A close PoV demands the reader to form an intimate relationship with that character. Asking the reader to form that level of empathy with many characters is asking a lot and liable to be self-defeating. Even as readers we cannot be many people at once, and trying to focus on too many characters is liable to make us either lose the plot (literally speaking), or only follow one or two characters that appeal to us and almost skip the rest, leading, either way, to a poor reader experience. It's worth periodically reminding ourselves that, in this process of self-editing, we are polishing the book to make it more readable, not necessarily to make it more technically adept. It may be possible to write a book with a huge cast of intensely and deeply realised characters, but whether the reader is going to appreciate that is open to question.

WHEN TO USE THIRD PERSON REMOTE POV

Third person remote PoV is ideally used in the situation mentioned above, where there are many characters pursuing their own plot and character development strands and it would be both unnecessary and unreasonable or self-defeating to ask the reader to follow all their stories in detail, or empathise with each character profoundly.

Because we are following many characters, even though not in any great depth, this PoV is sometimes called *third person multiple*. Here the pendulum has swung more firmly in the direction of plot above character. We observe a large cast of characters in their fight to realise their ambitions throughout the story, and dip from one character to another as necessary to further the plot. We are never particularly immersed in one character's thoughts or feelings and therefore the psychic wrench for the reader to assume the mantle of another character in the next scene or chapter is not that hard.

SUMMARY

When to use third person PoV

The story requires intimate connection with a character, or several characters, but also has plot-driven elements.

Third person PoV is common to all genres, but especially prevalent in crime, historical fiction and fantasy/sci-fi.

When not to use third person PoV

If the story is really about the development of one or two characters, third person narration might create barriers to the reader getting immersed in the character in sufficient depth for true emotional impact.

If the scope of the book spans generations, and many different places/worlds (as in some epic sci-fi), an omniscient narrator may be easier to manage.

Strengths

Flexibility, with empathetic immersion in the character possible, but also the ability to describe events and scenes from a more remote and objective perspective.

Good for narrating the personal stories of small groups by cycling through their various individual PoVs.

Weaknesses

Like first person PoV, close third person can also be potentially claustrophobic if maintained throughout.

Very easy to make PoV errors like head-hopping, lapsing into an omniscient PoV by mistake, and failing to manage the transition (in multiple third person PoV) between the different PoVs adequately.

Omniscient

The third significant option for PoV is omniscient, sometimes called "the God view," in which the story is told by an all seeing, all-knowing narrator. This PoV has fallen out of fashion somewhat in the modern novel. As I mentioned at the beginning of this section, the well-established trend (that started towards the end of the twentieth century) is for immersive fiction, in which the reader is encouraged to identify closely with the main character or characters. In an omniscient PoV, the reader rarely gets to feel deeply emotionally connected to individual protagonists.

However, balancing this, there are significant advantages in an omniscient PoV, notably one of flexibility in all sorts of directions. An omniscient narrator can traverse time and space, can describe events happening out of sight of any character, can speculate on events before they unfold, and describe every character motivation in any scene.

The narrator figure can be more or less "present," depending on the writing style. Some epistolary novels (novels written in letter or diary-entry form) have a very obvious and tangible narrator who forms, to all intents and purposes, a character with whom the reader can identify. This quite subjective narrator tells us of events but imposes their own interpretation of those events, and their own interpretations of character motivations and reactions. These may or may not be true, and we can be left to decide for ourselves whether the interpretation is correct. (In Kurosawa's film *Rashomon*, a samurai is murdered and his wife raped. Four different versions of events are told in sequence, from four different viewpoints: a bandit arrested for the crime, a woodcutter witness, the samurai's wife and the dead samurai himself. We are never told which is the true version.)

With objective omniscience, the personality of the narrator is muted. Narration is purely a mirror, held up to events as they unfold. We may dip in to any character's head at any point in the narrative, and the narrator neither condones nor condemns motivations or actions.

WHEN TO USE OMNISCIENT POV

Such is the ubiquity in modern literature of immersive close PoV fiction that it's difficult to recommend uses for the omniscient PoV, even though the vast canon of early (eighteenth and nineteenth century) novels were almost all written in it. However, in narratives that describe great epochs of time, geography and/or space, the omniscient voice can give the author the necessary freedom to tie in multiple threads of plot (a political thriller, for example), huge casts (sci-fi or fantasy epics), or many different geographic locations (a dystopian end-of-world zombie apocalypse type drama).

It might be the case that your story is far more plot-driven than character-driven, in which case profound immersion in the individuals who take part in the narrative isn't really necessary. In a war story, for example, it might be that the survival of the unit, a regiment or even entire army, is the main crux of the plot, and there is no particular focus on individual members of that unit. This is quite possible, but you should note the increasing frequency with which war stories are told from the very small unit or even individual solider perspective. Recent such films include *Fury*, about a lone tank crew, *American Sniper*, about the effects of war on one man, *Lone Survivor*, the story of a four-man Navy Seal team behind enemy lines, and multi-Oscar and Bafta award-winning *The Hurt Locker*, the story of one elite bomb disposal team. These are all films (mostly based on books) that distil the story of war down to a focus on a small team of characters with whom we get to identify closely. This is the modern trend: to break down an epic event, war, which might have previously been told in an omniscient voice, into the stories of individual protagonists whose stories we can then be deeply involved in.

SUMMARY

When to use omniscient PoV

The story is primarily plot-driven, and close identification with particular protagonists would be distracting.

The story covers great stretches of time and/or space, which can't be narrated by a reasonably small number of PoV characters.

When not to use omniscient PoV

The story includes a lot of character development and emotional interplay that would be very difficult to convey in a remote PoV.

Strengths

Flexibility. The narrator can go anywhere, in any time or place, backwards or forwards with narrative impunity, dipping in and out of character PoVs as necessary.

The omniscient narrator can be a character themselves, bringing subjectivity to an otherwise objective narrative.

Weaknesses

The omniscient narrator can feel dated to the modern reader.

Modern fiction demands more immersion of the reader in the story than an omniscient narrator can provide.

Second person PoV

Second person PoV is rarely used for novel-length fiction MSs, but it has been used before, and is a valid option.

In second person PoV, as its name suggests, the narrative is turned on its head and the reader is the character.

> You run down a blood-stained corridor, shoulder-slam the door and emerge into sunlight, Alice tumbling out after you. You stop, and there's a soft click as the door locks shut at your back.
>
> "Ah," you say, as Alice unslings her sawn-off shotgun from her shoulder and pumps a cartridge into the breech. "This is where the zombies were gathering."

It's an unusual choice of PoV, because of the obvious difficulty in getting the reader to suspend their disbelief to the extent that they see themselves in the story. This isn't a case of empathising with a character in a book; it's a matter of the reader being able to place themselves in the scenes and events in the book. If those events are particularly unusual, or far-fetched, or the character's actions in the book seem illogical or haphazard or hard to justify, then the reader may simply not be able to see themselves in that situation and making those choices, and therefore the transfer of identity will not work.

If you would like to read a full-length novel in this PoV, there are only two that are regularly recommended as examples by writing craft books, being *Bright Lights, Big City* by Jay McInerney, and *If on a Winter's Night a Traveler* by Italo Calvino.

WHEN TO USE SECOND PERSON POV

Some books for young children use the second person PoV, because the author, like a parent, is talking directly to the child (reader). In this sense it's an intimate PoV that emulates a parent-child relationship, and might be used to good effect in a book with some element of moral or practical teaching in it without taking on a preaching tone. "You," the child-reader, is making the decisions in the book rather than being told by another character.

There was a fashion for a time for "choose your own adventure" books, whose story consisted of a multi-branching narrative in which the reader, based on decisions they were asked to make in the text, followed different paths through the book. Many of those paths would terminate with the premature end and failure of the quest, and it was only by following the correct sequence of answers (there was possibly more than one route) through the narrative that the reader would reach the end of the story. Those books were invariably couched in second person PoV.

> You turn the corner to find a hobbit cowering at the end of the passage. Do you a) try and kill the hobbit, b) ask the hobbit what he has got in his pockets, c) ask the hobbit to join your group?

For each answer the reader would be directed to a different page. If the reader chose a), the entry on the page they were directed to might read:

> As you approach the hobbit with sword drawn, shouting, "Die, verminous furry creature with over-large feet," he reaches into his pocket and suddenly disappears. You have failed in your quest. The end.

For literary fiction, the idea of using a second person PoV might be useful in a situation where the character is a kind of Everyman, where events in the book (while being originally and uniquely described), are actually common to most people's life experiences. In this case the gap between reader and character is not so distinct as to cause problems with suspension of disbelief. Alternatively, the book could be written for, and speaking to, a particular group in society who would identify very closely with the protagonist's views and actions. The measure of whether it succeeds among the wider reading public would then be how compelling a story it is to bridge that self-perception gap.

For example, one might write a story in second person PoV about participation in a reality TV game show.

> You go through the door into the house and are temporarily disoriented. It's much smaller than you thought it would be. You walk through and out to the yard at the back. The other contestants are already there, lying around the pool. There's an overpowering smell of chlorine, which somehow you didn't expect ...

This PoV places the reader as contestant, learning about what goes on behind the scenes, backstage politicking in order to survive the regular culls of participants etc. Enough people would love to be in that position (bizarre though that ambition might be to some of us!) that a readership beyond those who actually had taken part in a game show would probably be assured. (In fact, why am I writing this book and not that one?)

Free indirect style

Sometimes called indirect free speech (which is misleading because it's nothing to do with speaking) free indirect style is a hybrid of close third person PoV and a more distant narrated style that was pioneered by, among others, Jane Austen in English, and Flaubert in French writing. It's a perfectly acceptable style in modern literature but it is more advanced and technically difficult to master. Elmore Leonard, who by the end of his career used free indirect style fluently and profusely, didn't start out his writing that way. It was only as he grew more proficient in his craft that he felt freer to use it in his characteristically scene-driven westerns and crime thrillers.

Perhaps the style you've written your book in didn't quite fit any of the previous PoV definitions I've listed? You might find that you've naturally written in a free indirect style, in which case, don't panic. Let's try and pin down what it is and why you might justifiably use it.

I mentioned one of the limitations of first person narrative as being of limited scope (the reader can only experience what the first person character sees and knows) and possible reliability issues. Conversely, a narrated third person PoV can be too distant, and while comprehensive enough to deal with a story epic in scope, not sufficiently immersive for what might still be a character-led novel.

Free indirect style aims to meld the two PoVs by including, in a narrated third person PoV passage, direct thought from the character in a seamless juxtaposition to the narrated story without the use of italics or tags or quotes or any other notation. In this way a narrator can tell the story, dipping in and out of any character at will to illustrate how they feel and what they are thinking about the situation they are in, but without the use of endless he felt/she thought tags (known as filtering, which we'll cover in another section in Part II). It's essentially fake—we are not the character, we are still with a narrator, but the character has taken over the role of narrator, or the narrator is speaking with the character's voice. An example is probably the easiest way to show this.

CLOSE THIRD PERSON POV

> He pushed on to the train. *God it's crowded.* In the middle of the carriage raucous cheering started up. "Ar-sen-awwwl. Ar-sen-awwwl." *Must be a match on. I should have waited for the next one.* The doors slid shut behind him. "Excuse me. Sorry. Sorry," he said, squashing up against a small Japanese man trying to read a book. *How can he try and read? Can't he see the carriage is jammed full?*

DISTANT THIRD PERSON POV

> He pushed on to the packed train, the normal passenger numbers swelled with a crowd going up to the Emirates for the match that night for a crucial cup tie. Why hadn't he waited for the next one, he wondered? The doors slid shut behind him. He apologised for squashing up against a small Japanese

> man who was trying to read a book, although he didn't mean it. He actually rather resented the man trying to make space for his book in the crowded carriage.

FREE INDIRECT STYLE

> He pushed on to the train, oblivious to the fact that the normal passenger numbers were swelled with a crowd going up to the Emirates for a crucial cup tie. In the middle of the carriage raucous cheering started up. "Ar-sen-awwwl. Ar-sen-awwwl." There must be a match on. Why on earth hadn't he waited for the next one? The doors slid shut behind him. "Excuse me. Sorry. Sorry," he said, squashing up against a small Japanese man who was trying to read a book. Who has the audacity to try and read a book in the rush hour?

You can probably see the difference between the close third person and the distant third person PoVs clearly enough. The close PoV has interior monologue, is very much written from the perspective of the man squashing on to the train. The distant PoV tells us, rather than shows us, how the man is feeling. The free indirect style example is a blend of the two. Instead of showing the character's thoughts in italics as interior monologue, the thoughts are directly expressed, as if they were the narrator's own thoughts. Although the passage is in the past tense, the character's irritated thought "Who has the audacity..." is written in present tense, further differentiating it from the general narrative.

Free indirect style is a subtle PoV. It does allow you to bring in details that the character might be oblivious to. In this case, he's not a football fan, because he didn't anticipate the football crowd on the train. But the free indirect style, like the distant PoV, allows the author to mention the fact that it's a crucial cup tie. (Of course, the author would only do this if the fact that it was a crucial cup tie becomes relevant later in the story.)

As you can see from the above examples, it does tend to be a wordier style, using both narrative and expressed direct thought, so if word count is an issue, it may be that one of the other more straightforward PoVs would be a better fit.

Unusual points of view

It's not necessary, or course, to restrict your story to a human narrator. There are plenty of children's stories narrated by animals. On closer examination however, many of these are simple anthropomorphic substitutes for a human PoV—there are obvious practical difficulties in writing for animals in what we might perceive to be that animal's own voice.

Rarer are books for adults written from an animal PoV, and rarer still are books with an inanimate object as PoV character. It used to be a common exercise in junior school English lessons to write the story of a penny, from being minted and travelling from hand to hand until, presumably, getting lost down the back of a sofa or thrown down a well. Such inanimate object narrators do exist though, in books such as *Anatomy of a Soldier*, by Harry Parker (in which each chapter is written from the perspective of a different inanimate object associated with the main character, the wounded soldier Tom Barnes), or *My Name is Red*, by Orhan Pamuk, in which objects such as a corpse, a coin and even the colour red share narrative duties.

Whether these more experimental PoVs work is a matter of opinion; certainly it's a brave author who writes one as their debut, but then Harry Parker's bravery is not in question, and Orhan Pamuk went on to win the Nobel Prize in literature some years later.

Shifting points of view

Is it possible to use more than one type of PoV within a book? The short answer is, yes, of course it is. There are no laws written in stone about such things. Best practices would tend to suggest that a book written solely in one type of PoV is best, as I said at the beginning of this chapter, but if the story demands a more flexible approach, then the story requirements must be met.

A change in PoV that occurs quite naturally in large-scale fantasy epics is a switch from an omniscient narrator at the beginning of a chapter or major scene, down to a more intimate third person PoV when the action or dialogue starts. In this way an author can describe a scene quickly and efficiently, to allow the reader a mental image of the surroundings, without laboriously "showing" this information through the eyes of the third person PoV character.

> Flags fluttered from every tower in a stiff southerly breeze. Guards ran hither and thither, strapping on armour and picking up weapons as they ran. The

> blacksmith roared at the boys on the bellows. "I need the fire hot, lads. We've some oil to boil."
>
> A few miles east, Sir Henry, at the vanguard of the column, smiled grimly as they emerged from the forest. *Just as I remember it.*
>
> "Do you still intend a frontal assault, my lord? Those walls are high," said Lancaster, trotting beside him.
>
> "All the further to fall," he snapped.
>
> "How so, my lord?"
>
> "A new invention called gunpowder," he said. "I have seen its power. No longer is any castle safe harbour." *That includes yours, Lancaster.*
>
> "Magic?"
>
> "Science, my dear Lancaster, science."

I'm sure you can imagine this as a film: the aerial shot panning over the battlements, then down to a tracking shot through the castle courtyard, following different extras as they struggle into their armour and grab spears leaning up against the wall. Then into the forge where the blacksmith is yelling at his assistants; and then back out again, over the walls, straight towards the forest where a column of soldiers emerges from the gloom, Sir Henry and his pal Lancaster at the head. Then we have close-ups of each man as they talk and possibly, at the end, a cut to a wagon rolling along at the back of the column, weighed down with sacks from one of which a little black powder is leaking.

In terms of writing and PoV, this entire passage could be an omniscient PoV (since an omniscient narrator knows everything) but when we "zoom in" on Sir Henry we begin, seamlessly, to interpret the world from his perspective. He smiles grimly. We hear his inner thoughts. He snaps at Lancaster. There's clearly some tension in their relationship ("that includes yours, Lancaster," he thinks to himself) and we are now firmly in his PoV rather than an omniscient but remote narrator who might merely observe "Sir Henry snapped at Lancaster, seemingly irritated at his lack of enthusiasm for the attack."

In terms of the opening scene-setting, it would be quite difficult, if not impossible, to describe what is going on in the castle through the eyes of the protagonist, Sir Henry. He can't see inside the castle walls. What is happening inside is happening at the same time as he is emerging from the forest so, since this is presumably before the age of mobile phones, he can't possibly know exactly what is going on. Perhaps he might imagine?

> Sir Henry eased in his saddle. The forest was getting lighter as they neared the edge of it. *Not long now.* They would have heard of his army's approach, and if they hadn't, they would soon know.
>
> They emerged from the shadow of the trees. The warmth of the sun was welcome on his face after so long in the gloom of the wood. There it stood, Castle Florid, with all its flags flying in a pathetic attempt at bravado. *Just as I remember it. The drawbridge is up; the*

> *gates closed. They knew we were coming*. The forge would be at full blast, the guards trying to find their weapons. The courtyard would be chaotic, livestock underfoot, farming families huddled for shelter inside the castle walls.
>
> He smiled grimly.

This version conveys pretty much the same information, but is rooted much more firmly in Sir Henry's PoV. Observations are coloured with his opinions ("a pathetic attempt at bravado," "the warmth of the sun was welcome on his face"). There is not the same sense of an aloof observer, or the aerial camera shot over the castle walls. What is going on inside the castle is left to Sir Henry's speculation, rather than the reader being told in exposition, but either version is perfectly acceptable. The danger with the initial omniscient fly-by approach is that you spend too long on the exposition and description, and the immersion of the reader in Henry's story, and the pace, both suffer as a result.

I hope that's given a pretty comprehensive overview of the various PoVs and the terms used, what type of book each PoV lends itself to and the pros and cons of each. If you've already written your book, then, as I say in the chapter on PoV, it would be a major job to rewrite. But with the next book, you're now fully informed about the choices you have available.

Appendix III: Hiring an editor

Having worked through this book you've now hopefully got a really tight, well-written MS. Bearing in mind what I said at the very outset, you have a couple of options from this point. You could settle for what you have and start the process of self-publication, or you could go that further step and have a professional editor go over your MS. With luck, all it needs is a proofread (there will be mistakes you've not noticed—missing words, homonyms, punctuation problems etc.). What is the process for hiring an editor—what should you expect?

In my editing inbox, a typical first-time enquiry from a novice author often runs along these lines: "I've written a book. It's 200,000 words long and has taken me ten years to write, on and off. I've sent it to agents but got no responses, so I know it's got some problems. How much would it be to edit it?"

What happens next? Writers who've had no experience with the publishing industry often don't know what to expect. Here we demystify the process, which, although it might not be absolutely identical with all editors, should be pretty similar.

First things first

Firstly, let's roll back a stage. Have you done your homework? Always contact an editor who someone else can vouch for. That might be a professional organisation like the CIEP or ACES, or a reputable writers' resources group like ALLi, or a personal recommendation from someone you can trust. There are too many charlatans out there to run the risk of giving your money to someone who doesn't know what they're doing.

Having been given a few names, google them. A professional editor will have a website, a corporate email address (not edityourbook@yahoo.com, or you'll get a yahoo of an editor), a consistent social media and online profile (perhaps a blog, some evidence of testimonials, membership of professional organisations). Have a read of their site or blog. They might mention particular genres that they work in, particular genres they avoid. They may only work in a specific English version, US English or European English, or they might work in both. They'll have a style of communication, chatty and friendly, or business-like and professorial, that may or may not appeal to you.

Satisfied that they look competent, there's some evidence that they've had some training, they work in your genre and your language version, you send them your enquiry.

How quickly do they reply? Immediately? Hmm. They could be very diligent, or they might just be sitting at the centre of a very dusty web waiting for a fly. Not for weeks? Well, they've sent their message—you're not that important to them, and that lack of interest will probably play out in your ensuing relationship. Some editors are just too busy to take on new clients—that's no reflection on you. Somewhere in between? I think it's courteous to answer all new enquiries within a couple of days, but editors are humans too, and sometimes they're giving birth, or burying a parent, or accepting a Pulitzer on behalf of their famous client, so cut them some slack!

What's their response to your enquiry?

Thanks for your enquiry. I'll edit your book for $500. Walk away. This "editor" is a chancer of the first order.

Thanks for your enquiry. I'll edit your book for $50. Walk away. This "editor" is a chancer of the second order. Just because they're only stealing $50 and not $500 doesn't make their crime any less heinous.

Any editor who knows what they're doing will not be able to quote you a firm price on an edit without seeing at least a sample of the MS. Further, any editor who knows what they're doing knows that there are all sorts of edits, all priced differently. A developmental edit takes much more time and is therefore much more expensive than a proofread, for example. They can't possibly know what your MS needs until they see it, and any smart editor knows that an author who comes to them saying their MS "just needs a proofread" isn't necessarily the best judge.

The response you should be looking for is polite interest, probably a few questions establishing who you are and what your ambitions about writing are, and the crucial "Send me your MS, and I'll have a look."

Plagiarism—does it happen?

Another common worry among novice authors rears its head here. What if the editor steals your masterpiece and passes it off as their own? If you've done your homework and got in touch with a reputable editor with a real business, this won't happen—the chances of plagiarism are vanishingly small. You may eventually turn out to be the next J.K. Rowling or Dan Brown with a multimillion-dollar bestseller on your hands, but at the moment, you're an unknown author with a debut MS that no one has heard of. The idea that an editor with an established business and reputation is going to gamble their entire livelihood on the success of your book by stealing it and claiming it's their own is an outlier. Even so, it's a big step, pushing your baby out into the world, so, heart in mouth, you email a few chapters.

Triggers

A word of warning: If your MS contains content of an explicit nature, either violence, abuse, rape or other potentially triggering passages, it's only courteous to tell the editor this in advance. Editors are humans too, don't forget. Some don't work with books which contain certain types of graphic content, and they won't appreciate being blindsided.

Initial feedback

Normally an editor will give you some idea of when they will be able to give you some feedback, but again, if three weeks go by and you've heard nothing, then this editor is implicitly telling you something. "I'm really busy. Your enquiry is not that important to me. Please hold." If your heart is set on that particular editor (perhaps they come highly recommended?) you might be prepared to wait.

On the other hand, if they respond immediately with a ten page dissertation on what they saw wrong with your first few chapters then ... okay. That strikes me as a little needy, but perhaps you've caught them in a slow patch (even the best editors suffer them) and maybe the dissertation is insightful and resonates with you.

Let's assume you get a response from your chosen editor in a reasonable timeframe. What are they likely to say? "Your work is an abomination in the eyes of the Lord." Well, okay—time to just tiptoe quietly away. "Your work is good to go—it doesn't need editing." Unfortunately, that's extremely unlikely, but if it does happen, thank your editor profusely.

It's more likely to be somewhere in the middle. "Your first few chapters are good, but have some significant structural problems that really need sorting out. I'd recommend some developmental work on this," or, "Your work is excellent. It does need a proofread, but otherwise should be good to go to agents."

Pricing

When your chosen editor has told you what type of editing they think your book needs, they'll give you a price. Editors fall into two camps. Some price by the word, others by the hour. Editors who price by the word like that method because it's easy for authors to calculate their likely costs. Other editors charge by the hour. They know the rate at which they edit, in thousands of words per hour. They assess the number of hours they will need to edit your MS and multiply that hour count by their hourly rate. Editors who work a lot with publishers tend to like this method—it's the way the industry works. Both sets of editors will vary their rate per word or per hour for books that require more editorial intervention than others. The standard of books that self-publishing authors submit to editors for tidying up varies greatly. If you've been diligent and spent weeks and months rewriting and revising, self-editing many drafts until you have a highly polished story, you should be rewarded for that effort. That reward takes the shape of reduced editing costs. It simply won't take an editor as long to whip your MS into shape as it will an MS of identical length that's a rough first draft on which the ink is still wet, therefore they should be quoting you a fee per word towards the lower end of their per word or per hour range. This is where this book should earn you its cost many times over.

Quite often an editor will use a kind of hybrid method to arrive at a fee. Instead of quoting a flat rate per word, they'll quote a range of rates per word, reflecting the difference in quality that they see across writing samples. This is the process I use. Clients can get a rough idea of a range of prices just from looking at the website, but I have a certain amount of flexibility in what I actually quote per word, looking to reward those authors who have sent me a really polished MS with a lower quote.

How *much?*

So how do you know, as a novice author, if the fee your editor has quoted you is reasonable? Most professional editing organisations (of which your editor is a member, right?) publish rates guides. Although by their nature they are only rough guides, they do give some guidance to authors as to whether the rate they're being charged is reasonable. The other alternative is to ask several editors for a quote. Editors do charge differently—they have different overheads, some are more experienced, some are only starting out, some have prestigious client lists and years of working with top publishers. Ultimately it's the author's choice and budget.

Sample edits?

And what about sample edits? You've got in touch with an editor. They've assessed your MS and given you a price. In spite of all their qualifications and experience, how do you know they're going to be a good "fit" with you and your book? It's an intensely close relationship. An editor really does get inside your head when they're critiquing your work. How do you know that you want them in there, poking about?

Look again at their website, Facebook groups they belong to, writing websites they may contribute to (or run). Some editors are rather prescriptive ("you should do it this way ...", "the rule is ..."). You might like that approach. Having been struggling with a writing problem on your own, you may want to be told what to do. Others are very laissez-faire ("there are no rules ...", "rules are made to be broken ..."). That more flexible approach might appeal, or it might feel as if perhaps the editor's own grasp of the rules isn't that strong.

An alternative method of finding out whether they would be a good "fit" is to ask for a sample edit. The editor "edits" a few pages of your submission and sends it back. You can see what they pick up (and what they miss!), how they couch their suggestions for changes (vague, or polite, or didactic), what their general communication style is like. There's one caveat with sample edits. If your book needs structural work it's practically impossible to give a sample developmental edit, because by its nature such an edit looks at the book as a whole, and not at just a few pages.

You can then compare sample edits from the different editors and arrive at an informed opinion as to who is going to gel with your book and you. (One minor point. Please don't try and get your book edited for free by asking thirty different editors to edit thirty different chapters! It's called a Frankenstein Edit, for obvious reasons, and it has been attempted more times than you'd think. It always causes us editors, most of whom know each other online if not personally, enormous amusement.)

Timing

Finally, timescales. Some editors are booked up months in advance. If you're happy to wait for the right editor, just join the queue. If you have a deadline (a self-imposed publishing date, or perhaps a competition entry), some editors are able to be more flexible with their schedules and fit you in earlier. If it's really urgent you might struggle to get a decent editor, or they will charge you a "rush fee" because they've had to put aside work they were immersed in.

Conclusion

I hope that's shed some light on the process of hiring an editor and given you some idea as to what to expect, and the likely pitfalls. It's a hugely important relationship in your writing career, so it's worth taking some time over finding the right editor.

Appendix IV: Editing terminology

Following on from Appendix III, I thought it might be useful to define some of the editing terminology used to describe the work editors do. Because editing isn't a globally regulated profession, the terms may differ from one English-speaking jurisdiction to another. I'll try to accommodate those differences in this list.

Proofreading

Many first-time writers believe editing is just checking an MS for spelling mistakes and missing or (more often) unnecessary apostrophes. Would that it were that simple! Proofreading is only the very last look at a final draft MS before it goes for printing. It might include things like checking punctuation and spotting missing words or typos, but it will also include things like checking for consistent indentation, layout and correct labelling of images, consistency in headings and subheadings and so on.

Proofreading is more about presentation than content—all the issues such as a character having blue eyes in chapter one and brown eyes in chapter ten should have been picked up in an earlier stage of the editing process, copyediting, but it is the last chance to pick up little errors that have been missed, or introduced, at the copyediting stage.

Copyediting

The stage before proofreading is called copyediting. This term used to be hyphenated, at least in the UK, but some editors got together recently and decided that maybe it shouldn't be hyphenated (this is the kind of thing that gives us editors sleepless nights), so you might see "copyediting" begin to creep onto editor websites in the near future. "Copyediting" is more common in Canada and the US. Neither is wrong.

Precisely what is covered by copyediting varies slightly from editor to editor, but they will all agree that this is the process of making a text flow at sentence-level. This is where any errors in punctuation should be sorted out, so those comma splices corrected, rogue apostrophes exterminated, colon and semicolon usage reviewed, and also where spelling mistakes, homonyms, missing words and plain wrong words should be detected. The idea is to make the sentences flow correctly, to eliminate those little errors which can trip a reader up and remind them that they're sitting on the train reading a book, not actually wading through a swamp full of piranhas in search of a missing temple (which is where you want them to think they are).

COPYEDIT SCOPE

The scope for copyediting can cover more than these simple changes, however, and this is where editing terminology can differ slightly. An editor might feel that some words aren't needed. An example might be:

> He sat nervously, drumming his fingers
> on the desk.

"Nervously" isn't an error here, but it's not needed. It's a common mistake to both tell the reader something, "He sat nervously," and also show it, "he drummed his fingers on the desk." An editor might suggest deleting the adverb.

> He sat, drumming his fingers on the desk.

Sometimes it can be entire phrases that the book is better off without:

> Nigel carefully carried his tray of glasses making sure that it remained horizontal.

In this sentence the entire phrase *"making sure … horizontal"* is pretty redundant, considering he is "carefully" carrying the tray of glasses, so an editor might suggest deleting it.

The list of things that might be picked up in this type of copyediting is too long to enumerate, but would include things like intrusive alliteration (*"Tim's ratty Ray-Bans were really wrecked"*) odd phrasing (*"the sun had turned blue the sky"*) faulty parallelism (*"Elizabeth was brilliant at horse-riding, embroidery, and to snowboard"*), PoV issues, those descriptive inconsistencies that I mentioned earlier (blue eyes/brown eyes) and so on.

HARD AND SOFT COPYEDITS

Some editors draw a distinction between the more objective corrections that we mentioned at the beginning of this section, spelling and grammar mistakes, PoV and tense shifts, and things like treatment of numbers and capitalisation, and the latter more subjective issues, like the use of filter words, descriptive inconsistencies, elimination of clichés and so on. This latter type of copyediting they term line editing, and it can also be termed, since it is more to do with an author's style rather than actual content, stylistic editing.

Other editors talk of "hard" and "soft" copyedits. A soft copyedit focuses on the objective changes we mentioned, whereas a hard copyedit includes not only those objective changes but also the more subjective issues like the use of filter words in close PoV, or the use of too many adverbs, or over-elaborate dialogue tags. In this instance, a hard copyedit is the more intrusive of the two types.

Developmental editing

Developmental editing, also termed "substantive editing," looks at the major structural issues in a book. Here, instead of suggesting that an individual sentence is wrong or a particular scene could be shorter, the editor might be suggesting wholesale changes to the book that will involve significant rewriting.

These suggestions might be; "could you make this character female, perhaps a love interest for the main character?" or, "there was one bank raid at the beginning of the book. This second one is nearly identical. Does it need to be included, or if it does, do you need to go through all the details?"

The editor might have a less specific recommendation, like; "these middle chapters are very slow, with nothing much happening—just the main character crying over her broken heart. Can you introduce a subplot to retain the reader's interest?" or, "I don't see how the main character really changes over the course of the story. He's still as selfish as he was when the book started. How has he matured?"

In the course of a developmental edit, most editors will also comment on the style of writing, the issues picked up in a hard copyedit or stylistic/line edit above. They will comment on PoV and tense handling problems, use of filtering or excessive adverbial description, inconsistent dialogue styles, use of language, cliché, and the balance of exposition to plot.

OVERLAPS BETWEEN DEVELOPMENTAL EDITING AND COPYEDITING

How much overlap there is between developmental editing and copyediting relies a great deal on what state the MS is in. If there are significant big-picture problems the editor is dealing with, they are unlikely to be able to dig down to the nitty-gritty sentence-level problems in your book, and those will have to wait until the copyediting stage.

Summary

In summary, editing terminology generally describes three different tasks:

Proofreading is the final detail-level look-through after the content of the book has been thoroughly edited.

Copyediting is the general fine-tuning of the technical side of the book, grammar, punctuation, spelling—all the basic issues—but also might involve changes to words, word order, sentence-level changes and even the restructuring or reordering of paragraphs.

(*Line editing* is a subset of copyediting that deals exclusively with the more subjective issues that arise, things like the use of clichés, adverbs, filter words, and the problems that sometimes crop up in the handling of PoV or tense. This might also be referred to as *stylistic editing*.)

Developmental editing is the comprehensive overview of the book, taking into account every facet of the story including plot structure, character arcs, pacing, rhythm, development of conflict and tension, and resolution of all the story strands in a good climax. Depending on the editor, it will also overlap to some extent with copyediting, looking at use of language, writing style, scene level details. It might also be referred to as *substantive editing*.

Doing it all at once

Why these separate stages? Why shouldn't the editor do all kinds of editing at once?

For one thing, copyediting chunks of text that might have no place in the final book is a waste of the editor's time and your money.

Secondly, concentrating on big-picture issues means that, being human, editors will miss quite a few of the smaller more detailed problems that they would catch in a dedicated copyedit.

It's best to do one type of editing at a time. If you think about the way this book is structured, I try and break down the self-editing process into clearly defined stages. In practice, those stages overlap to some extent (filtering problems bleed into PoV discussions, and so on), but working on specific areas of your book generally helps you focus on each type of issue with more clarity. It's like starting a jigsaw by finding all the edge pieces, instead of starting in the middle of the picture and working out. If there are very few major structural problems to comment on in a developmental edit, it might be that your editor will address some of the copyediting issues at the same time, but even then, the issues addressed are likely to be of the more subjective variety, the line editing or stylistic editing type of problem.

Cost

Cost increases with the more work involved, so expect to pay more for copyediting than proofreading, and more (sometimes much more) for developmental editing than copyediting. Judge it on the basis that an editor might be able to proofread a fairly clean book in a week, but it might take them two weeks to copyedit a similar length MS, and four weeks or more to perform a developmental edit.

Summary

The evolution of the publishing industry has caused some of these terms to evolve along with it. Proofreading, for example, used to mean literally looking at the page proofs of a book going to print. These days it is generally accepted to have a slightly wider meaning, that of the final check on a text that might be going to print, but equally well might be being converted to ebook format. Whenever you intend commissioning an editor, read the small print on their website or have a conversation, because sometimes the terminology will differ. If comparing editors on pricing, you'll want to be sure that you are comparing a similar service, whatever that editor happens to call it.

Appendix V: Beta readers, uses and misuses

What is a beta reader? What do you use beta readers for, and when do you try and find some?

Historical role

An author writes a book and sends it to his publisher. His editor suggests some revisions, the author redrafts. The editor discusses the new draft with her colleagues. Together, they're not sure. It's a good book, but is it going to appeal? They'd like some reader opinion. They send the draft out to some trusted readers they have on call, asking them "What do you think of this?" These readers would have been called "alpha readers," the first people outside the actual production team to see the draft.

The MS comes back with approving comments. Encouraged, the publisher pushes the book in to production, copyediting, proofing, cover design, promotion campaign ... "But hang on," the marketing team says. "Is this book literary fiction, or romance, or historical fiction? It has all three elements, but in order to promote it efficiently, in the right media and in the right way, we need to know which market sector it is the most likely to appeal to." "Send the final proofs out to some beta readers," the managing editor says. "See what they make of it."

So beta readers were only involved at the very last stage of the process. They took no part in shaping the book; they were like the screen-test audience in a film pre-release screening. "Is this movie a turkey, or is it worth spending a big chunk of our promotion budget on?"

Indie publishing and beta readers

The accepted role of the beta reader in indie publishing circles is very different. An author completes the first draft of a book. When the delight of typing "The End" wears off, they are usually assailed with doubt. "Is it any good? Will people want to read it? Are there any glaring problems? Is there something I missed? Am I really a writer?" At this stage, authors could turn to an independent editor, and get a professional opinion on their work. Few do. For a start, that costs money. Secondly, it's not about critique at this stage. It's more about validation. Authors haven't grown that thick skin that they need to develop in order to hear a professional's frank and honest opinion about their writing. Remember what I said about Hemingway's reputed quote: "The first draft of anything is shit." The fragile newbie-author ego is not likely to be resilient enough to hear this unwelcome news just yet.

So the author researches online, hears about "beta readers" and turns to their writers' group, or asks a friend, or their old high school teacher, and asks for their opinion. "Will you be a beta reader? Tell me honestly what you think."

Evolution

How the role of a beta has evolved should be clear. The beta reader is now getting involved in the very first stages of the book, when it is still an early draft. What are they likely to say? A beta reader might say: that they got a bit bored in the middle, that they didn't like this particular character, that this bit of plot seemed a bit too coincidental or contrived. They're no longer merely commenting on what they liked or didn't like about a finished book. Suggestions they make might have a critical impact on how subsequent drafts of the book develop. Arguments as to whether this is a good thing or not are missing the point. This evolution has already happened. The key thing to consider is that in this new role beta readers are potentially far more influential in the development of a book than they ever used to be in their traditional role.

What should I look for?

Yikes! So you are that newbie author, and you've heard about beta readers, and you were going to recruit a few for feedback on your book. What should you look for in a beta reader?

WELL-READ ...

Firstly, they should be well-read. There's not much point in giving your draft to someone who hasn't read a book since leaving high school. You're going to be asking them their opinion on the structure of your book, whether the plot holds water, whether the characters are believable.

They need to have something to compare it to. The more books they've read, especially of modern literature, the more they'll have to compare it to.

... IN YOUR GENRE

Ideally, they should be well-read in your genre. If you're writing for a specific audience, ideally your beta reader should like that genre, have some prior experience in reading books of that genre, and/or even better, be a member of that target readership. There's not much point giving your YA LGBTQ steampunk mermaid romance to your rather dusty and conventional classics professor and asking her opinion.

OBJECTIVE ...

They should be capable of being fairly objective in their analyses. Here's the hard thing. Potential beta readers may be unaware of their own biases. If someone tells you that your tragic ending really doesn't work, it might just be that their preference is for Happily Ever After endings. Your dystopian "everybody dies" Analysis of the Human Condition that is truly the best thing since "On the Beach" is not going to go down well.

... BUT NOT TOO OBJECTIVE

A beta reader who claims that the inciting incident must occur on the first page, that all the major characters must have been introduced by page four, and that adherence to the three-act structure is mandatory, has read too many books on the craft of writing, and worse, memorised them.

A CONFIDENT COMMUNICATOR

And finally they should be capable of communicating what they thought to you, clearly, concisely and unambiguously. Ideally they should be able to give you their feedback in writing (it helps to be able to mull over critique in your own time) so they need to be able to communicate ideas and thoughts in writing in a clear and ordered fashion. Rambling monologues, where one idea blurs into another, are hard to read and difficult to learn from. Comments should be as specific as possible (you're trying to isolate particular problems so that you can fix them—"I found it a bit boring" isn't going to help you do that).

Their prose needn't be polished and perfect, but it should be clear what they mean. The most insightful beta reader is no help if they can't communicate their ideas about your book. They should also know, if they have critical things to say, how to phrase criticism so that it isn't personal, and is always constructive. This helps defuse the emotional baggage of what otherwise can be quite a sensitive conversation.

How many beta readers?

Truly? As many as you can cajole, entice, bribe. As you can see above, getting the "right" beta reader is fraught with complexity. You're unlikely to achieve a perfect audience at the first attempt. That doesn't matter too much, if you've got a reasonably wide range of opinions to choose from. What you're hoping to get from your beta readers is a loose consensus. Five out of ten betas saying that "the chapter where she goes on a road trip through New Mexico with her pet lizard is a bit boring," is useful feedback. One beta saying "I wanted to know what the lizard thought. Lizards are cool," is perhaps not so useful.

Should you heed what they say?

Statisticians routinely take a sample, (in a survey, for example), and discard the bottom 5% and top 5% of results. They are outliers. They are that person who was more interested in a book about a lizard. You're not writing a book about a lizard, so their opinions, while possibly entertaining, are not much use to you. What you're looking for is clues as to how "most people" would rate your book. If the majority (or even a significant minority) of your beta readers suggest that one particular facet of your book grated with them (be it one character's motivation, or a plot device that seemed unlikely, or a section that they skipped) then you have a good clue as to something you should take a second look at.

Can I use a beta reader as an editor?

You mean, skip paying an editor to edit your books and rely solely on beta reader feedback? Well, I'd say no, but I'm obviously biased. I should have to justify that opinion. Why would I say no? After all, many authors swear by their beta reader feedback when drafting their books.

There are a couple of issues.

OBJECTIVITY

However well-intentioned a beta reader is, they bring their own biases. Perhaps they dislike first person narrative, or they don't like New Mexico. Maybe they don't like lizards. Perhaps they dislike cynical protagonists, and you fancy yourself as the next Raymond Chandler. Professional editors get the subjectivity of their analyses beaten out of them (!) either by training and then continuous professional development (which any editor who's a member of a professional organisation is encouraged to participate in), or by repeated exposure to the wonderful world of fiction and its authors. I've edited countless books. If I ever thought there was only one way to write a novel, I would have had the error of that opinion forcibly demonstrated to me by many talented and diverse authors. Beta readers rarely have that objectivity, or that depth of experience.

MISSION CREEP

Secondly, some beta readers come to see their role as an editor. They might start handing out advice about not using adverbs, avoiding passive voice, showing and not telling. All of these can be valid criticisms of writing, in their place. But that's not what you're giving your work to a beta reader to find out. Professional editors treat developmental analysis, the big issues about plot structure, character arcs, pacing, voice and so on, completely separately from the nitty-gritty copyediting functions looking at technical issues of sentence structure, expression, word choice and so on. There's a good reason for that. You can't competently do both at the same time. If your beta reader points out that your spelling is appalling and your punctuation needs an overhaul, that's a useful aside that you might want to take a look at before you give your book to a professional editor, but it's not what you've asked them to do, and it's not generally a beta reader's role. If they're looking for spelling mistakes, they can't be appreciating your wonderful prose.

Summary

Beta readers, within the modern definition, are very useful to authors looking for layman reader opinion. While strictly speaking "alpha readers," the distinction is rather irrelevant these days. I'd have the following suggestions:

> Have more than one beta reader. If possible, many.
>
> Don't give too much weight to one beta reader's opinion that isn't mentioned by others.
>
> Choose your beta readers carefully.
>
> Don't use your beta readers as proxy editors, unless, of course, they're qualified to be so.
>
> Be specific about the kind of advice/opinion you want from your beta readers. At an early draft stage you're concentrating on the big issues about plot and character and pacing and voice, not the detailed level of word choice and sentence structure. The more clearly you brief them with particular issues ("I'm worried about the dialogue—is it realistic?" "I'm worried about the main character—is she empathetic, or just

pathetic?") then the more likely that you'll get opinions really focused on areas you want help with.

Finally, you can do your bit to get the most out of the experience:

Give your betas a tidy MS, with as few errors as possible.

Don't send them a revised first ten chapters, after they've been reading for a few weeks, and expect them to start again.

Remember to be grateful! Although the paid beta reader market is growing, beta readers are often still doing it for free, for a love of books and writing. Good beta readers genuinely want to help.

Don't take it personally, and don't be personal. They're expressing an opinion about your book, not about you. And if you really don't get on with a beta reader's opinion, don't rant and argue and tell them they're idiots who know nothing about writing. Say thanks for the feedback, and quietly drop them off your beta reader list.

Appendix VI: Editing software

There are several companies producing web-based grammar checkers—Grammarly and ProWritingAid are the two market leaders at the moment—but the market is constantly changing, and those two companies frequently evolve their products and alter their pricing strategies, so any detailed review I prepared here would be quickly out of date.

Opinions about such programs in the writing community are varied, but editors are consistently more negative than those of writers. That might be expected—no one likes to think that their job might be replaced by a machine in the near future! But do they have valid reasons? What are the problems with writing software apps, and what are the benefits for self-publishing, self-editing authors?

Algorithms

All writing software (any kind of software, in fact) depends on algorithms to do its job. An algorithm is a set of rules. In order for software to detect something wrong with your text, a programmer must have entered a rule in the software for that program to check your writing against. Whether that's detecting passive voice construction, verb-noun agreement, spelling or punctuation, each error that the software finds is a result of comparing your text to a set of rules. That's writing software's biggest positive, and its biggest failure.

If you gathered anything from working through this book, it's probably (because I repeated it so many times) the fact that there are very few rules in writing. There are some things that are universal. Sentences begin with a capital letter. They end with some form of punctuation, a point, or a question mark perhaps. It's very straightforward for a computer program to check, in milliseconds, that all your sentences start with a capital letter, and that they all have some kind of final punctuation. These are simple objective tests, for which there is a right and a wrong answer. Computers, if you strip away all the operating systems and cloud-databases and networking that they are wrapped in, deal in data that can be in one of two states, a 1 or a 0. Tests that are either right or wrong are perfect for a computer to work on, and here they excel, and will save you endless hours of manually checking through your manuscript.

Nuance

What no software can do that has yet evolved is detect the nuance that a writer wants to convey in writing. It can see the words in the file, and the more sophisticated programs will perform some level of contextual analysis (the depth and accuracy of that analysis usually depending on whether you buy a "premium" package or opt for their free or basic package). If one of your lines begins, "They all ran to the bike sheds and got on ..." and you've written "they're" as the next word, contextual spelling analysis is going to flag that as a likely error. However, cast your mind back to when I was discussing passive voice.

> Women are often paid less for doing the same work.

This statement is a passive construction. Who pays women less for doing the same work is, for the purpose of this statement, irrelevant. It's a generalisation—an opening statement perhaps. The document might go on to discuss which industries in particular uphold this sexist differentiation, which have taken steps to combat it and how successful they have been. But before we get to any of this detail, the writer is stating their opening position. There's no reason to change it. If you put this into one of the writing software apps mentioned above, it flags it as an error. To add insult to injury, it suggests the following replacement phrases: "It often pays women are often less for doing the same work," or perhaps the even more nonsensical "I often pay women are often less for doing the same work."

Outcomes

There are two things that have happened here. One is that the software has flagged as an error something that isn't an error. The second thing is that I've then had to go in and evaluate whether the alternative proposed solutions are better than what I've actually written. In this particular case, they make no sense, so that's a fairly easy decision to make.

Since this type of software has been programmed to detect passive voice and flag it as an error, and since as far as computers are concerned there can only be two states, "an error" or "not an error," it will record every occurrence of passive voice as an error. You will have to evaluate, for each of those occurrences, whether the computer is right or if you are. The more you are right, the more time of yours the software is wasting.

Further, if you're not too sure about your writing and your voice, and a software program (that in its promotional material asserts that it is state-of-the-art, and used by editors worldwide) is telling you that you're wrong, do you have the confidence to ignore the program, or are you going to start editing your voice out of what you've written and substitute it with generic computer-speak?

Errors of omission

Algorithms can only inform you of the likely accuracy of what is there. They can't anticipate the fact that you might have left something out. We might check one of our vocative comma examples from earlier.

"If I drove over Jack, can you pay me?"

There's no error flagged here. It's a perfectly grammatical sentence, so the computer, assessing text by its binary metrics of wrong/not wrong, can't appreciate that we didn't mean to imply that we were going to assassinate Jack for money.

Editor viewpoint

This is, ultimately, what exhausts a human editor's patience with these programs. When you've run the algorithm over a text, you're faced with a list of errors, many of which, if the original text was written by a competent author, are not mistakes. Each one will have to be evaluated on its merits. Further, just because you've run the algorithm over the text doesn't mean that there are not errors still to be found. The editor will still have to manually go through the entire text, looking for errors of omission rather than errors of commission—it really hasn't saved them much time at all.

It's very easy for a professional editor to detect whether a manuscript has been properly edited, or whether it has merely had one of these grammar checkers run over it, and I'll tell you the secret.

In a text that has had little human editing input, there will be no passive voice, there will be next to no sentence fragments, there will be commas in, and only in, prescribed places, such as after a prepositional introductory phrase. And there will be lots of errors of omission still remaining that the software didn't pick up.

Costs

Writing software packages have costs. Without going in to the exact payment structure of each package, which may change at any point after this book goes to print, it's difficult to compare those costs but, let's be clear: they are a fraction of a professional editor's fees.

There are free versions of most packages. They generally have word count constraints and functional limitations and some, at time of writing, depend on your uploading text into a browser in small sections while online. None of these issues are optimal for a novelist whose work might run into hundreds of thousands of words. The "free" packages don't include the possibly more value-added checks like contextual spelling (to pick up some homonyms).

For the paid versions, check the minimum subscription period, if there is one, weigh up the cost of a monthly licence with a one-off fee (if available) and bear in mind that even small subscriptions per month can add up pretty quickly, as you would when contemplating any overhead. $30 per month is $360 per year, and two years of that is well into professional editors' proofreading fee levels, although not perhaps the more advanced copyediting.

What you already have

Finally, I'm no Microsoft salesman, but if you're using Word, how about trying the tools buried in the software you already own before contemplating buying anything else? In the proofing section of the Review tab, there's a function called Spelling and Grammar. This has a comprehensive text checking system which, among other things, checks for the following:

Grammar:

- Capitalisation
- Commonly misused words
- Possessives and plurals
- Punctuation
- Subject-verb agreement

Style:

- Clichés, colloquialisms and jargon
- Use of contractions
- Identifying sentence fragments
- Gender specific words
- Hyphenated and compound words
- Commonly misused words
- Passive voice (of course!)
- Possessives and plurals

- Stylistic punctuation issues
- Sentence structure and length, and "readability" scores

That is a fairly comprehensive list of what most of the paid writing software packages offer, and if you're using Word, is already embedded in your writing software, with no software translation issues, no cutting and pasting in small sections and no necessity for an online connection. Be careful that you aren't paying extra for something you already have, or, if comparing prices of word-processing packages generally, consider that these review options are already included in the price of Word.

Conclusion

Before you buy any writing software, evaluate what you have already if you're using Word. I'd bet a decent sum that most of the errors a paid package will highlight would be covered by Word's own grammar and spell-check function.

Of course, Word's checker has exactly the same foibles as the paid software. It will throw up many objective errors on a first draft, missing or incorrect punctuation and spelling mistakes, but it will also highlight every sentence fragment and tell you to "Consider revising" and wag a finger at every example of passive voice. Try it, though. If you find yourself spending more time hitting the ignore key than the accept key, then software isn't for you.

If you decide to go ahead, evaluate the packages on offer. Bear in mind that the more complex software becomes, the more it will start intruding on your sentence structure, suggesting changes not only to the errors, but to what it considers poor writing. Adverbs and adjectives, especially modifiers like "really" and "very," will get short shrift. Sentence fragments will be rejected as wrong. Complex sentences will be flagged as confusing. There are truths buried in all of these suggestions, but never forget that these packages are really intended for copywriters writing vacuum cleaner manuals, businesspeople writing annual reports and marketing execs drafting publicity material for their new widget factory. You will have to fight tooth and nail to keep your prose looking how you wrote it, and in the frustration of having to defend your writing to a machine, you might well miss sound advice buried among the false negatives.

Also, don't forget that everything covered in Part II of this book won't be picked up by writing software anyway. It won't pick up plot holes. It won't pick up unbelievable characters. It won't tell you that "this chapter is a bit boring, frankly." It might tell you that your dialogue is incorrectly punctuated, but it won't tell you that "a real human being would never say that." Even if you do subscribe to some writing software and find it really useful, you're still going to have to self-edit!

Further reading:

This isn't an exhaustive list—there are hundreds of books out there on the various aspects of writing craft—but a selection of those that I think offer something rather unique:

As I said at the outset, there are few books specifically on self-editing. There is one notable exception, *Self-editing for Fiction Writers*, by Renni Browne and Dave King. This venerable text was first published in 1993 and a second edition published in 2004. Although it predates the entire self-publishing explosion, it's still full of good sensible writing advice. It does fall more into the arena of how to write, rather than how to edit, but it was instrumental in opening my eyes to the concept that self-editing could (and should) be a process quite distinct from writing.

Stephen King's *On Writing* is another inspirational book, again, more to do with writing than editing, but combining dispensing solid advice with an inspirational story of how he came to success. Be careful not to interpret his advice too literally, however. Although he can invent a neat aphorism ("the road to hell is paved with adverbs"), he doesn't stick rigidly to that advice himself, and admits that candidly.

Beth Hill's *The Magic of Fiction* goes into far more comprehensive detail about the specifics of writing than I felt the necessity to do here in a book on self-editing. If you have a technical question that I haven't covered, it's surely answered in that huge book.

Into the Woods by John Yorke is a fascinating insight into story structure, for those of you for whom my brief mention of the subject in Part II of this book only piqued your curiosity.

REEN PUBLISHING

Index